MOUNTAIN HIGH

MOUNTAIN HIGH

Europe's greatest cycle climbs   Daniel Friebe and Pete Goding

Quercus

Contents

PAGE 1: The view back down the Valle Varaita from high on the Colle dell'Agnello, Europe's third highest main road pass.

PREVIOUS PAGE: Even though Austria doesn't have the same historic links with professional cycling as France and Italy, the Großglockner Hochalpenstraße is one of the great cycling highways.

THIS PAGE: The Edelweißspitze on the Großglockner – not only one of Europe's greatest and most historic climbs, but also among its most vaunted mountains.

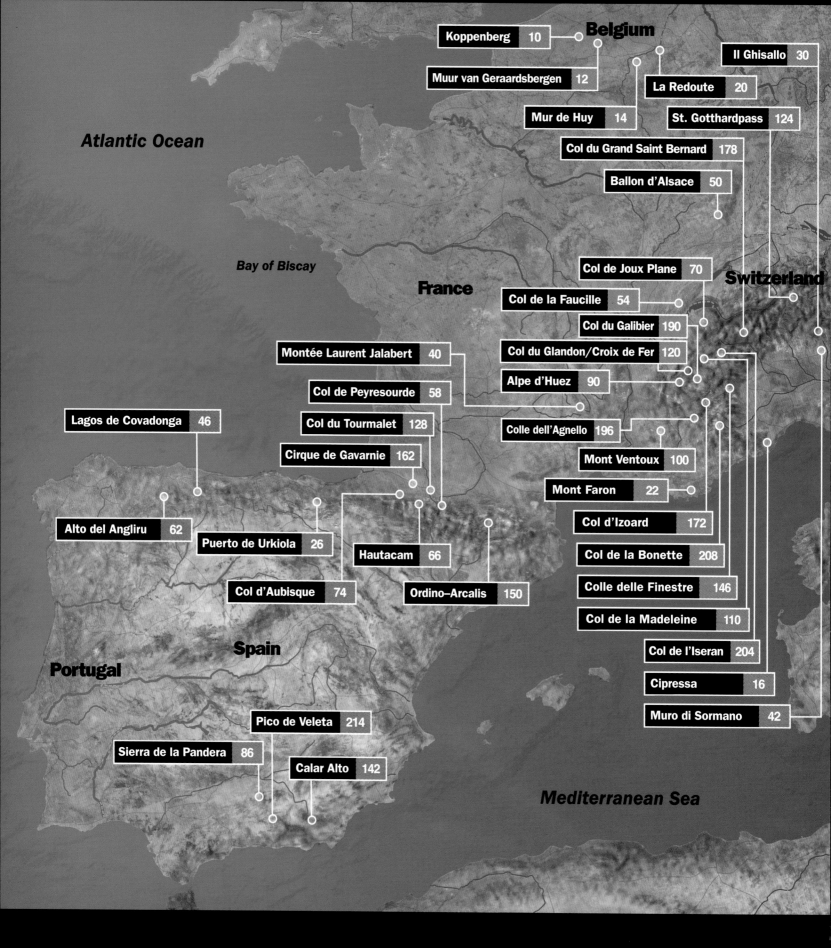

Atlantic Ocean

Bay of Biscay

France

Belgium

Switzerland

Spain

Portugal

Mediterranean Sea

Koppenberg 10

Muur van Geraardsbergen 12

Mur de Huy 14

Il Ghisallo 30

La Redoute 20

St. Gotthardpass 124

Col du Grand Saint Bernard 178

Ballon d'Alsace 50

Col de Joux Plane 70

Col de la Faucille 54

Col du Galibier 190

Col du Glandon/Croix de Fer 120

Montée Laurent Jalabert 40

Alpe d'Huez 90

Col de Peyresourde 58

Colle dell'Agnello 196

Lagos de Covadonga 46

Col du Tourmalet 128

Cirque de Gavarnie 162

Mont Ventoux 100

Mont Faron 22

Alto del Angliru 62

Puerto de Urkiola 26

Hautacam 66

Col d'Izoard 172

Col de la Bonette 208

Colle delle Finestre 146

Col d'Aubisque 74

Ordino–Arcalis 150

Col de la Madeleine 110

Col de l'Iseran 204

Cipressa 16

Pico de Veleta 214

Muro di Sormano 42

Sierra de la Pandera 86

Calar Alto 142

Europe's greatest cycle climbs

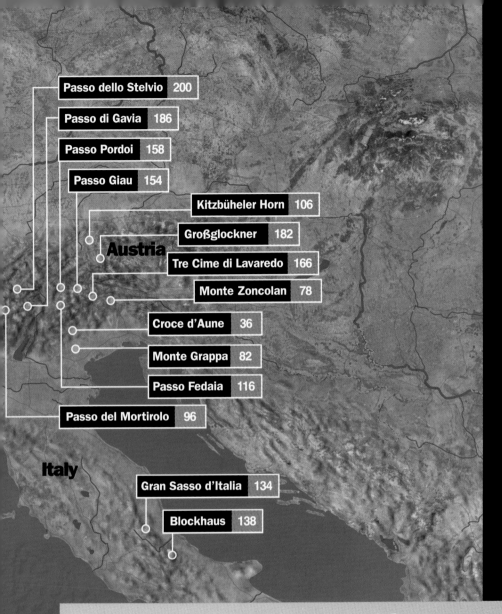

Passo dello Stelvio	200
Passo di Gavia	186
Passo Pordoi	158
Passo Giau	154
Kitzbüheler Horn	106
Großglockner	182
Tre Cime di Lavaredo	166
Monte Zoncolan	78
Croce d'Aune	36
Monte Grappa	82
Passo Fedaia	116
Passo del Mortirolo	96
Gran Sasso d'Italia	134
Blockhaus	138

Austria

Italy

This book is the first to provide both a practical and historical guide to 50 of Europe's legendary cycling climbs. Previous volumes on the topic have concentrated on route information, spectacular photography or a mountain's impact on professional cycling's great races, but never have all of those ingredients been assembled on the same pages... until now.

Mountain High is, then, both a bible for those who wish to take on giants like the Tourmalet or Galibier, and the ultimate reference book for connoisseurs of these climbs' history and mystique. The concepts of place and topography are integral to cycling at any level, and both our text and pictures have been carefully planned and selected to reflect that symbiotic connection.

Notions of difficulty and beauty are so subjective that they become meaningless in a context like this. All of the climbs in *Mountain High* are special for their own unique reasons, and so we decided to classify them in the only way that nature intended – by the height to which they rise from the earth.

Understanding the graphics

Each climb or variation thereof is summed up within a detailed fact box, giving the reader all the essential facts as well as a locator map. The profile of each climb uses clear colours, ranging from green to black, to illustrate the gradient steepness in per cent.

REGION: The region in which the climb is located

ACCESS: Short directions to the start of the climb

HEIGHT: The maximum altitude of the climb

LENGTH: The overall length in kilometres

ALTITUDE GAIN: The difference in altitude between the start and top

AVERAGE GRADIENT: The average gradient of the climb given in per cent

MAXIMUM GRADIENT: The maximum steepness as well as its kilometre mark, given in per cent

OPEN: The months of the year the road is open

REFRESHMENTS: Where, if any, refreshments are to be had

ALTERNATIVE ROUTES: Sometimes, alternative, less well-known routes to the summit will be given

Monte Grappa 8.2

1745m
1500m
1000m
500m

9.0
4.2
4.3
2.8
8.8
5.4
2.6
10.3
20.5
9.7
7.5
9.4
8.6
3.3
9.5
Possagno 6.0
2 4 6 8 10 12 14 16 18 20 22

Monte Grappa — Key locations along the way
1,500m — Altitude

0 – 4%   4 – 8%   8 – 10%   10 – 15%   15 – 25%

SS50
SEREN DEL GRAPPA
ITALY
metres
1500
1000
500
SS47
SS550bis
SP148
Alano di Piave
MONTE GRAPPA
Pederobba
POSSAGNO
SS47
SS348
PADERNO DEL GRAPPA
(Salto della Capra)
SEMONZO
ROMANO D'EZZELINO
N
0   5 km
0   3 miles

▷ – Direction of the climb
— All possible ascents and descents
SP148 – Route Nationale/autostrada/B-roads
◐ – Starting point(s) of the climb
◑ – Finish and also normally highest point of the climbs

Introduction

A t the time when J. K. Starley and Rover produced what was the first recognizably modern, two-wheeled bicycle, the notion that any such device would one day transport mortal men and women into the mountains seemed, by some distance, more preposterous than the notion that dragons, witches and gods lurked among the peaks of the Alps and the Pyrenees.

Starley's *tour de force* was dated 1885. The first Tour de France was still 18 years away. Alpine giants such as Mont Blanc and the Meije had been conquered, but the mountains still evoked terror.

This book and its photography are as much about the emotions those roads and mountains have bestirred as the physical climbs themselves. Riding a bike uphill is always hard, so there is no need to reaffirm that here, many times over. Instead, our goal is to piece together the features, the stories, the quirks and unique attractions of 50 of Europe's most famous and compelling cycling ascents, from the 78-metre-high Koppenberg to the gigantic 3,384-metre Pico de Veleta in Spain's Sierra Nevada.

Mountain High does not, then, set out to classify definitively Europe's

Koppenberg
Belgium
78m

Love or loathe the Koppenberg – and it has its share of detractors – this 600-metre upturned mogul run in the west of Belgium occupies a unique place in professional cycling: whatever the year or the weather, and however much training methods and technology evolve, this is the only climb on earth where you're as likely to see the world's best cyclists get off and walk as grind to the top.

The Koppenberg is controversial for this reason. Its history is as turbulent as the journey to its summit, chequered with sporting debacles and ensuing periods in quarantine. Between 1988 and 2002, it appeared on the Tour of Flanders route not a single time and looked destined never to return. Having already caused rumblings of discontent as well as of bikes and bodies in 1985, when the Belgian Eric Vanderaerden was the only rider not to walk, two years later the Koppenberg provoked outrage and the end of the Dane Jesper Skibby's chances in that year's Tour of Flanders. The Dane led the race by ten seconds when, halfway up the climb, he lost momentum and veered from the right-hand gully into the centre of the road. The race director's car hit Skibby as he drifted left, then, as the Dane lay prostrate on the cobbles, drove over his bike and up the road. After years of complaints and near misses – not to mention the undignified spectacle of the great Eddy Merckx staggering to the top, bike over his shoulder, in 1976 – this was the last straw. Indefinitely exiled, the most infamous cobblestones outside Paris–Roubaix fell even further into disrepute and disrepair.

Return to centre stage in the nineties

That 1976 race, infamous for Merckx's struggles, had also been the Koppenberg's Flanders premiere. Merckx's countryman and rival Walter Godefroot had earlier 'discovered' it, or at least brought it to the race organizers' attention, and onto the 1976 race course it went between the Oude Kwaremont and the Taaienberg hills. Its precise collocation was tweaked over the next decade, but almost invariably it signalled only the beginning of hostilities spread over a succession of short, steep cobbled climbs or *bergs* in the last 60 kilometres. This was the critics' other issue with the Koppenberg: it was a lot of hassle, a few cheap thrills, for very little tangible outcome. Even those who had to dismount often regained contact with the leaders on the flat road before the next hill.

OPPOSITE: Rugged, rickety and brutally steep, the Koppenberg is in many ways the quintessential Belgian *berg* or cobbled climb. Having been declared too treacherous for professional racing and banished for over a decade, it has once again become a fixture of the Tour of Flanders.

Nonetheless, during its years of exile and particularly in the 1990s, support for the Koppenberg's reinstatement became stronger and more vociferous. First, its devilish cobbles had to be refurbished – and they were, one by one, at a cost of 6,000 euros. The road was also widened, the ruts filled in, and 200 more metres of cobblestones added. In total, the 'cosmetic surgery', as the Belgian press dubbed it, cost the Oudenaarde town council around 150,000 euros.

And so, finally, in 2002, the Koppenberg made its return, not without a little trepidation on the part of the riders and organizers. Four years passed without serious incident or complaint before, in 2006, only two riders in a breakaway and seven from the main peloton made it to the top on their bikes. Race chief Wim Van Herreweghe had been warned: the Belgian star Philippe Gilbert was among several riders who came up short of the summit in a pre-race recce. In response, Godefroot, by now the T-Mobile team manager, had sniffed that anyone who'd struggled on the Koppenberg in training merely 'lacked motivation.' The reality, of course, was that the cobbles had deteriorated again and Van Herreweghe had no choice but to once again remove the offending article, the Koppenberg, at least temporarily. 'There's too much space between the stones and if it rains it would be a catastrophe,' he said, to the sighs of the thrill-seekers at the side of the road.

Restored to the Flanders route in 2008, but no doubt on permanent probation, the Koppenberg packs more history and intrigue into those 600 short metres than many Alpine and Pyrenean passes have amassed over a century of Tours de France. If the notion of 'famous Belgians' has become a running joke, the same could be said, literally, about what is possibly Belgium's most famous road: if you don't laugh you'll probably cry; and if you can't ride, then you can at least run… or perhaps just walk.

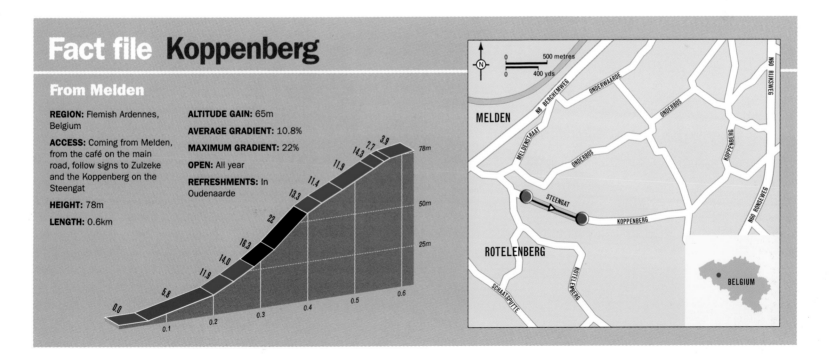

Fact file Koppenberg

From Melden

REGION: Flemish Ardennes, Belgium

ACCESS: Coming from Melden, from the café on the main road, follow signs to Zulzeke and the Koppenberg on the Steengat

HEIGHT: 78m

LENGTH: 0.6km

ALTITUDE GAIN: 65m

AVERAGE GRADIENT: 10.8%

MAXIMUM GRADIENT: 22%

OPEN: All year

REFRESHMENTS: In Oudenaarde

Muur van Geraardsbergen
110m
Belgium

The people of Geraardsbergen have an old saying. It goes, 'There are three walls in the world – the Great Wall of China, the Berlin Wall and ours.'

While pedants may suggest that the Western Wall of Jerusalem has rather stronger claims, those familiar with the Tour of Flanders and its iconic Muur can be seen nodding in agreement. Or, if they're real nitpickers, pointing out that, of the three, Geraardsbergen's is the only one whose legend is still very much in the making.

An aggregation of five roads heading in and out of Geraardsbergen – in order, Brugstraat, Markt, Vesten, Oudebergstraat, then the final 20 per cent ramp to the Chapel of Our Lady of Oudeberg – the Muur has established itself as the totem of Belgium's favourite sporting occasion in the space of just 60 years. Or even fewer if one considers that, while it was first included on the Flanders route in 1950, just weeks after also making its debut in the race known then as Het Volk, only since the 1980s has it been a permanent feature of cycling's grimmest, but in many ways most fascinating, one-day event.

Culminating just 15.8 kilometres from where the Tour traditionally finishes in Meerbeke, the Muur is the place where Flanders is, more often than not, won and lost. Every one of the 15 or so (depending on the year) *bergs* sprinkled through the last 120 kilometres is vital, each one provoking a miniature stampede, but this is where the posturing and, for many riders, all chance of victory ends. As the smooth cobbles of the Oudebergstraat pucker into what looks like a medieval bridleway, the gradient ratchets up to 20 per cent, and aspiring winners come face to face with their destiny as well as the cobbled road. A last, sharp, right-hand bend and the riders enter a corridor of noise like nothing else in the sport. 'Unless you've experienced it, you really can't understand what it's like when you first glimpse the chapel at the top,' said Alessandro Ballan, who attacked on the Muur en route to victory in 2007. '"You can't hear yourself think" is supposedly just a figure of speech, but I realized what that means on the Muur. It's a sensation and a noise that you'll never recreate anywhere else.'

OPPOSITE: The final push to the top of the Muur and the Chapel of Our Lady of Oudeberg. On the day of the Tour of Flanders, the grass bank is crammed with baying Belgian fans.

RIGHT: Eddy Merckx, the greatest cyclist ever, 'only' won the Tour of Flanders twice, but this bronze monument near the top of the Muur leaves no doubt as to the mark he made here.

Under threat

It goes without saying that climbing the wall isn't quite the same for amateur riders, however many memories of past Flanders come flooding back. From the 1990s, in particular, most fans associate the Muur with Johan Museeuw, the so-called Lion of Flanders. Museeuw's attacks on the Muur launched him to victory in 1993, 1995 and 1998. Only half-joking, he later compared leading the Tour over the top of the Muur to having an orgasm.

The following decade saw the Muur extensively refurbished. Several pros agreed that the improved surface also made the ascent easier. At around the same time, Tom Boonen and Fabian Cancellara inherited Museeuw's mantle as the new demons of the Muur. So powerful was Cancellara's acceleration away from Boonen in 2010 that eagle-eyed observers – call them that or conspiracy theorists – suspected there was a motor hidden in the bottom bracket of his bike. The Swiss's alleged 'mechanical doping' soon became the hot topic of the racing season. Video clips of Cancellara's winning moves in Flanders and Paris–Roubaix the following week were pieced together and posted on YouTube,

the Italian editor of one even presenting his evidence in a book the following year. The sport's governing body, the UCI, took note and even scanned competitors' bikes at the 2010 Tour de France, without ever extending the measure to other races, and despite declaring a year later that they believed the rumours to be nonsense.

If nothing else, the controversy added to the romance of the Muur, as does every edition of the Tour. That mystique seemed set to grow as long as the climb retained its position on the Flanders route – but the long-mooted threat of an impending change was duly realized in 2012. The town of Oudenaarde managed to wrest the race finish from Meerbeke, and the entire route underwent a major overhaul. Not only that but the unthinkable happened: the Muur was removed from the course. Vocal protests followed and didn't die down when Tom Boonen won over what most agreed was a far inferior layout, climaxing on the nearby Paterberg. Only time will tell whether the race organizer heeds the clamour for the Muur's immediate reinstatement; In the meantime, somehow, absence will make the heart grow fonder and the legend even richer.

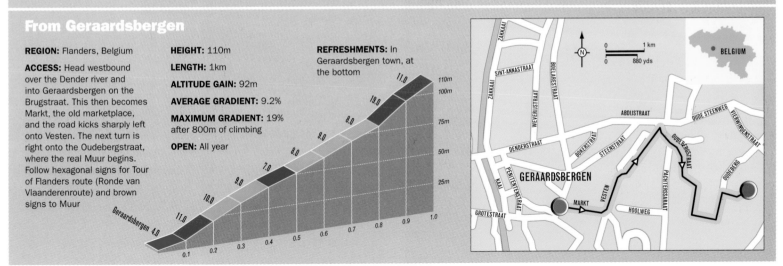

Fact file Muur van Geraardsbergen

From Geraardsbergen

REGION: Flanders, Belgium

ACCESS: Head westbound over the Dender river and into Geraardsbergen on the Brugstraat. This then becomes Markt, the old marketplace, and the road kicks sharply left onto Vesten. The next turn is right onto the Oudebergstraat, where the real Muur begins. Follow hexagonal signs for Tour of Flanders route (Ronde van Vlaanderenroute) and brown signs to Muur

HEIGHT: 110m

LENGTH: 1km

ALTITUDE GAIN: 92m

AVERAGE GRADIENT: 9.2%

MAXIMUM GRADIENT: 19% after 800m of climbing

OPEN: All year

REFRESHMENTS: In Geraardsbergen town, at the bottom

Mur de Huy
204m **Belgium**

How bad can a 1.3-kilometre climb be? Philippe Gilbert, the local Walloon hero, said that to one day conquer the Mur and win the Flèche Wallonne, the Belgian one-day race to which its folklore is inextricably linked, he would have to endure 'two minutes of suffering.' And therein lies the problem: what for Philippe Gilbert was two minutes of torture, for anyone not among the finest riders in the world might mean an agony of double or triple the duration – not to mention equal, if not more excruciating, pain.

'The Tour of Flanders has the Muur, Amstel Gold has the Cauberg and Liège–Bastogne–Liège has La Redoute... but the Mur de Huy is by far the hardest of the lot,' opined Claude Criquielion, winner of the first Flèche to finish atop the Mur, in 1983.

The road or wall's significance, of course, far predates and transcends its sporting legend. Historically and still officially known as the Chemin des Chapelles or Chapel Way, the road soars out of the Rue du Marché in Huy and towards Notre Dame de la Sarte, the last of seven chapels dotted up the hillside and supposedly the scene of a miracle in 1621. Pilgrims stop at all seven before ending their journey at Notre Dame. For cyclists, a glimpse of the church steeple heralds the imminent end of the climb and their deliverance.

An encyclopedia of Belgian cycling climbs published in 2004 rated the Mur only the country's 34th hardest ascent, well adrift of the 4.6-kilometre, six per cent Col d'Haussire in La Roche-en-Ardenne. The Mur's extreme and unorthodox proportions, though, render any such ranking system meaningless; while only 800 metres of its 1.3 kilometres are truly difficult, that stretch is steeper and more brutal than anything else in professional cycling. The Frenchman Laurent Jalabert, who triumphed twice on the Mur, reckoned that only the Mont Saint-Clair above Sète in the south of France (1.7 kilometres long, average ten per cent, maximum 24 per cent) could compare or compete. Flèche Wallonne race director Christian Prudhomme called the Mur 'the longest kilometre of the racing season' and 'basically a mountaineering competition.'

'Like the middle of a rock concert'
A mazy cavalcade through the wooded mining valleys of the Belgian Ardennes, the Flèche's route has been tweaked in recent years, but the Mur remains its centrepiece. Depending on the year, the peloton climbs its ramps either once or twice before a final, frantic scramble to the summit. Since Criquielion's victory in 1983, Lance Armstrong, Michele Bartoli, Moreno Argentin, Cadel Evans, Maurizio Fondriest and Laurent

FAR LEFT: The notorious chicane where the Mur's gradient rears up to over 20 per cent. This is the section that inspired Frenchman Laurent Jalabert to call the Mur 'essentially a staircase'.

LEFT: The famous bridge over the Meuse river in Huy, the town that acts as base camp for the 'longest kilometre in the racing season', in the words of Christian Prudhomme.

OPPOSITE: No photo can do it justice, but a name like the Mur (wall) perhaps does.

> **" AMSTEL GOLD HAS THE CAUBERG AND LIÈGE–BASTOGNE–LIÈGE HAS LA REDOUTE....** but the Mur de Huy is by far the hardest of the lot. **"**
>
> Claude Criquielion

Fignon have all won here; other Classics legends such as Paolo Bettini, meanwhile, have repeatedly tried and failed to get the measure of the Mur.

In 2002, unfancied home rider Mario Aerts was clear in a six-man breakaway group when the Mur loomed for the last time. The next few minutes, which culminated in the Belgian crossing the line with arms aloft, Aerts will never forget.

'It's just an incredible feeling,' he recalled in 2011. 'There are so many people – it's like being in the middle of a rock concert or football match... Once you start the climb it's not that steep, but you know what's coming. The climb is basically only two corners, but if you take them on the inside, they're 25 per cent, and if you go on the outside you're obviously penalizing yourself because it's further. After the bends, the road straightens and the slope eases for the last 200 metres, but they last an eternity. The key is to really dose your efforts and keep something back for those last 200 metres. If you're lucky and strong, having gone up the climb in a 39x21 gear or even 23, you can manage that final bit with a 39x19.'

Victorious in gripping duels with Maurizio Fondriest and Luc Leblanc on the Mur in 1995 and 1997 respectively, Jalabert agreed in 2005 that economy was the key. 'The difficulty of the Mur is its length and its gradient – but also the altitude you gain with every step, because it's essentially a staircase,' the Frenchman explained. 'You have to know how to use your gears to save energy. You always just have to hold a little bit back and be aware of how far you've got to go to the summit. That said, on the steepest parts, it's purely a question of strength and energy. Everyone is in their smallest gear. Later, when it eases slightly at the end, you can get away with a 39x21 or 39x19.'

While Aerts and Jalabert can blithely compare notes about gear ratios, and Philippe Gilbert console himself with the brevity of the ordeal, amateur cyclists should be aware that, for them, the Mur will be a test of survival. On the two bends that give the climb the feel and gradient of a helter-skelter in its middle section, merely staying upright can be a challenge. Even bike fans familiar with TV pictures of the Flèche Wallonne and its Mur are often astonished when they stand at its base for the first time.

Short but steep, not sweet, the Mur may very well be Belgium's most fearsome climb. It is certainly among its most infamous. Bettini used to say it was simply 'too hard.' He had no Flèche Wallonne in his *palmarès* – but the Italian may have had a point.

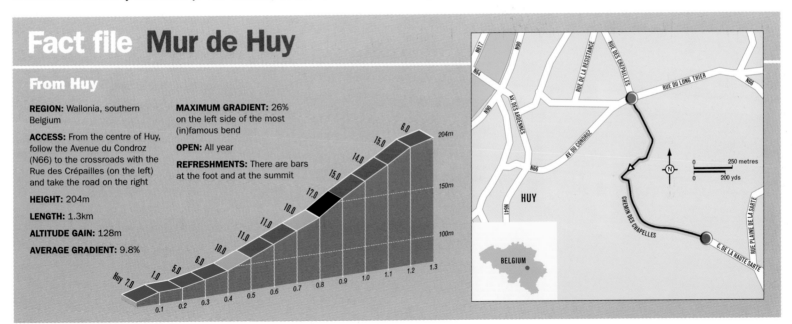

Fact file **Mur de Huy**

From Huy

REGION: Wallonia, southern Belgium

ACCESS: From the centre of Huy, follow the Avenue du Condroz (N66) to the crossroads with the Rue des Crépailles (on the left) and take the road on the right

HEIGHT: 204m

LENGTH: 1.3km

ALTITUDE GAIN: 128m

AVERAGE GRADIENT: 9.8%

MAXIMUM GRADIENT: 26% on the left side of the most (in)famous bend

OPEN: All year

REFRESHMENTS: There are bars at the foot and at the summit

Cipressa
234m Italy

❝ **EFFECTIVELY AN EXTENSION OF THE CÔTE D'AZUR JUST ACROSS THE BORDER IN FRANCE,** this is an equally dramatic and beautiful coastline, with homespun charm and faded grandeur in place of garish glitz. ❞

Why the Cipressa and not the Poggio? Two climbs define the most romantic, beguiling, longest and most famous Italian one-day Classic, the Milan–San Remo, and of the two the Poggio is both the longer-established and more decisive. Added to the route in 1960 by race director Vincenzo Torriani, and topping out six kilometres from the finish line in San Remo, its brief was to end the sequence of sprint finishes that risked becoming a cliché. It worked, often if not always – at least until the rot set in again and Torriani added the Cipressa in 1982 – and so the Poggio grew into a Classicissima's icon. The Cipressa, by comparison, was a topographical *arriviste*, an interloper, which too often flattered to deceive.

The answer to our question, then, is purely unsentimental: the Cipressa is simply a much better climb. At 5.65 kilometres long and rising to 234 metres above the neighbouring Mediterranean, its dimensions are those of a hill, not a mountain – but this still gives it the clear edge over its 3.7-kilometre-long, 160-metre-high older yet smaller adoptive brother. In Italian *poggio* means hillock or mound. And San Remo's version is truly nothing more.

Suicide mission

With just a shade under nine kilometres between where the descent off the Cipressa ends and the right-hand turn off the Via Aurelia onto the Poggio, the climbs have in common a dreamy setting on the Ligurian Riviera. Effectively an extension of the Côte d'Azur just across the border in France, this is an equally dramatic and beautiful coastline, with homespun charm and faded grandeur in place of garish glitz. While on the Poggio, figs, almond trees, vines and olive groves have slowly ceded their place to terraced flower plantations, the Cipressa retains the olive trees and cypresses from which it takes its name. The olive oil from here and particularly nearby Taggia, generically known as Olio Taggiasca, is especially prized. Locals claim it owes its bright yellow colour and mellow flavour to the salty sea air and southern exposure of hills precisely like the Cipressa.

Mellow is also an adjective one might use for the ascent of the same panoramic hillside by bike. In 2005, the Milan–San Remo peloton broke the record of nine minutes, 36 seconds set by Francesco Casagrande five years earlier, registering a new mark of nine minutes, 30 seconds. That gave them an average speed of

ABOVE: Exiting the village of Cipressa and beginning the
fast, at times perilous, descent back onto the Via Aurelia.

35.6km/h. Otherwise stated, a group of professionals working in
unison will devour the Cipressa at a rate only 5km/h slower than
their usual cruising speed on the flat, even after 270 kilometres of
racing. Tackled from a standing start, the Cipressa appears even
more benign.

The surface is smooth, the gradient steady and innocuous apart
from a 100-metre stretch at nine per cent midway through the
fourth kilometre, when the road doglegs right and away from the
Mediterranean. The only other challenge here can be a headwind
which has often deterred attacks in Milan–San Remo. Mirko
Celestino, who was born in a hospital overlooking the route in
Albenga on the day of the 1974 race, once remarked that attacks
on the Cipressa rarely amounted to anything more than suicide
missions. 'There should be no reason why a group of six or seven
can't attack here and produce a race winner. The reality is that, for

all sorts of reasons, that just never happens,' Celestino lamented.

More often, Milan–San Remo has been lost in the last two
kilometres before the road loops into the village of Cipressa and
towards the summit, now barely even gaining altitude. Mario Cipollini,
the finest sprinter of the 1990s but perennially frustrated in Milan–
San Remo, saw his chances of victory disappear here along with the
wheels of better climbers on numerous occasions. Conversely, in
2009, one sprinter, the young Manxman Mark Cavendish, diligently
picked his way through the stragglers, including some who had
ridiculed his chances in the build-up. To pundits' amazement, the
self-declared former 'fat bank clerk' went on to survive the Poggio
and become one of the youngest ever winners of Milan–San Remo at
the age of 23.

Trapdoor for losers

'You can't win San Remo on the Cipressa but you can lose it' has
thus become a great cycling truism, as formulaic as those sprint
finishes Torriani wanted to mitigate if not abolish. News of him
including the Cipressa arrived barely a week after the 1981 race,

meeting with almost unanimous approval. 'It was about time,' wrote Maurizio Caravella in *La Stampa*. Torriani had flirted with the idea of adding the 485-metre Testico, but considered the climb too difficult and too great a detour from the Aurelia coastal road. Instead, he took the advice of a flower seller and some-time collaborator from San Remo, Mimmo Filippi, who pointed him towards the Cipressa. And thus ended Torriani's 'desperate search for some idea to enliven the most famous race in the world' as Caravella hubristically described it.

The riders were impressed by the theory, less so by the reality. In the weeks and days leading up to the 1982 race and the Cipressa's world premiere, they converged on San Lorenzo al Mare, where the roads flicks right off the Aurelia and the climb begins. 'A climb like that 270 kilometres into the race is fraught with danger, but it's the descent that's most frightening,' said the Italian Francesco Moser. Moser's long-term foe, Beppe Saronni, echoed him, rating the descent off the Cipressa 'much more dangerous than the Poggio.'

Moser duly delighted the Italian fans by shattering the peloton on the Cipressa – but by that time a freak breakaway containing the unfancied Frenchman Marc Gomez had already barrelled by. Gomez's winning move, or rather the two costly skids by his only remaining challenger, Alain Bondue, came at the start of the descent off the Poggio. It wasn't entirely the dénouement that Torriani had dreamed of.

Over subsequent years, though, Cipressa quickly established itself on the Classicissima route, if not always in the public's affections. Less launchpad for winners than trapdoor for losers, it eliminated the weak without exalting the strong. In the late 1990s and early 2000s in particular, it was the focus for fans' frustration as the sprinters resumed their stranglehold. The 1999 race saw Marco Pantani's blistering attack on the first hairpin – followed by a clamour for yet another route change when not even that resulted in victory. There was talk of a new climb, the Pompeiana, harder and closer to the Poggio, replacing the Cipressa.

ABOVE: A typical Ligurian scene, low down on the Cipressa. Olive trees and Mediterranean pines, more than the cypresses from which the village at the top takes its name, adorn the hillside.

Instead, race organizers RCS opted for a tougher middle section of the race, retaining the Poggio, the Cipressa and the three *capi* that precede them, but adding the 4.7-kilometre, 6.7 per cent Le Manie after the Passo del Turchino.

No doubt there'll be more changes, but with any luck the Cipressa will remain, as tantalizing and enigmatic as the race that made it famous. Torriani's legacy to professional cycling included the Muro di Sormano, the Passo Fedaia and countless other temples to the sport's obsession with mountains. In 1982, on a sleepy stretch of Ligurian coastline, he and the sporting world discovered that small could also be beautiful.

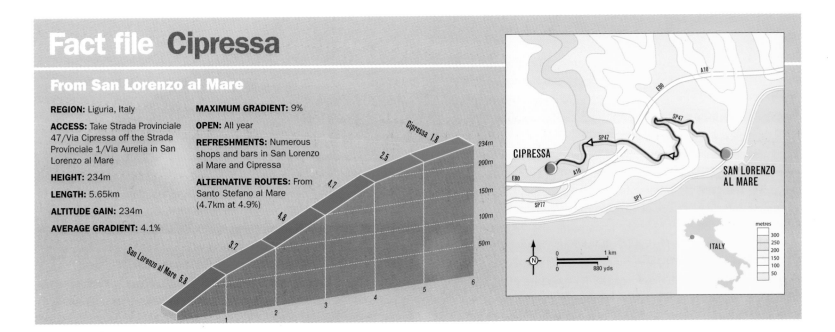

Fact file Cipressa

From San Lorenzo al Mare

REGION: Liguria, Italy

ACCESS: Take Strada Provinciale 47/Via Cipressa off the Strada Provinciale 1/Via Aurelia in San Lorenzo al Mare

HEIGHT: 234m

LENGTH: 5.65km

ALTITUDE GAIN: 234m

AVERAGE GRADIENT: 4.1%

MAXIMUM GRADIENT: 9%

OPEN: All year

REFRESHMENTS: Numerous shops and bars in San Lorenzo al Mare and Cipressa

ALTERNATIVE ROUTES: From Santo Stefano al Mare (4.7km at 4.9%)

La Redoute
292m   **Belgium**

It comes as a disappointment that the most aptly named of Europe's iconic climbs owes its appellation to events unrelated to cycling. The Côte de la Redoute, or just La Redoute as it is more commonly known, is indeed among the most redoubtable ascents in Belgium, but the moniker has zero to do with the 1.7-kilometre, 9.8 per cent bluff hoisted to legendary status by cycling's oldest one-day Classic, Liège–Bastogne–Liège. Since the climb's introduction to the route of La Doyenne in 1975, its banks have hosted many epic duels – but none as bloody as the conflict that occurred here over two days in September 1774 between French revolutionaries and the Austrian

imperial army. The Redoute in question was in fact a redoubt, or fort, erected in preparation for that battle which resulted in victory and the definitive withdrawal of the Ancien Régime from Belgium.

Two centuries on, this slither of rural lane had long since established itself as one of cycling's most hallowed locations. First organized in 1892 and often considered cycling's unofficial world championship, Liège–Bastogne–Liège was viciously undulating and venerable before acquiring La Redoute, but gained lustre with its addition. Former rider, journalist and Tour de France director Jean-Marie Leblanc proclaimed it the most beautiful of professional cycling's five Monuments – an exclusive category within the already elite club of Classics – in order of appearance in the calendar, Milan–San Remo, the Tour of Flanders, Paris–Roubaix, Liège–Bastogne–Liège and the Tour of Lombardy.

'Liège–Bastogne–Liège has always been my favourite race, the most beautiful of all without question,' Leblanc said in 2005, his final year as the organizer of the Tour, Roubaix and Liège. 'Paris–Roubaix is emotional. But Liège is the most exacting on an athletic level, and the most beautiful, with the majestic backdrop of the Belgian Ardennes. Those hills bring back so many memories from my journalistic career – especially Bernard Hinault's victory in the snow, in 1980.'

That day, by the time Hinault swung into Remouchamps, the village on the banks of Amblève river and the doorstep of La Redoute, he was already alone. 'The Badger' had woken that morning, glanced at the snow falling outside his bedroom window and 'wanted to go back to bed'; having secretly intended to abandon just after the halfway mark, instead, purely in an effort to keep warm, Hinault accelerated and proceeded to drop the field 80 kilometres from Liège. Either side of La Redoute, he pulled alongside his *directeur sportif* Cyrille Guimard's car to warm his hands on the heater. 'Go f**k yourself… or get on the bike and pedal yourself,' Hinault had snarled at Guimard when, at one point, Guimard told him to dispense with an unseemly red balaclava. Even insulated like a yeti (sure enough, the nickname with which some papers immortalized his performance), Hinault suffered such bad frostbite that he permanently lost all feeling in two fingers.

OPPOSITE: The Liège–Bastogne–Liège Classic has turned an otherwise anonymous rural lane into a place of painful pilgrimage. The council of Aywaille has paid homage to its pride and joy with this monument.

RIGHT: This roadsign under the A26 motorway bridge near the beginning of La Redoute has nothing to do with cycling – but is highly apt in this setting.

FAR RIGHT: In recent years La Redoute has become a shrine to Philippe Gilbert, who grew up at the foot of the climb and delighted the locals in 2011 with victory in the Liège–Bastogne–Liège.

Hinault's victory had been consolidated but not constructed on La Redoute. Far more often, and particularly prior to the inclusion of the Côte de la Roche-aux-Faucons between La Redoute and the Côte de Saint Nicolas in 2008, Liège has been decided here – on what has been called cycling's equivalent of the Hillary Step, the formidable rock wall just beneath Everest's summit.

A monument – a myth

'You won't necessarily win Liège–Bastogne–Liège on La Redoute, but it's there that most riders lose it. The light goes out and it's goodnight from him,' said Claude Criquielion, a man who knew 'every millimetre of the climb' according to his one-time nemesis, the four-time Liège winner, Moreno Argentin.

Dirk de Wolf, the champion in 1992, called it a 'simple' climb. With one proviso… 'It's very straightforward: you just need to be strong, as strong as a bear,' De Wolf said in 2011. 'You always hear stories about riders having gone up it in the big chainring, but that's poppycock. In training, maybe… but in the race, after 240 kilometres, it'd kill you.'

De Wolf ought to look closely at pictures from the 1999 race:

before blowing away the last of his opposition on the Côte de Saint Nicolas, Frank Vandenbroucke had indeed achieved the unthinkable and powered up La Redoute in his 53-tooth chainring; Vandenbroucke's dominance that year was surpassed only by his arrogance. On the eve of the race, he'd told journalists not only on which climb he would land his knock-out punch, but in front of which house on the Saint Nicolas. Best or worst of all, Vandenbroucke had kept his promise.

In 2009, the new darling of the Belgian fans, Philippe Gilbert, who grew up in Remouchamps, lobbied hard and successfully against a proposal to remove La Redoute from the race route. Gilbert argued that the climb is a 'monument, a myth', on a par with the Poggio in Milan–San Remo or the Muur van Geraardsbergen in the Tour of Flanders – but he may just as convincingly have pleaded that, *per se*, La Redoute is a jewel of a climb, situated in a superlative region for cycling. A land of emerald hills and valleys, yet bellicose history, the French-speaking Ardennes delight and amaze, and for those on two wheels, challenge and reward.

La Redoute is their totem. Redoubtable and unmissable.

Fact file La Redoute

From Sougné-Remouchamps

REGION: Belgian Ardennes

ACCESS: From Sougné-Remouchamps, follow signs for La Redoute off N.697, towards N.666-R.P

HEIGHT: 292m

LENGTH: 1.7km

ALTITUDE GAIN: 161m

AVERAGE GRADIENT: 9.5%

MAXIMUM GRADIENT: 17%

OPEN: All year

REFRESHMENTS: Numerous shops and bars in Remouchamps

Côte de la Redoute 4.0

BELGIUM

SOUGNÉ-REMOUCHAMPS

Mont Faron
508m
France

> ❛ **AN ASTONISHING, SINGLE-LANE BALUSTRADE CURLING AROUND SHEER LIMESTONE ROCK.** It's hard to imagine three more dramatic kilometres of road than the middle section of the 'real Faron'. ❜

'The Mont Faron is to the people of the Var what the Eiffel Tower is to the Parisians. Just as the Parisians wake up and see the Tower, or people from Clermont Ferrand draw the blinds every morning and look out over the Puy de Dôme, for people like me who have spent their life in the Var, the Faron is something you grow up with, something you carry with you for the rest of your life. For a cyclist, it's more than that: it's an honour, a rite of passage in a career.'

When Lucien Aimar speaks of the Mont Faron, he does so with the authority and affection of a man whose name has become

OPPOSITE: The bay of Toulon is 'the third most beautiful bay in the world after Hong Kong and Rio', according to the tourist board, and it is foregrounded by one of those famously hideous hairpins of the 'real' Faron.

RIGHT: The Trou du Diable, or Devil's Hole – hard going uphill, as it used to be tackled in the Tour Méditerranéen, and positively diabolical on the way down.

synonymous with the 584-metre 'hill or mountain… depending on whether you're from the Camargue or the Tourmalet.' Born practically in the shadow of the Faron in Hyères in 1941, Aimar became a Tour de France champion in 1966, but today is known as much for his association with the rugged 'Lord of the Toulon' as for his career as a cyclist. The two also went hand in hand: as Aimar points out, he may well be the only rider to have won on the Faron 'as a junior, as an amateur and a professional.'

His first victory there came as a teenager in the Trophée du Faron, a mountain time trial organized every year and with separate races spanning ages and abilities. For 'any kid in the region with a bike and interest in racing', Aimar says, it was the 'highlight of the year'. For the pros, it was also a 'key fixture in the spring-time calendar' – and one that had accumulated a stellar roll of honour. The Italian-born Frenchman Jean Dotto triumphed three times in the 1950s, thus becoming Monsieur Faron the first; Aimar, his heir, went on to win the pro race and set a new record for the climb in the 1960s – only to have his mark beaten by the greatest cyclist who ever lived, the Belgian Eddy Merckx.

The death of the 'real Faron'

As the legend of the Faron grew, so, inevitably, in the early 1970s, Aimar entered the twilight of his career. He could and did leave the professional peloton – but would never escape the allure of the Faron, so much so that he was soon scheming to prolong both his own and his sport's love affair with the mountain. 'There was a lack of early-season races for pros at the time so, together with my cousin

and the two local cycling clubs, we started thinking about maybe doing something in the region,' he recalls. 'We'd run it in several stages and the Faron would be its centrepiece. That's how, in 1974, the Tour Méditerranéen was born.'

Those were the days, he says with a sigh, of the 'real Mont Faron'. By this Aimar means that there are two routes up the Faron – or two sides to the same road that lassos the summit – and the 'superior' ascent is the eastern one from Valette. Unfortunately, since the Toulon councillors made the road over the Faron a one-way street a few years ago, this has also been the 'wrong' or forbidden way to climb the Faron. As a result, both the Tour Méditerranéen and normal traffic head up the Faron on the still steep, still spectacular, still sinuous – but slightly less 'real' western flank.

'The real Faron is a bit shorter, and steeper,' Aimar explains. 'On that side, there is one bend in the middle section called the Trou du Diable, or the Devil's Hole, where the gradient is 16 per cent. It's brutal on the way up and the way down.'

An astonishing, single-lane balustrade curling around sheer limestone rock, it's hard to imagine three more dramatic kilometres of road than the middle section of the 'real Faron'. The views over Toulon, the port where Napoleon Bonaparte masterminded his first major military victory in 1793, are sublime. Not that it would be wise to look anywhere but straight ahead: if uphill it used to be brutal, then the descent of this side is utterly treacherous – far too narrow and steep to ever feature in modern races.

The Faron hasn't changed, but cycling clearly has since the mid-1960s, when the downward corkscrew off the eastern side of the

Faron was briefly one of the highlights of the Paris–Nice stage race.

'I can remember one year when we went down the Trou du Diable side and Jean Leuillot, the Paris–Nice organizer, had put up a prize of a pair of skis for the fastest descender,' Aimar remembers. 'My team captain, Jacques Anquetil, had been dropped on the way up, so I went down at what I thought was a pretty slow pace so that he could catch up with me, but I still apparently did the fastest time. Jacques was miffed at me getting the skis. He couldn't believe that I was the fastest. I think we mislaid them before the end of the race anyway.

'In 1967, when Tom Simpson won Paris–Nice, we also went down that way,' Aimar continues. 'There was a group of us clear at the top, with me and Tom and Bernard Guyot – and Bernard overshot one of the bends and went flying. You've got about a three-metre window in which to break before the hairpins and, if you don't, you're in trouble…'

Aimar admits with regret that the 'real Faron' as a climb may be lost forever. While local authorities would theoretically allow the Tour Méditerranéen or for that matter Paris–Nice to ascend from that side to a summit finish, they would also demand safety measures way

beyond Aimar's already stretched budget. In 2011, even organized on a shoestring, the race almost had to be cancelled due to lack of funds.

The most beautiful bay in Europe

'We always used to go up the Trou du Diable side in the Tour Méditerranéen, but then the police saw the Paris–Nice climb from the other side a few times and said "Hang on, why should you get special treatment? You can go up that side like them". As for the likelihood of the Faron ever featuring in the Tour de France, I have major doubts. We've tried but a Tour finish has to be accessible to about a thousand vehicles, and there's no way that would be allowed. The Office National des Forêts – the National Office for Forests – already put restrictions on us when we go up with the Tour Méditerranéen. They would never let the Tour up there – the environmental impact is too great.'

Aimar can take heart from the fact that even from the east, Mont Faron remains a gem of a climb, with its five hairpins slashing across the limestone rock face like the flourish of Zorro's blade. While the 'real Faron' spent its final third zigzagging through pines, the climb from the

east enters the same forest blanketing the summit only at the end of its journey. The majority of the trees, predominantly cedars, Aleppo pines and oaks, were planted at the beginning of the 20th century. Prior to that locals referred to the Faron simply as Le Caillou (The Pebble). Now, for some, it is Toulon's Poumon Vert or Green Lung.

The Faron's summit is home to a zoo famed for its colony of big cats. Nine disused military forts also dot the mountainside. The third, time-honoured ascent of the Faron is via the cable car inaugurated in 1959. While the road passes just beneath the summit, pedestrians can walk all the way to the Faron's highest point, 584 metres above sea level, and admire what the local tourist board calls the most beautiful bay in Europe – and the third most beautiful in the world behind Rio and Hong Kong. While the view here is truly spectacular, Monte Carlo has reason to feel aggrieved.

The Faron is, though, far more than just a beautiful vantage point or imposing backdrop. For the people of Toulon and Lucien Aimar it is nothing short of the mountain of a lifetime – as well as indisputably one of the cycling world's most romantic destinations.

OPPOSITE: The western ascent of the Mont Faron – still scenic, spectacular and challenging, but perhaps less impressive than the way down what is now a one-way system off the summit.

ABOVE LEFT: A glimpse of the forest planted at the start of the 20th century that now carpets the upper slopes of the Faron, earning it the moniker of Toulon's Poumon Vert or Green Lung.

ABOVE: A different perspective on the Trou du Diable, where ace descender turned Tour Méditerranéen boss Lucien Aimar more than once proved his credentials as one of cycling's top 'divebombers'.

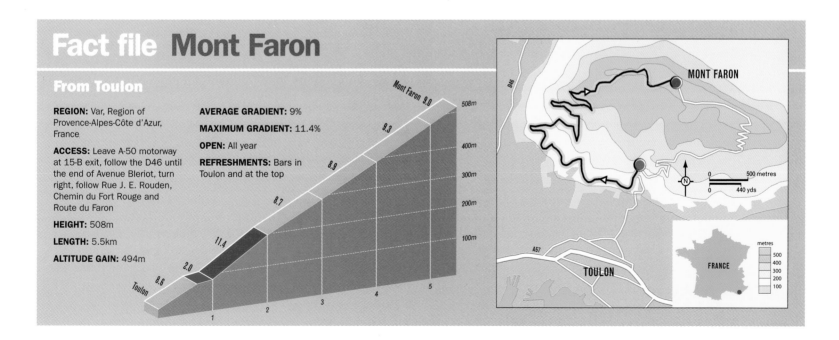

Fact file Mont Faron

From Toulon

REGION: Var, Region of Provence-Alpes-Côte d'Azur, France

ACCESS: Leave A-50 motorway at 15-B exit, follow the D46 until the end of Avenue Bleriot, turn right, follow Rue J. E. Rouden, Chemin du Fort Rouge and Route du Faron

HEIGHT: 508m

LENGTH: 5.5km

ALTITUDE GAIN: 494m

AVERAGE GRADIENT: 9%

MAXIMUM GRADIENT: 11.4%

OPEN: All year

REFRESHMENTS: Bars in Toulon and at the top

Puerto de Urkiola
713m
Spain

ABOVE: The sign says 'Welcome to the Urkiola National Park', and it is also from around this point that some of the climb's hardest ramps begin, climaxing with the 14 per cent Txakurzulo stretch.

Peaking at 713 metres above sea level, the Puerto de Urkiola is over 100 metres shorter than what in 2011 was the world's tallest building, the Burj Khalifa in Dubai – and yet in Basque culture and cycling, the climb known simply as the Urkiola has a towering reputation.

Urkiola is, in fact, the name of an entire mountain range and national park in the Spanish Basque Country, which for hundreds of years has been traversed by one main north–south highway, the Puerto or pass. Historically a vital supply line linking the Cantabrian coastline to the plains towards Madrid, it was for generations the route of choice for Castilian wool merchants heading for the Bay of Biscay in one direction and for the transport of Mañaria marble

" CYCLING IS ANOTHER ESSENTIAL INGREDIENT in the fascinating melting pot of Basque culture, and the Urkiola is the sport's crucible here. **"**

ABOVE: A wheel's-eye view of the 14 per cent Txakurzulo ramp, overhung by the *sirimiri* – the damp, grey mist that is a frequent visitor to the Basque mountains.

in the other. Midway through the 18th century, the bridleway was still used by between 200 and 400 carts a day between April and October, but its disastrous condition prompted governors in Durango, the regional capital, to approve an upgrade which they hoped would stem the town's increasing economic isolation. The work started in 1777 and would take 12 years and nearly three times the money originally budgeted.

So far, so unremarkable. Nothing, though, in the Basque Country, is quite what it seems – or what it would be anywhere else in Europe. At least that's what non-Basques like to think – as Joseba Zulaika put it in his *Basque Violence: Metaphor and Sacrament* in 1988, 'Their being a mystery people is what seems to be of most interest about Basques to outsiders' – and it is also largely true. Although the topic is fraught with conjecture, latest research still supports the theory that the Basques are a distinct ethnic group, quite different from the Spaniards who are technically their compatriots. Their language and its origins also continue to bamboozle linguists, who have tried for centuries to find related vernaculars in every corner of the globe, never with convincing results.

Thunderbolt and lightning

Paddy Woodworth wrote in another fine book on the Basques, *The Basque Country: A Cultural History*, that Victor Hugo's characterization of the Basques as 'the people who sing and dance at the foot of the Pyrenees' drives them crazy, and yet traditions that perpetuate the image of a mystical and superstitious bunch continue to flourish. Mari, the Basque deity who appears as a thunderbolt, a white cloud or a girl with long blonde hair, remains a central figure. She is said to lurk on the mountain overlooking the Urkiola from the east, the 1,331-metre limestone cone of the Anboto. People in the Basque Country who claim to have sighted Mari in one of her various guises are ten to the dozen. Zulaika, for example, wrote that his mother had seen her represented in a fireball. Her features are also recognizable, her followers maintain, in a rock formation at the end of the tiny grotto where she's said to reside on the eastern side of the Anboto.

Cycling is another essential ingredient in the fascinating melting pot of Basque culture, and the Urkiola is the sport's crucible here. The Basque mountains aren't high, but the roads to their summits are often steep, very much like the Urkiola. Professional cycling has three major tours – of France, Italy and Spain – but if the passion of the local population was the qualification criterion, the Tour of the Basque Country would join them, and stages over the Urkiola would be elevated to the same status as the Tour de France's trips to Alpe d'Huez and Mont Ventoux, or the Giro d'Italia's to the Dolomites. As well as being the Basques' national race, the climb's legend has been enriched since 1931 by the Subida a Urkiola one-day race,

LEFT: The road out of Mañaria climbs gradually at first before stiffening near the summit, with few kinks or corners to break the misery.

OPPOSITE: The view back down the Urkiola towards Mañaria and, beyond that, Durango. This is the very heart of Basque cycling country.

traditionally featuring a double ascent of the Urkiola and finishing opposite the religious sanctuary at the top.

The Irish rider Daniel Martin rode over the Urkiola in the 2011 Tour of the Basque Country and said afterwards that two things struck him about the climb: one, its difficulty, and two, the atmosphere there on race days.

'The climb is horrible,' Martin said. 'It's steep and it just goes pretty much straight the whole way up. It reminds me a bit of the Navacerrada outside Madrid: it's a big road with two lanes and a bit of a shoulder, but that creates an optical illusion, makes you think it's less steep than it turns out to be. The other thing that really surprised me about the Urkiola was the crowd. We're used, in Europe these days, to pretty small, aging crowds at most stage races outside the major tours, but on the Urkiola at the Tour of the Basque Country there was a massive, young and passionate audience. You can tell how much cycling means to them in this part of the world.'

The Basque Ventoux

Steep and straight is how the Urkiola begins its course out of Mañaria, with the summits of the Mugarra and Untzillaitz as natural grandstands. The gradient here is around ten per cent, which is roughly where it stays for the remainder of the ascent. The toughest stretch of the first half comes when the road darts left and then right up the Kalero wall in the second kilometre, then uncreases to face the second of the four ramrods that make up almost all of the Urkiola's 5.7 kilometres. The longest of these sections is the third one – two-and-a-half interminable kilometres through woodland ending with a kink to the right, then left to face one of the most feared stretches on any Spanish climb: the 400-metre, 14 per cent Txakurzulo ramp. In 2009, as has often been the case, the Subida a Urkiola was decided here, with the Basque rider Igor Anton's solo

attack. As a boy in the mid-1990s, Anton had stood at the roadside and watched his idol, the great Italian climber Marco Pantani, suffer a rare defeat at the hands of a fellow tragic hero, the Spaniard José Maria Jiménez. On winning in 2009, Anton said that he had fulfilled a dream that took root that day. Speaking for all Basque cyclists, he also said, 'The Urkiola is our Galibier, our Mont Ventoux.'

Like the Ventoux, the Urkiola can seem both sinister and sacred, particularly when the Anboto is shrouded in what they call here *sirimiri* – the dense, dank mist that often collects over the Basque mountains. The pass itself is situated at 713 metres above sea level, but the road continues to rise sharply for another 400 metres before peaking at the *Urkiolako Santutegia*, or Urkiola Sanctuary, at an altitude of 752 metres. The neo-medieval church is now the centrepiece of an assortment of religious buildings and monuments huddled around the summit, some of which have been traced back as far as the 13th century.

Political tension and the threat of attacks from Basque separatist groups kept the Vuelta a España out of the Basque Country for 33 years, but the race finally returned to the region, and the Urkiola, in 2011. It was a timely reinstatement, not least because the Subida had hit financial difficulties that led to the race's cancellation in 2010.

The most noteworthy performance on the Urkiola in that year, in fact, may well have come from a 22-year-old Basque gentleman by the name of Alexander de la Huerta. He wouldn't have broken any speed record – it took de la Huerta one hour and eight minutes to reach the summit – but he was the first cyclist ever to climb the Urkiola... sitting on the handlebars of his bike and pedalling backwards.

De la Huerta claimed to be 'very proud' of his achievement. He may also have been smarter than people first thought: on a climb as hard as the Urkiola who wouldn't, after all, rather contemplate what's already accomplished, and not what tortures lie in wait?

Fact file Puerto de Urkiola

From Mañaria

REGION: Biscay, Basque Country, Spain

ACCESS: From Mañaria follow the BI-623 through the Calle de Solaguren

HEIGHT: 713m (to Puerto – road continues to climb to 752m)

LENGTH: 5.7km (to Puerto – road continues 400 metres to Urkiola Sanctuary)

ALTITUDE GAIN: 524m

AVERAGE GRADIENT: 9.19%

MAXIMUM GRADIENT: 14% (at km 4.7, in Txakurzulo)

OPEN: Depending on weather

REFRESHMENTS: At the bottom and at the top

ALTERNATIVE ROUTES: From Otxandio (5km at 2.9%)

Puerto 10.7 7.0
10.4
Txakurzulo 9.8
9.9
7.7
9.8
Mañaria 7.9

752n
500n
250n

1 2 3 4 5 6

Durango E70 A8
BI-623
MAÑARIA
PUERTO DE URKIOLA
BI-623
N
0 2 km
0 1 mile
SPAIN
metres
1000
750
500

Il Ghisallo
754m Italy

❝ A CENTURY OF CYCLE RACES HAS GIVEN US MANY 'SACRED' MOUNTAINS – but one just a little more holy than all the rest. ❞

At the risk of lapsing into hyperbole, there are pockets of Europe where the sport of cycling evokes not only the fanaticism but also the language of religion. More than in football or indeed any other sport – perhaps owing to the dual canons of dedication and sacrifice, as well as cycling's divine natural canvases – the lexicon overflows with notions of sanctity and veneration. Thus, a century of cycle races has given us many 'sacred' mountains – but one just a little more holy than all the rest.

The climb from Bellagio to the Santuario della Madonna del Ghisallo on a southern spur of Lake Como took its first communion in the 1919 Tour of Lombardy. Considered brutish at the time, particularly in its first and final thirds, the Ghisallo's merits were twofold: firstly, eight years after the Giro d'Italia's first trip to over 2,000 metres at Sestriere, the Ghisallo introduced cycling's one-day Classics to the joys and agonies of the mountains; secondly, nowhere in Lombardy were the essence and colours of autumn more vividly condensed than in the Triangolo Lariano, between the southern tentacles of Lake Como, or in particular on the misty peaks above the village of Magreglio.

That maiden ascent saw the first of the Italian *campionissimi*, Costante Girardengo, triumph, and so began a long and star-studded tradition.

Six years later, in 1925, a young Italian plasterer living over the border in France arrived on the train from Nice, attracted by the 500-lire prize for the first rider over the Ghisallo. No one knew Alfredo Binda. Reputation, though, counted for little on the Ghisallo, as the *nouveau venu* attacked and dropped the peloton. On finally catching him, the defending Lombardy champion Giovanni Brunero demanded, 'So who are you?' With hindsight, Binda might have replied that he was a future winner of five Giri d'Italia and four Tours of Lombardy.

A spiritual journey

An old folk tale had it that the Santuario had been built by the Madonna herself in the Middle Ages, at the (last) request of a gentleman named Ghisallo as he was attacked by brigands. As time went on, in the 1930s and '40s, the climb's decisive role in the Tour of Lombardy and, more occasionally, the Giro, turned the chapel into a place of pilgrimage for cyclists. In 1949, Pope Pius XII proclaimed the Madonna del Ghisallo their patron saint. Pius blessed a torch that was then carried by the nation's best riders all the way to the Ghisallo. The unofficial pontiffs of Italian sport, Fausto Coppi and Gino Bartali, were the last to bear the flame.

Nine years earlier, almost on the eve of the Second World War, a young man whose name would later become inextricably linked to the Ghisallo scaled it for the first time with the Italian national

amateur team. Hailing from Monza, just outside Milan, Fiorenzo Magni would later go on to win the Giro three times and become the 'third man' on the margins of the Coppi–Bartali duopoly. Half a century later, in his 80s, he would also lobby hard and eventually obtain permission for the construction of a museum to house the vast collection of memorabilia that cyclists had donated to the Santuario over the decades. In 2006, after years of difficulties and disputes, the splendid museum finally opened. It now welcomes visitors from all over the globe and boasts pearls including bikes ridden to victory on the Tour de France by Eddy Merckx, Coppi and Bartali.

Cyclists whose spiritual journeys are more concerned with the climb itself remark that it is harder than either its statistics or reputation suggest. The first six kilometres out of Bellagio are, for the most part, horribly steep. They clamber in serpentine squiggles through dense woodland, with some vicious 14 per cent slopes in the third and fourth kilometres out of Bellagio. In the village of Guello, a kilometre-and-a-half of false flat followed by an equal portion of downhill do, it's true, draw the sting from what would otherwise be an unpleasant last two kilometres. The Santuario and museum lie off the road to the left at the summit, before the ramrod-straight descent towards Canzo and, if you wish, a right turn after seven kilometres towards the Colma and the Muro di Sormano.

ABOVE: A view across Lake Como to Bellagio and, behind it, the Ghisallo. In recent years the lake's shores have become a magnet for the glitterati – actor George Clooney, among others, owns a property here.

Interviewed in 2011, Magni said that a climb that Paolo Bettini scooted up in 19 minutes, 30 seconds at the 2005 Tour of Lombardy was once considered 'a terror'. 'It's not the awful climb it once was, before the road was paved, but it's still a tough one,' Magni said. 'It was once one of the best-known mountains to cyclists in Lombardy – now it's one of the most famous climbs in the world. It's always held a very special place in my heart, ever since that first time in 1939. In the years after that, it became my favourite training climb, along with the Onno – the road that climbs up from the lake and intersects with the descent off the Ghisallo.'

BELOW: A sight of the summit and the famous chapel that became so full of memorabilia deposited by cyclists that a museum had to be built to house the more prized pieces.

MADONNA DEL GHISALLO

CARABINIERI
BELLAGIO
localita'
ind'rizzo
telefono   031-9503

The Superghisallo: a climb to oblivion

The Triangolo Lariano that was once Magni's playpen has served the same purpose for generations of cyclists in Lombardy. For years they longed for the Muro di Sormano to be restored to a decent state, which it was, and to the Lombardy route, which it almost certainly never will be. Today some of them harbour the same hopes for another climb even closer to the Ghisallo, the Superghisallo, which also figured briefly on the Lombardy route in the early 1960s, and which also provoked outrage.

Discovered by Lombardy and Giro chief Vincenzo Torriani in his never-ending quest for better races, harder climbs and more pizzazz, the Superghisallo combined the difficult first section of its sibling from Bellagio to Guello with a longer and tougher second portion accessed via a right-hand turn towards Monte San Primo. After a brief section of false flat, the road kinked up for four kilometres from Cernobbio to Pian Rancio, 975 metres above sea level, at an average gradient of seven per cent. A four-kilometre descent then returned the riders to the small square by the Santuario. From there they would descend to face the murderous Muro.

Described as 'a climb more suited to cyclo-cross' and 'even more exhausting than the Ghisallo' in pre-race previews, the Superghisallo was not, it's true, a great success. Perhaps wrongly entangled with the Muro in the blame game after that ludicrously difficult 1961 race, its stay of execution lasted just 12 months and one more race. It has never returned and probably never will.

Even the Ghisallo itself has rarely proved critical in recent years, with the Lombardy route an increasingly moveable feast, tweaked almost annually. Bettini's brace of wins, in 2005 and 2006, were rare reminders of the Ghisallo's glory years. The latter served up one of the mountain's most memorable days, as Bettini took charge on the climb then rode all the way to victory with tears streaming down his face. Three weeks earlier he had won the World Championship road race; nine days after that his brother had died in a car accident.

The 2006 season had also seen a more unseemly incident play out in the shadow of the Santuario, with Gilberto Simoni accusing the Giro d'Italia champion-elect Ivan Basso of trying to bribe him on live TV, then waving away Basso's offer of a conciliatory handshake.

It'll take more than that, though, to displace the halo that hangs in those mists above the Ghisallo's 'sacred' peak. When you go, more than a prayer, Fiorenzo Magni says, 'you'll need to pedal'. Because as the old man reminds us, 'in the mountains there are no secrets and no saviour except your legs.'

ABOVE: The road to the Superghisallo, the mutant climb unearthed by Tour of Lombardy boss Vincenzo Torriani in the 1960s, and which combines the difficult first section of the Ghisallo to Guello with a longer and tougher loop towards Monte San Primo.

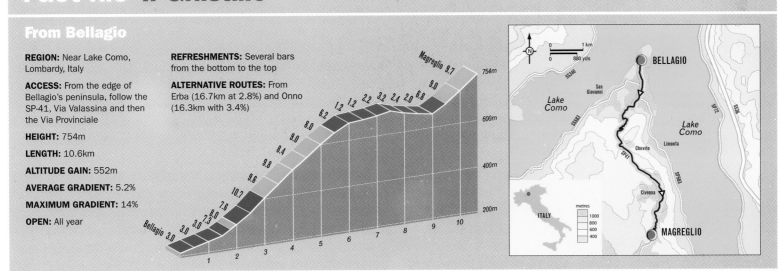

Fact file Il Ghisallo

From Bellagio

REGION: Near Lake Como, Lombardy, Italy

ACCESS: From the edge of Bellagio's peninsula, follow the SP-41, Via Valassina and then the Via Provinciale

HEIGHT: 754m

LENGTH: 10.6km

ALTITUDE GAIN: 552m

AVERAGE GRADIENT: 5.2%

MAXIMUM GRADIENT: 14%

OPEN: All year

REFRESHMENTS: Several bars from the bottom to the top

ALTERNATIVE ROUTES: From Erba (16.7km at 2.8%) and Onno (16.3km with 3.4%)

1,000m +

Croce d'Aune
1,015m   **Italy**

The Croce d'Aune looks to all intents an unremarkable mountain pass, overhung and overshadowed by many higher and more magnificent Dolomite peaks, submerged in woodland and, it seems, anonymity. It boasts neither legendarily steep slopes nor outstanding vistas, nor indeed any other great distinguishing features. As for the town where the least insignificant of the routes to the summit begins, Pedavena, well, it does own a brewery. And there the tourist attractions run bone dry.

Eight-and-a-half kilometres and just over 700 vertical metres away, though, at the summit of the Croce, rises a statue famed throughout the cycling world and commemorating a moment as important as any in the evolution of the racing bicycle. Its inscription bears a date, November 11, 1927, and a name, that of Tullio Campagnolo. The rest is engraved in cycling folklore.

The son of a hardware-store owner from Vicenza in northeast Italy, the young Tullio was a gifted and ambitious engineer who had turned his hand to building bikes and railroads in the years that followed the First World War. He was also a moderately gifted cyclist, not that races at the time were necessarily a pure test of athletic ability. Take this one, the Gran Premio della Vittoria: on the Croce d'Aune, Tullio might easily have been romping away towards victory – or at least lurching over the summit faster than his opponents – yet here he was barely able to detach his frozen fingers from the handlebars. This spelled trouble: changing gears in those days meant unscrewing the rear wheel by hand, flipping it through 180 degrees and using the single sprocket on the other side of the central hub. With numb hands, what was usually little more than a time-consuming inconvenience now became an impossibility. '*Bisogno cambiá qualcossa de drio!*' ('We need to change something back here!') cursed Tullio in his nasally Vicentino dialect as he wrestled furiously with the nuts holding the wheel steadfastly in place. Meanwhile, rivals sped by, and Tullio's chances of victory with them.

But so much more was at stake that day than local bragging rights or a cheap piece of silverware. Three years later, inspired by his misadventure on the Croce d'Aune and after endless tinkering, Tullio had perfected the quick-release wheel mechanism that remains *de rigueur* on all but the cheapest of mass-produced bicycles today. As with all great innovations, its genius lay in its simplicity: a skewer slotted through the hollow axle of the wheel, a cone nut at one end, a short lever for securing and releasing the wheel at the other, and cycling had its equivalent of the corkscrew or the can-opener.

As the popularity of the new quick-release mechanism spread, so did Tullio Campagnolo's reputation as an engineering visionary. It was destined to grow yet further; having registered his company in Vicenza's Corso Padova in 1933, Campagnolo set his sights on the next frontier of component design – gearing. Although not the first system to dispense with the old wheel-flipping rigmarole, Campagnolo's dual-rod solution was viewed as the gold standard by amateurs and professionals alike for much of the 1940s. Its successor, the Gran Sport, launched in 1950, can be considered to represent the last quantum leap in gear technology prior to the advent of electric gearing in the third millennium. It was also the first system to employ a rear derailleur of similar form and functionality to that still widely used post-2000.

Like a gnat in the presence of an elephant

Andy Schleck's skipping chain on stage 17 of the 2010 Tour de France notwithstanding (not made by Campagnolo, incidentally), few would ever argue now that choice of componentry is often the decisive factor in cycling's major races. In the years immediately pre- and post-war, however, as Fausto Coppi and Gino Bartali united Italy's collective obsession with their rivalry while also splitting its allegiance down the centre, the legend of Campagnolo soared not least because his was the age when components could also be kingmakers. Just as the infamous episode on the Croce d'Aune had cost Tullio Campagnolo, so Giri d'Italia and Tours de France were won and lost – in Bartali and Coppi's case, usually won – by the consistency or capriciousness of whatever gear system the rider had chosen, and his skill at using it.

ABOVE: Not one of the lovelier cycling monuments, the stone structure commemorating Tullio Campagnolo's eureka moment on the Croce d'Aune is nonetheless one of the more significant.

ABOVE: The region around the Croce d'Aune offers some beautiful cycling, with climbs such as the Passo Manghen, Cima di Campo and Monte Grappa all in close proximity.

ABOVE: Largely immersed in dense forest, the Croce d'Aune can be an asphyxiating climb, reminiscent in places of the Plateau de Bonascre in the Pyrenees and Prato Nevoso in the Italian Alps.

Culturally, as well, Campagnolo had begun to establish itself as an Italian national treasure. Vittorio di Sica's classic 1948 neo-realist film *Ladri di Bicicletta*, or 'Bicycle Thieves', featured bikes equipped with Campagnolo Corsa components. Some 40 years later, Tullio, who died in 1983, may or may not have been wheel-spinning in his grave when his now iconic signature appeared on caps and clothing in the cult American basketball movie, *White Men Can't Jump*. Either way, here was eloquent confirmation of how far and how loudly his legacy now resonated.

Julio Marquevich, president of Campagnolo USA, once said of meeting the company's founder, 'I felt like a gnat in the presence of an elephant.' Tullio's son, Valentino, must have felt similarly daunted upon stepping out of that elephant's shadow in 1983, yet went on to successfully consolidate Campagnolo's position as cycling's most fêted brand name. In his first decade at the helm, under growing threat from Japanese rival Shimano and the rise in popularity of mountain biking, the galleon teetered but stayed afloat thanks largely to continued success among the pro road-racing elite. In what since the 1970s had essentially been a duopoly, Shimano took until 1999 to break Campagnolo's stranglehold on overall victory at the Tour de France.

Times were tougher in the following decade, but the one constant with Campagnolo was and would always be the mystique whose origins nestled among the peaks to the north of Vicenza, on the Croce d'Aune. Campagnolo, in turn, nourished the legend of the climb by making it the centrepiece of their prestigious mass-participation ride, the Granfondo Campagnolo. Renamed the GF Sportful in 2009, the event and its thousands of entrants continue to visit the Croce d'Aune every year.

300 punctures

The Giro d'Italia has also made sporadic trips, once with significant consequences. Stage 8 of the 1964 Giro took the peloton over the Passo Rolle, the first Dolomite pass the race had ever climbed in 1937, before heading the 'wrong' way over the Croce d'Aune before a stage finish in front of, you guessed it, the brewery in Pedavena. Aptly, as in 1927, it wasn't the climb of the Croce d'Aune that posed problems but the demands it placed on the riders' equipment: arguably the best climber in the race and hence the pre-stage favourite, Vito Taccone, punctured seven times on the execrable gravel surface of the descent into Pedavena, losing all hope of victory. The *Corriere delle Alpi* later reported that Taccone had finished the stage possessed by a 'legendary rage' and that the Croce d'Aune had cost the peloton 'something like 300 punctures – definitely a record'. *La Stampa*'s reporter spoke of a 'hecatomb of tyres' caused by the 'disastrous conditions of the final descent'. 'A hecatomb, I tell you,' the outraged correspondent went on, 'with one poor soul after another, barely visible on the narrow dust road as they waved their wheels above their head, calling for assistance. The rider who didn't puncture was the winner.' Precisely – the unfancied yet fortunate Marcello Mugnaini.

The Giro returned to the Croce d'Aune in 2009 in its centenary edition. The road was now tarmacked and the ascent from Pedavena too far from that day's finish at San Martino di Castrozzo to induce any real drama, mechanically-induced or otherwise.

That climb, though, should not be underestimated. The first kilometre out of Pedavena is deeply unpleasant, and the road thereafter features long and straight sections affording little recovery from that initial battering. The climate in this corner of Italy is also uncomfortably clammy, even at relatively high altitudes, as anyone who has cycled on or around the nearby Monte Grappa will know.

On and among the surrounding mountains, though, lie undiscovered jewels such as the climbs of Cima di Campo or the Passo San Boldo for the cyclist, or for the tourist the exquisite town of Feltre and the Altopiano di Asiago, so evocatively described in the novels of Mario Rigoni Stern. *Per se* and in this company, Pedavena and the Croce d'Aune may be small beer; to aficionados of cycling's greatest inventions, however, there may be no more iconic destination.

ABOVE: The final metres of climbing before the summit of the Croce d'Aune, tackled from Pedavena. Note the smooth road surface: a far cry from the 1964 Giro d'Italia and the 'hecatomb of tyres' that saw around 300 punctures.

Fact file Croce d'Aune

From Pedavena

REGION: Veneto, Italy

ACCESS: Go to Feltre on the SS50. In Feltre, follow Via Carlo Rizzarda, then Viale Farra and Viale Pedavena. From Pedavena, follow Via Trento, turn left and take Via Belvedere to the top

HEIGHT: 1,015m

LENGTH: 8.57km

ALTITUDE GAIN: 665m

AVERAGE GRADIENT: 7.8%

MAXIMUM GRADIENT: 12% (short section between km 0.7 and 1.2)

OPEN: Depending on weather

REFRESHMENTS: Bars in Pedavena, at the Albergo Croce d'Aune (km 6.5) and at the summit

ALTERNATIVE ROUTES: From Ponte d'Oltra (11.5km at 5.3%)

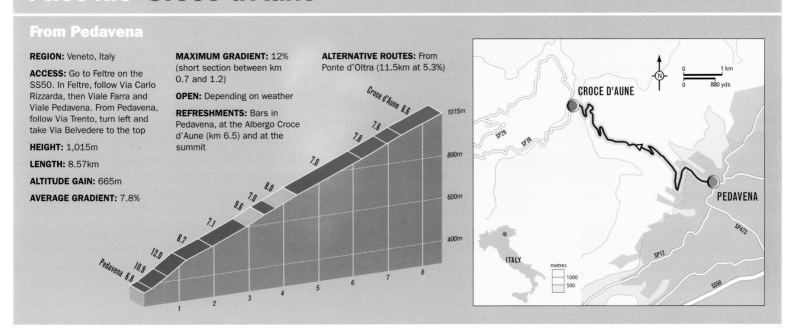

Montée Laurent Jalabert 1,057m

France

The two events were 29 years apart in time and even further in nature, yet somehow they each turned the aerodrome on the Mont Mimat above Mende, albeit briefly, into a beacon of French national pride.

The first was the filming of the last, memorable scene of Louis de Funès's 1966 comic masterpiece, *La Grande Vadrouille* (The Great Stroll) – still by some gauges the most popular French film ever. The second, aptly, occurred on an identical spot on Bastille Day in 1995.

If it was possible to capture and condense the essence of the Tour de France into a single stage, this was the day. The sun dazzled, the Massif Central throbbed and France was about to revel. Two hundred and six years on from the real thing, a Frenchman was about to storm the Tour's equivalent of the Bastille – four-time winner Miguel Indurain and his Spanish Banesto team's fortress. Laurent Jalabert's ONCE squad was professional cycling's revolutionary army, and Jalabert was about to single-handedly create the legend of a climb that, until that day, had never even featured in the Tour.

The previous year, the prodigiously talented, panda-eyed Jalabert had made the headlines for different reasons at the Tour. In a bunch sprint to Armentières on stage one, he had crashed shockingly into the roadside crash barriers, his ensuing somersault ending in a pool of blood and a chorus of gasps from the watching millions. The Frenchman was lucky to be alive – and he knew it. From that day on, fearing a repeat, he abandoned his flourishing career as a sprinter to focus on other disciplines – climbing, time-trialling and cultivating the 'punch', precisely, that would be perfect for a short, steep climb like the 3.32-kilometre, 9.5 per cent Côte de la Croix Neuve over the Mont Mimat above Mende. 'You have to go about this abrupt ascent like a *puncheur* (boxer),' wrote Dominique Julien of *L'Humanité* on the eve of the Tour's 2010 visit. 'Basically, Mende is a ring. A knock-out is in the air at any moment. The leaders will have to forget about their jabs, and unleash their left then right, with millimetre precision. There's some of Mike Tyson in this sharp incline.'

For one afternoon, Jalabert was Mike Tyson, and by the end of the day it would be Indurain, the so-called Tourminator who lay bloodied, if not beaten on the canvas. Wearing the green jersey reserved for the leader of the points competition, Jalabert attacked on a descent 24 kilometres into the 222.5 stage from Saint-Étienne to Mende and was joined by the Italian, Dario Bottaro. Twenty kilometres later, the pair of kamikazes were going nowhere fast, their advantage having plateaued at around 30 seconds – a heartbeat in professional cycling terms. Bottaro suggested they were doomed. But for reasons that escaped even his understanding, Jalabert seemed possessed – or at least inspired. 'I was getting cheesed off. I said to myself that I was maybe making a big mistake. But not being able to get away was hacking me off, so I said to myself: if they want to come back, they'd better hang on for dear life.'

Jalabert's glory, Indurain's record

The game changed when four more riders, including two of Jalabert's ONCE team-mates, attacked from the main bunch and bridged the gap to the two leaders. Indurain's Banesto were thrown into disarray. The fugitives' advantage had rocketed to nearly 11 minutes by the time they reached Pradelles, with 130 kilometres covered. Jalabert was now *maillot jaune virtuel* – the theoretical leader of the Tour. By the time he sailed into Mende, through an avenue flanked by plane trees and euphoric Frenchmen, up the chemin des Tilleuls, past the cemetery, then onto the first 12 per cent ramp of the Côte de la Croix Neuve – the Mike Tyson climb – it was time for Jalabert to deliver his *coup de grâce*. He did so with an uppercut that floored his fellow escapees and sealed Mende, the Mont Mimat and the Côte de la Croix Neuve's place in French sporting affections forever.

Jalabert hadn't won the yellow jersey and neither could he or ONCE prevent Indurain from winning his fifth Tour title. His victory also came with the same caveats as almost any other exploit in the doping-addled age of the early and mid-1990s. Two key figures in his metamorphosis were, after all, ONCE doctor Nicolas Terrados and the team's manager, Manolo Saiz. Three years later, Terrados would be charged with importing doping products in the Tour's biggest ever scandal, the so-called Festina Affair. Meanwhile, Saiz withdrew the entire ONCE team from racing that year with the parting message: 'I've stuck my finger up the Tour de France's a**e.' Saiz was arrested in the even more sordid Operación Puerto drugs bust in 2006.

Jalabert's greatest ever day at the Tour did, though, remain so synonymous with the climb of the Croix Neuve that in 2005 the mayor of Mende, Jean-Jacques Delmas, announced that it would be renamed the Montée Laurent Jalabert. Not only that, but amateurs could now

stamp a ticket at the bottom of the climb and then again at the top and compare their time to those of leading pros in the Tour and other races that have finished here. As of 2011, the record was thought to belong to the trio of Indurain, Marco Pantani and Bjarne Riis, who shot up in eight minutes, 40 seconds in their belated pursuit of Jalabert in 1995. Alberto Contador took just over a minute longer on both of his triumphant ascents in the 2007 and 2010 editions of Paris–Nice. Laurent Dufaux, Alexandre Vinokourov and Sven Montgomery also all won on the Croix Neuve in the now discontinued Midi Libre stage race.

The mountains of the Massif Central and in particular the Cévennes haven't often had a major impact on the Tour de France. Mont Aigoual, the highest peak in the range and centrepiece of Tim Krabbe's fictional *The Rider*, offers more variety than the Croix Neuve

ABOVE LEFT: Low down on the Côte de la Croix Neuve, before a tight left-hand bend sends the road soaring over Mende and onto a magnificent terrace above the town.

ABOVE RIGHT: The *Croix Neuve* or New Cross at the summit. The finish line for Tour de France stages has traditionally been placed a few hundred metres further on, in the middle of the aerodrome where *La Grande Vadrouille* was filmed.

and more in the way of aesthetics, yet has featured in the Tour just once, in 1987. By contrast, thanks to an unforgettable afternoon of sport in 1995, what turned into the Montée Laurent Jalabert also became the Cévennes' *montée emblematique*, not to mention the cycling Bastille that was nearly the scene of a French revolution.

Fact file Montée Laurent Jalabert

From Mende

REGION: Lozère, southern Massif Central

ACCESS: From Mende, Route du Faubourg-Saint-Gervais, then Route de l'Aérodrome

HEIGHT: 1,057m (1,050m at Tour de France finish line)

LENGTH: 3.3km

ALTITUDE GAIN: 317m

AVERAGE GRADIENT: 9.5%

MAXIMUM GRADIENT: 12.4%

OPEN: All year

REFRESHMENTS: Numerous bars at the bottom, in Mende

Muro di Sormano
1,107m

Italy

'A two-kilometre-high spiral staircase… A torment. A joke. Impossible. Absurd,' swooned *Procycling* magazine of the Muro di Sormano, not skimping on rhetoric, but accurately describing the awful reality lurking in the verdant peaks above Lake Como.

For 40 years, even for many cyclists growing up in the bike-besotted region of Lombardy, the Muro with its average 17 per cent gradient seemed to belong to the realm of legend – its name uttered only in hushed tones of fear and reverence. Forty years was also how long it had languished in near disuse and disrepair after a rise to notoriety as short and steep as the climb itself at the beginning of the 1960s. Miffed at the Tour of Lombardy's sudden inability to produce a winner worthy of one of cycling's monumental Classics, one day in 1960, race organizer Vincenzo Torriani set off with *Gazzetta dello Sport* journalist Rino Negri to see for himself a climb that, according to the Legnano team's director Eberardo Pavesi, would make their eyes boggle and stomachs lurch. 'More than a road, it was a kind of goat track,' Negri later recalled. 'I told him that the riders would have to go by foot because there were sections at 25 per cent. Torriani rubbed his hands and said that everyone would be talking about the race.'

Torriani got his wish, but Negri was right – any riders who didn't hop off and walk or run were pushed by spectators when the race officials weren't looking. What he also got were protests from those who believed that the Muro had turned the race into a farce. Yet far from heeding them, Torriani switched the finish of the following year's race from Milan to Como, much closer to the Muro and the apocalypse it would once again provoke.

'I can't fathom the reason why Torriani wanted a novelty like this,' huffed Ercole Baldini after that 1961 race won by Vito Taccone. 'I understand that the Ghisallo didn't offer the guarantee of breaking the race up any more, but frankly he's gone overboard in the opposite direction. This climb is simply beastly, impossible to get up.'

The irony was that no one went faster up the Muro than Baldini, not that year and not ever in the Tour of Lombardy. Years later Baldini would admit to Torriani that he was 'ashamed to hold the record'. 'Having lots of fans meant getting lots of pushes… and I had lots of fans,' he grinned. After just two years, the Muro had become a theatre of savage cruelty and the tragicomic. Thus, in 1961, various newspapers reported that Taccone had overcome the 'frightening Mauro di Sormano', mistaking the mountain for a man. The same year, Ottavio Cogliati recalled of his ordeal on the Muro: 'When I got there, everyone was too worn out to push the riders, especially someone two metres tall like me. I screamed "Puncia!" at one fan, which means 'push' in my local dialect, but he confused it with 'punch'. "Sorry," he said, "I've only got Coca-Cola". I didn't know whether to laugh or cry.'

Torriani had created a monster – and one that would soon rear up and bite him on the backside. In 1962, the Muro figured on the Lombardy route for the third straight year, and fans flocked to what they now knew was cycling's most spectacular circus. Which would have been fine, except that whole troupes of *tifosi* (fans) had now come with the sole aim of pushing their favourite rider over the summit. Critics of Torriani's 'silly gimmick' had been vindicated; the Muro had to go, which it did, and over the next four decades the road but not the folklore it inspired slowly crumbled.

Open-air museum

In perhaps any other region of Italy, or indeed the world, that would have been that, but the sport's roots in Lombardy grow strong and deep. On the cusp of the millennium, a group of local cyclists set about lobbying support for the climb to be rescued from the disintegrating state that made it accessible only to mountain bikes. The Region of Lombardy also pledged 150,000 euros to resurface and reinvent the Muro. In its second coming, it would be more than a *muro* (wall) and more than even a road. Instead, local architect Franco Tagliabue Volontè drew up plans for what *Procycling* magazine called 'part hill, part hell and part open-air museum'. In fact, when the Muro reopened in 2006, riders from the Como area and much further afield discovered that the context for their uphill agony was a work of art – just over two kilometres of pristine asphalt, entirely closed to motorized traffic, and beautifully stencilled with notice of every metre gained in altitude, names and diagrams of the native foliage, plus the split times and terrorized soundbites of *campioni* who came and wilted on the Muro in those three Tours of Lombardy in the 1960s.

Thus, by now moving so slowly that, as *Procycling* put it, '[one] can not only read what's written on the road, but also check the punctuation, spelling and grammar', the Muro-defying masochist rounds the final hairpin onto a stunning natural balcony adorned with the words of Gino

TORRIANI HAD CREATED A MONSTER – and one that would soon rear up and bite him on the backside.

BELOW: One of a series of soundbites from the Muro di Sormano's golden age, now stencilled onto the tarmac to provide a running commentary of the uphill ordeal. This quote was from the legendary Italian rider, Gino Bartali.

Bartali. The adjective *difficilissimo* will require no translation, but used here by Bartali it seems almost euphemistic; more vivid and accurate is his description of the 'frightful' ramps that abate only in Colma – that is, when the ordeal ends and the Muro rejoins the *strada provinciale* connecting Asso and Pian del Tivano.

The chances of the Muro ever returning to the Tour of Lombardy are, alas, somewhat slim. A number of professionals have tackled the climb in recent years and reached a unanimous verdict: used in a pro race, the climb would cause a bloodbath. Perhaps unsurprisingly given the precedent set by Torriani, current Lombardy and Giro d'Italia chief Angelo Zomegnan seemed dubious about the Muro ever featuring in either race when quizzed in 2010.

'The Muro di Sormano is still a really appealing and unfortunately improbable idea,' Zomegnan, usually someone with a taste for the extreme, sighed. 'If we put it on the Lombardy route, together with the Ghisallo, the race would be decided a long way from the finish line; and if we put it on the Giro route, it would have to be very close to the stage finish, unless we considered it for a mountain time trial. Nevertheless, if the local authorities show their interest, we'll be ready to look into possible solutions.'

While amateur riders savoured that prospect, they could also enrol in the annual time trial, La Carica dei 101, that now takes place on the Muro every autumn. In 2009 local rider Matteo Cappè slashed the record for the climb to seven minutes, 38 seconds. That was nearly two minutes faster than Baldini managed in 1962.

Those not satisfied with such short doses of self-harm can also combine the Muro with the nearby and more famous Ghisallo, climbed from Bellagio, or its Siamese twin the Superghisallo. The alternative approach to the Ghisallo from Canzo in the south, and particularly the five kilometres from Canova to Sormano and the foot of the Muro, represent a stiff test of climbing in themselves. They are also, though, the tiny door into a miniature wonderland of wooded mountains – and one to which the frequent morning mists can lend an almost ethereal allure.

Impossible, absurd, but also beautiful and unique, the Muro has risen again. Oh, how it has risen.

LEFT: Just beyond the halfway point, with only 70 more metres of altitude still to gain, the vista opens up towards Canzo and the Ghisallo. The top ten split times from the 1962 Tour of Lombardy, the Muro's last, are painted on the road.

ABOVE: The gradient now nears 25 per cent as the Muro creeps above the 1,000-metre mark. The worst is nearly over – not that what follows will come as any comfort.

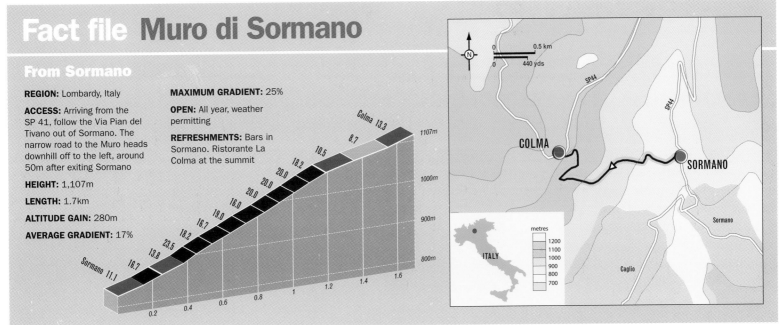

Fact file Muro di Sormano

From Sormano

REGION: Lombardy, Italy

ACCESS: Arriving from the SP 41, follow the Via Pian del Tivano out of Sormano. The narrow road to the Muro heads downhill off to the left, around 50m after exiting Sormano

HEIGHT: 1,107m

LENGTH: 1.7km

ALTITUDE GAIN: 280m

AVERAGE GRADIENT: 17%

MAXIMUM GRADIENT: 25%

OPEN: All year, weather permitting

REFRESHMENTS: Bars in Sormano. Ristorante La Colma at the summit

Lagos de Covadonga
1,135m
Spain

Spanish journalist Juanfran de la Cruz observed a few years ago that, like all sports, cycling has many myths and legends, but also the peculiarity that some are made of flesh and bone and others of tarmac road. 'The ascent to the Lagos de Covadonga,' de la Cruz wrote in *20minutos*, 'belongs to the second category, like Alpe d'Huez or the Tourmalet in France, like the Mortirolo or the Marmolada (Passo Fedaia) in Italy.'

If he was reading, Vuelta a España boss Victor Cordero at the time would have smiled. In the early 1980s, Cordero's predecessor Enrique Franco set out to find Spain's answer to Alpe d'Huez – the climb that had become a Tour de France icon in the space of a few years since the mid-1970s; never mind the mercury, iron and magnesium mined at La Bufferera near the summit, at Covadonga, Franco sensed he'd struck gold. Not long but devilishly steep and with two evil ramps at La Huesera and the Mirador de la Reina (literally The Queen's Look-Out), the Lagos could also boast something with which the Alpe wasn't particularly blessed: unspoilt natural beauty. With its two lakes beneath the summit, the Enol and the Ercina, and stunning views over the Picos de Europa, the site seemed the perfect antidote to the barren and indistinguishable summits of the deep south and the Sierras around Madrid.

PREVIOUS PAGE: The Lago de Enol, one of the two Lagos de Covadonga – or three if you count the 'phantom' Bricial Lake, which only appears about once every five years.

THIS PAGE: Above the clouds and the Mirador de la Reina, where the gradient ratchets up above ten per cent.

The 1983 Vuelta would, then, see two firsts: the first trip to the Lagos and the first stages broadcast live on Spanish television. Franco's new discovery would therefore get maximum exposure. Ironically, it also turned out to be the last ever stage that his successor Cordero's wife ever watched from the race course and not in front of the couple's television set at home. 'On the first left-hand bend, our car's front right wheel went over the edge and we nearly fell into the ravine,' Cordero, manager of the Zor team in that 1983 Vuelta, remembered in 2008. 'It really shook up my wife, so much so that she never went to watch a bike race live again.'

Lagos de Hinault

If Cordero was relieved, Franco was perhaps also glad to see a Spanish winner in Marino Lejarreta and, in world number one Bernard Hinault, a champion elect who had clearly relished the new climb. The Lagos had been wrongly identified as the Lagos de Enol before the race and now journalists took a further linguistic liberty, rechristening them the Lagos de Hinault. Hinault returned the favour by comparing the climb to, you guessed it, Alpe d'Huez. The Frenchman hailed the ascent as 'one of the hardest in the world'. Lejarreta admitted later that, more than the image of him lurching to victory ahead of Hinault and home favourites Julián Gorospe and Alvaro Pino, 'the Lagos really left their mark on the public'.

According to Victor Cordero, quite simply, 'a star was born that day'. 'It's a very spectacular ascent, the Vuelta's first trademark,' he added. In another interview with *20minutos*, Cordero spoke of the Vuelta's 'obligation to visit the Lagos at every possible opportunity'.

In 2006, that year's Tour de France champion Oscar Pereiro expressed similar sentiments, while also contributing to a fun, if meaningless debate that has exercised Spanish cyclists and fans

since the turn of the millennium: if, as Pereiro said, the Angliru was Spain's K-2, did that mean the Lagos was the superior (albeit inferior in height) Everest of the Iberian peninsula? Cycling writer José Carlos Carabias had asked more or less the same question in *ABC* newspaper during the 2001 Vuelta: 'In a radius of 100 kilometres, two colossi compete for the title of the most famous mountain in Spanish geography,' he wrote. The contenders, Carabias said, were in one corner the Angliru and its 'temple of pain' and in the other the 'symbolic' Lagos de Covadonga.

While the Angliru had the wow factor, by this time the Lagos could boast a short but memorable highlights reel. Spain's best and most cherished rider of the 1980s, Pedro Delgado, had laid the foundations for his 1985 Vuelta success here, then won again at the Lagos in 1992. The Colombian Lucho Herrera had also triumphed twice at the Lagos. And another brace of victories, from Laurent Jalabert in 1994 and 1996, confirmed the Frenchman's remarkable metamorphosis from sprinter to climber.

That 1996 race also represented Covadonga's consecration, not that it was a happy occasion for Spanish cycling. Miguel Indurain had lost the Vuelta leader's jersey to Delgado at the Lagos in 1985 and now, 11 years and five Tour de France victories later, Indurain's career ended not exactly on the climb to the Lagos, as has often been reported, but in front of the El Capitán hotel in Cangas de Onís, where his Banesto team was due to stay that night. There were 24 kilometres still to ride that day and nine stages in the Vuelta, but Indurain had had enough. Enough of the Vuelta, which his team had forced him to ride, enough of struggling in vain against the irrepressible ONCE squad, enough of the chest infection that had blighted him for nearly a week and enough of cycling, full stop. Almost 11 years later, fate would have it that the last of Indurain's former team-mates still racing, José Luis Arrieta, felt compelled to call time on his own career in an identical spot.

The phantom lake

As Spanish cycling lost Indurain, it acquired a new graveyard of champions, an imagined sanctuary to go with the real, neo-romantic Basílica de Santa María la Real at the foot of the climb and the Santa Cueva de Covadonga, the Holy Cave of Covadonga, hidden in the rocks above the church. The name Covadonga is derived from the Latin *cova dominica* – literally cave of the lady, in this case the Virgin of Covadonga, around whom assorted myths involving a hermit, a swarm of bees and local villains continue to mushroom. More importantly, Covadonga was reputedly the scene of the Asturian King Pelayo's defeat of the Moors in the eighth century and hence the beginning of Christianity's reconquest of Spain.

Another intriguing tale centres on a third lake, or at least 'phantom lake', the Bricial. Most who climb the Lagos will never see it, not because the Bricial is hidden behind an outcrop of the same name, 500 metres southwest of the Ercina, and not because it doesn't exist – but because it does so only rarely, or about every five years, according to the director of the Picos de Europa National Park, Rodrigo Suárez Robledano. The reason is that the lake forms, as if by magic, only after copious rainfall or the thaw following heavy falls of snow. When it does appear, Suárez Robledano says, the Bricial is a 'marvellous sight'.

Similar things had been said about Indurain during his reign at the Tour de France, but now his aura of invincibility had evaporated much in the same way as the Lago Bricial. Without even laying a wheel on the climb, still, somehow, Indurain had secured the legacy of the Lagos forever.

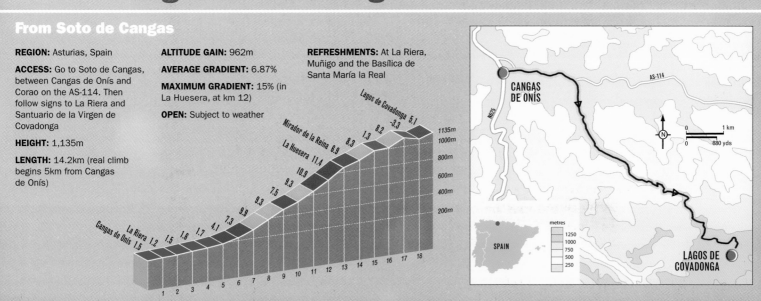

Fact file Lagos de Covadonga

From Soto de Cangas

REGION: Asturias, Spain

ACCESS: Go to Soto de Cangas, between Cangas de Onís and Corao on the AS-114. Then follow signs to La Riera and Santuario de la Virgen de Covadonga

HEIGHT: 1,135m

LENGTH: 14.2km (real climb begins 5km from Cangas de Onís)

ALTITUDE GAIN: 962m

AVERAGE GRADIENT: 6.87%

MAXIMUM GRADIENT: 15% (in La Huesera, at km 12)

OPEN: Subject to weather

REFRESHMENTS: At La Riera, Muñigo and the Basílica de Santa María la Real

Ballon d'Alsace
1,178m   **France**

The Ballon d'Alsace was not, contrary to popular mythology, the first mountain ever climbed by the riders of the Tour de France. That distinction fell, on the first day of the first Tour in 1903, to the 759-metre Col du Pin Bouchain near Roanne, whose sole claims to fame before or since are a visit from Napoleon Bonaparte at the start of the 19th century and his brief *contretemps* over the price of eggs in the Auberge du Perroquet. 'Are eggs so rare in this region that they justify such a bill?', the Little Corporal asked the owner of the hostelry. 'It's not the eggs that are rare, it's Emperors,' came the reply.

On day two of that inaugural 1903 race, *les forçats de la route* or 'convicts of the road' as journalist Albert Londres would later dub them, had scaled the 1,161-metre Col de la République near Saint Étienne, two full years before they would take on the Vosges mountains and the Ballon d'Alsace. Why, then, the Ballon is routinely cited as the col to which the Tour lost its mountain virginity in 1905 is anyone's guess. The most probable explanation is that Tour chief Henri Desgrange had got carried away in his own hype in the columns of *L'Auto*, billing the Ballon as more than just a mountain, the race's arrival as more than just sport; ever since 1871, when another Napoleon, the third, had lost a war and a large chunk of eastern France to Germany, the Alsace-Lorraine region and the Vosges highlands had, in fact, been the objects of patriotic yearning. More than a summit, more than a road, the Ballon also now marked the frontier with the cruel invader, and by venturing to its summit, the Tour was defying not only nature but Germany as well. The first man to the top (and the only one who stayed on his bike the whole way), René Pottier, would thus become an instant national hero – not to mention 'the first of the true climbers' in the words of Tour historian, Serge Laget.

Pottier, incidentally, committed suicide in January 1907, the victim of a broken heart. Six months earlier, in July 1906, he'd crossed the Ballon first once more in the Tour, again in a time of around half an hour from Saint Maurice sur Moselle, on his way to a 48-minute winning margin in Dijon.

Perhaps most significantly from the Tour's point of view, the Ballon continued the upward inflation that five years later culminated in the race's first trip to the Pyrenees, to be followed in 1911 by its maiden ascent of the Galibier in the Alps. In truth, the discovery that even the bigger ranges could be conquered by bike, albeit with great difficulty, rather stole the Ballon's thunder as far as the Tour was concerned.

Barely over 1,000 metres in altitude, it offered three access roads, but none that were genuinely difficult by the standards of most competent climbers. Most often, the race has headed from north to south over the route dating from the 18th century, climbing from Saint Maurice sur Moselle and descending into Malvaux. From Saint Maurice, the road to the pass measures just 9.5 kilometres in length and 6.9 per cent in gradient; from Malvaux it is three kilometres longer and on average 1.7 per cent less steep.

To say, then, that the Ballon was and is still easier than the legendary cols of the Alps and Pyrenees would be stating a fact. To say it is plain easy would, equally, be a gross misrepresentation. Marking as it does either the Tour's first or final highwire act, depending on whether the race is heading clockwise into the Alps or anticlockwise towards Paris, the Ballon has almost invariably caused some jitters if not substantial time gaps. A bad day on the Ballon before the Alps portends impending agonies; problems a day or two before Paris could mean losing everything.

On the highlight reel: Eugène Christophe's stage victory in Belfort in 1912, having tamed 'twists and turns that would make a bald man's hair stand up' on the Ballon, which the novelist-turned-Tour hack for a year Georges Rozet described as 'a giant, a sort of redoubtable god'; the revelation of Gino Bartali and his 'transcendent class on the Ballon' in the words of Tour director Desgrange in 1937; an epic stage ending atop the Ballon in 1967, with Raymond Poulidor floundering and his team-mate Roger Pingeon taking control of the Tour; another summit finish and Eddy Merckx's first Tour de France stage win on the way to the first of his overall Tour victories.

Ullrich on the brink

Stage 18 of the 1997 race could also be considered a miniature classic, albeit one nearly belonging to the second category of eleventh-hour disasters on the Ballon. The young German Jan Ullrich had dominated the Tour in the Pyrenees, consolidated in the Alps, then entered the Vosges with Frenchman Richard Virenque still champing but with worsening symptoms of bronchitis. More alarming still, unbeknownst to pretty much anyone outside his team, Ullrich's nerves were shredded. On the night before what ought to have been a straightforward stage over the Ballon and its neighbour, the Grand

PREVIOUS PAGE: Early on the road out of Malvaux, a typical Alsacian scene, with the road disappearing into the thick woods so characteristic of the Vosges mountains.

BELOW: Looking back down the Sewen road, two kilometres from the summit. This is perhaps the least well-known of the three ascents of the Ballon.

Ballon, so concerned were Ullrich's Telekom team bosses that they phoned around rival teams to solicit their pace-making help.

The next day, sure enough, Virenque attacked on the Grand Ballon, plunging Ullrich further into panic. Aided by his team-mate Udo Bölts, he would catch the Frenchman by the time they reached the foot of the Ballon, but in doing so teed Virenque up for the perfect, potentially lethal counter-punch: with two team-mates in the leading group, and Ullrich isolated but for Bölts, all Virenque had to do was attack repeatedly with his Festina cohorts Didier Rous and Pascal Hervé until the Telekom pair cracked. This is what any normal rider would have done; Virenque, though, as was confirmed to us the following year, was not only drug-

addled but also woefully dim-witted. As Rous and Hervé bolted out of the group and towards the most hollow of stage victories, Virenque glanced expectantly towards Ullrich, who looked in disbelief back at Virenque. Under no pressure to chase and with Virenque now outnumbered, he could coast towards Montbéliard and an emphatic first – and for Ullrich last – overall Tour crown.

In his autobiography *Ganz oder Gar Nicht*, Ullrich deduced from that day that 'the moderately difficult stages are the hardest ones to control' – and indeed the Vosges excel in unpredictable racing as well as sumptuous scenery. Like most of the major passes in the area, the three roads up the Ballon zigzag through dense and often misty woodland, like converging paths to the centre of an enchanted forest in a Grimm brothers' fairytale. From the clearing at the plateau, on relatively rare clear days, the Jura mountains to the south and beyond them the high Alps and Mont Blanc, line up magically along the horizon.

For Henri Desgrange, surveying the scene from the Ballon may well have been like glimpsing the Tour's future, nestling somewhere in among those higher peaks. The Pin-Bouchain had come first, but what did that have to do with the price of eggs – except where Napoleon had been concerned? At the Tour, Henri Desgrange played God; he decided what was a mountain, what was the first mountain, and what was not.

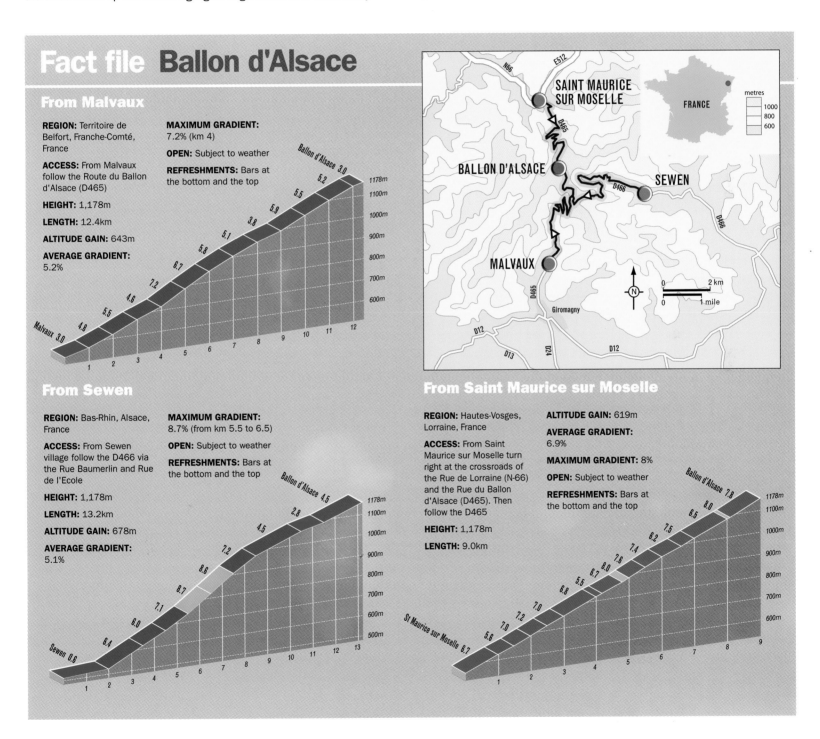

Fact file Ballon d'Alsace

From Malvaux

REGION: Territoire de Belfort, Franche-Comté, France

ACCESS: From Malvaux follow the Route du Ballon d'Alsace (D465)

HEIGHT: 1,178m

LENGTH: 12.4km

ALTITUDE GAIN: 643m

AVERAGE GRADIENT: 5.2%

MAXIMUM GRADIENT: 7.2% (km 4)

OPEN: Subject to weather

REFRESHMENTS: Bars at the bottom and the top

From Sewen

REGION: Bas-Rhin, Alsace, France

ACCESS: From Sewen village follow the D466 via the Rue Baumerlin and Rue de l'Ecole

HEIGHT: 1,178m

LENGTH: 13.2km

ALTITUDE GAIN: 678m

AVERAGE GRADIENT: 5.1%

MAXIMUM GRADIENT: 8.7% (from km 5.5 to 6.5)

OPEN: Subject to weather

REFRESHMENTS: Bars at the bottom and the top

From Saint Maurice sur Moselle

REGION: Hautes-Vosges, Lorraine, France

ACCESS: From Saint Maurice sur Moselle turn right at the crossroads of the Rue de Lorraine (N-66) and the Rue du Ballon d'Alsace (D465). Then follow the D465

HEIGHT: 1,178m

LENGTH: 9.0km

ALTITUDE GAIN: 619m

AVERAGE GRADIENT: 6.9%

MAXIMUM GRADIENT: 8%

OPEN: Subject to weather

REFRESHMENTS: Bars at the bottom and the top

Col de la Faucille
1,323m
France/Switzerland

If the gauge of a mountain's importance were the influence of a life it altered, the Col de la Faucille's place in any anthology of European elevations would be beyond dispute.

John Ruskin was the pre-eminent art critic of the 19th century, as well as one of its foremost social commentators, and the view of Mont Blanc from the Faucille changed his view of the world. In 1835, the London-born Ruskin was 16 years old and a newly published writer courtesy of the *Magazine of Natural History*. He had also, two years earlier, returned from a first family visit to Switzerland with memories and passions that threatened to overwhelm him, particularly of his first glimpse of the Alps from the town of Schaffhausen. Not even this, though, prepared Ruskin for the scene that awaited him, as it does anyone cresting the Faucille from the north in clear weather, on his next trip in 1835.

'The Col de la Faucille, on that day of 1835, opened to me in distinct vision the Holy Land of my future work and true home in this world,' Ruskin wrote in his unfinished autobiography *Praeterita*. 'My eyes had been opened, and my heart with them, to see and to possess royally such a kingdom!'

Ruskin's subsequent eulogies – his tableau of the 'sapphire lake' (Léman), the 'narcissus meads of Vevay [sic], the living plain, burning with human gladness, studded with white homes, a Milky Way of star-dwellings cast across its sunlit blue'– will mean little to those who have never crossed the Faucille and maybe also to many of those who have. His contention that most travellers arriving from Paris were too tired and too eager for their dinner and a rest in Geneva to let their gaze linger no longer applies; what persist are the vagaries of the weather which meant that Ruskin 'never [saw] that view perfectly but once – in this year 1835'.

Low cloud over Lac Léman below, or a fluffy veil across the entire chain of the Alps, are the most frequent saboteurs. In the absence of either, though, the skyline is the one that inspired Ruskin and many after him. Théodore Rousseau's *View of Mont Blanc, Seen from La Faucille* was described in the artist's biography as nothing short of 'one of the most beautiful pages of modern art'.

The road approaching the pass from Gex in the south is visible in the bottom right-hand corner of Rousseau's *chef d'oeuvre*. The other route to the top begins in Morez, deep in the Jura, the densely wooded, sparsely populated range of mountains sandwiched between the Vosges and the Alps on France's eastern extremity. It was from this direction that the Tour de France took on La Faucille for the first time in 1911, on the eve of the race's first ascent of the Col du Galibier. The Tour returned to Faucille 40 times over the following century, often with consequences greater than the climb's modest dimensions would suggest.

The first *domestique*

First to glimpse the Alps from the Faucille's regal lookout in that 1911 Tour was Maurice Brocco, who days later was also to become cycling's first ever *domestique* or 'servant'. Now a generic and sometimes noble term referring to any rider who forsakes personal glory to work for a team captain or leader, *domestique* was the most scathing insult Tour director Henri Desgrange could muster for Brocco and his antics in that Tour de France. Having capitulated and lost almost an hour on the other side of the Faucille, Brocco had seen his chances of overall glory disappear that afternoon in Chamonix, leaving him to plot other ways to enjoy a 'profitable' Tour. His solution was to illegally 'auction' his services to other riders. Desgrange lacked the proof to enforce a disqualification, but not the platform to shame him, and so dismissed Brocco as an 'unworthy *domestique*' on the pages of *L'Auto*. Brocco duly claimed revenge by winning the Pyrenean stage to Bayonne, and Desgrange in turn by finally excluding him; if Brocco had the strength and talent to win in the Pyrenees, he reasoned, only shady and ulterior motives could explain his lowly finishes in the earlier stages.

The first name on the Faucille's roll of honour was, then, an infamous one. In subsequent years, again in spite of the climb's modest difficulty, it favoured the strong and illustrious, with early Tour legends Eugène Christophe, Ottavio Bottechia and Antonin Magne all first across the summit in the pre-Second World War years. In 1931, the weather was so bad on the approach to the Faucille that the stage was neutralized for three minutes while the riders stopped

RIGHT: The sublime view of Mont Blanc from the summit of the Faucille that inspired John Ruskin in the 19th century. The Faucille's may be among the finest views of Europe's highest mountain.

THE COL DE LA FAUCILLE, ON THAT DAY OF 1835, opened to me in distinct vision the Holy Land of my future work and true home in this world. "

John Ruskin

to warm up. Conditions were again treacherous in 1936. Years later, Tour director Jacques Goddet would remark that, 'in the rain, the Faucille glistens'. The climb's name, Goddet clearly knew, referred to its shape – like a *faucille* or 'scythe' slicing into and behind the rock face, narrowly missing where France meets Switzerland 20 kilometres further along the D1005 at La Cure.

The Italian job

The Italian Gino Bartali twice led the Tour over La Faucille, in 1938 and 1951. In different circumstances his countryman Filippo Simeoni might well have emulated him in 2004; instead, having attacked from the main peloton and joined a breakaway group early in stage 18 of that year's Tour, as he neared the Faucille, Simeoni looked around to see champion-elect Lance Armstrong chasing him. When Armstrong caught Simeoni, he allegedly threatened to 'destroy' him and ordered him back to the peloton. Well aware that Armstrong's actions had

nothing to do with sport, and everything to do with Simeoni's court testimony against the American's doctor in a doping trial two years earlier, the Italian did as he was told. The only water at the summit that day came from Simeoni's tears.

The Faucille is unlikely to elicit any such anguish in amateur cyclists, be it from Morex or Gex. Of the two, the latter is the harder and more 'Alpine' in nature, consisting mainly of wide hairpins, cool pine forest and a regular gradient. Early on, in particular, the views over the Mont Mussy and Lac Léman are a fine diversion. Later, the more difficult ninth and tenth kilometres require lower gearing before the pass appears in a gulch between two outcrops and the gradient lessens to scarcely more than a false flat. It doesn't need us to tell you which is the more noteworthy attraction at the summit: a tacky souvenir shop or, glancing back towards Geneva, John Ruskin's magic place where 'a sweep of the road, traversed in five minutes at a trot, opens the whole Lake of Geneva, and the chain of the Alps along a hundred miles of horizon'.

On the other side of the Faucille, the Jura beckons. Largely neglected by industry and, blissfully, traffic, these docile mountains are a bike rider's nirvana, albeit one that excels more in scenery than in extreme challenge. The climb of the Faucille from Morez is typical of the region: a relatively abrupt, but still untaxing, hike up through pristine woodland to cross-country skiing haven Les Rousses, then almost 20 kilometres of gentle incline on the plateau beneath La Dôle. Ruskin claimed La Dôle had 'enormous influence… continually and calmly' on his life. To the inhabitants of the Jura, Geneva and all along La Côte stretching to Lausanne, it is famous for one thing: the huge, silver sphere housing a weather station on its summit.

As for the Faucille and, for that matter, its Swiss neighbour the Col de la Givrine, a picture, like Rousseau's, or a view, like Ruskin's, is worth a thousand words. Or for that matter, 11.8 or 26.8 kilometres of expectant climbing.

OPPOSITE: Lac Léman and, behind it, Mont Blanc in all its majesty. These, more than the gradient or difficulty, are the real defining features of the Faucille climb.

BELOW: A memorial to the First and Second World Wars on the Faucille. As is the case on many of the great passes, the surrounding slopes have a bellicose history.

Fact file Col de la Faucille

From Gex

REGION: Ain, France, near the Swiss border

ACCESS: From the centre of Gex, go north, following Rue de Harent and Rue de Paris

HEIGHT: 1,323m

LENGTH: 11.8km

ALTITUDE GAIN: 703m

AVERAGE GRADIENT: 6%

MAXIMUM GRADIENT: 8.1% from km 8.5 to km 9.5

OPEN: April to November

REFRESHMENTS: In Gex and at the summit

From Morez

REGION: Jura, France, near the Swiss border

ACCESS: From the centre of Morez, take the Rue de la République for 800m and then the Route de Prémanon for 1.4km

HEIGHT: 1,323m

LENGTH: 26.8km

ALTITUDE GAIN: 618m

AVERAGE GRADIENT: 2.3%

MAXIMUM GRADIENT: 5.9% from km 7 to 8

OPEN: April to November

REFRESHMENTS: In Les Rousses, La Cure or at the summit

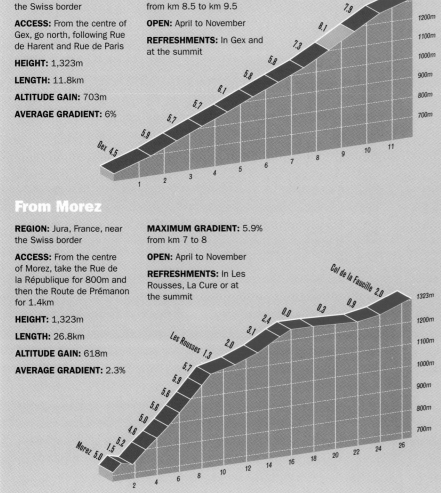

Col de Peyresourde
1,569m
France

'The Circle of Death', not life, was the epithet the locals had been using for decades to describe the Col du Tourmalet. Of the five Pyrenean passes on the Tour de France's second ever day in the range, the Col de Peyresourde was the first and far from the most deadly, yet its collocation before the lethal spiral would guarantee this smaller mountain a privileged place in cycling folklore. In a 2010 'factional' account of precisely that momentous 1910 stage of the Tour from Luchon to Bayonne, French novelist and cycling nut Christian Laborde noted the portentous echoes in the Peyresourde's three syllables: 'It's pitch black in the hairpins of the Col du Peyresourde. Peyre means *pierre* [stone] and the stone is *sourde* [deaf] to the pain of men, of these riders who advance painfully on the cambered road.'

Although almost equidistant from the Atlantic and Mediterranean coasts, right in the middle of the Pyrenees, the Peyresourde has rarely occupied centre stage in anything other than geography. At just 1,569 metres, it is far overshadowed by its more feared neighbours the Aubisque and the Tourmalet. Higher, harder, more forbidding – not to mention more frequently traversed by the Tour (respectively, the Tourmalet, Aubisque and Peyresourde had been visited 77, 71 and 62 times up to 2011) – those were the climbs that prompted Octave Lapize to yell 'Murderers!' at Alphonse Steines in 1910 and perhaps also what motivated Steines' boss Henri Desgrange to beat a hasty and unexplained retreat to Paris before the stage had even begun, maybe for fear of reprisals.

By comparison, the Peyresourde was a mere *amuse-bouche* that day, as it has often been for stages heading west out from the spa town of Luchon. Even for the pedestrian or car-bound traveller, its lush and placid green flanks lap like gentle tides in the foreground of some evergreen coastal storm. 'Beyond Tourmalet the valleys are again green with forest, grain and gardens, sparkling with bright white villages, and, after the sky-ride of that pass, even the Col d'Aspin and the Col de Peyresourde are taken easily, powerless to give the thrill they otherwise might,' Paul Wilstach wrote in his 1952 book, *Along The Pyrenees*. In 1898 another writer, Harold Spender, had also described the climb out of Luchon in mellifluous terms quite unlike the usual, daunted prose of early Alpine and Pyrenean travel writers. Spender spoke of a climb 'that makes abruptly westward from the old town, through smiling wooded country, dotted with villages and musical with streams.'

Sabotage in 1937?

As for former rider, journalist and Tour de France director Jean-Marie Leblanc, well, the Peyresourde was quite simply his favourite of all Tour climbs 'with its moss carpet'. 'It's a climb that doesn't inspire fear,' Leblanc went on. 'It makes you want to lie down on the grass next to the sheep and the cows.'

Here, in Leblanc's description, was all the charm of the Peyresourde. Like a kindly concierge, and like the neighbouring Aspin, it beckoned (or baited) the traveller forwards into a land of giants that it also helped to demystify. After all, it was not that much shorter or lower or easier than the Tourmalet – just a lot less menacing. The first eight kilometres up to Garin threaded through a geological formation called a moraine – in layman's terms, the leftovers of a melted glacier, before road and landscape unfolded via five loping hairpins into a sumptuous, pastoral postcard. At the summit, the Louron valley, the full panoply of the western Pyrenees and, yes, somewhere over there the Tourmalet, composed an awe-inspiring skyscape, but also one that seemed safe when viewed from this distance.

That first journey over the summit in the 1910 Tour passed largely without incident. The weather was 'tropical' according to one of the few journalists present, stage winner Octave Lapize rode first over all the climbs except the Aubisque, and only ten riders made the time limit. At midnight, 22 riders still hadn't made it to Bayonne, only 13 of whom were later confirmed to have abandoned.

The Peyresourde returned to the Tour route in 1911 – and indeed didn't miss another *Grande Boucle* until 1928. In 1923, the order of the original 1910 death march from Luchon to Bayonne was reversed, and with it the image of the Peyresourde as a preamble, almost literally, to the horrors that lurked around and beyond: having bickered with the official handing out food rations halfway up the Tourmalet, finally scoffing just a banana, breakaway leader Robert Jacquinot fell victim to the dreaded 'hunger knock' or *fringale*, plus the not-so-innocuous slopes of the Peyresourde's western side, and collapsed into a ditch. A sandwich revived him… but by then 15 minutes had slipped by and with them Jean Alavoine. In losing the stage, Jacquinot had at least retained his sense of humour – or maybe just his manners. 'I salute you, Jean, my boy,' he reportedly called out as Alavoine chugged by.

BELOW: Conquered by the Tour de France before its more daunting neighbours the Aubisque and Tourmalet on the same day in 1910, the Peyresourde has become one of the classic Pyrenean climbs.

The Peyresourde wouldn't always be the backdrop for such chivalry. In a 1937 Tour riddled with cheating, like many before and after him ahead of stages kicking off with the Peyresourde, French team leader Roger Lapébie headed out of Luchon with his team-mates for a morning warm-up. At Cierp-Gaud, 15 kilometres out of town, Lapébie plunged inexplicably off the road. Or not so inexplicably: closer examination revealed that Lapébie's handlebar stem had been sabotaged, presumably by the Belgians who had been squabbling with the French riders all race. 'Who did this to me? Bring them to me. I'll kill them!' Lapébie fumed. His body intact but his morale shattered, when the stage finally rolled out of Luchon the Frenchman was dropped almost immediately on the Peyresourde and trailed his Belgian nemesis Sylvère Maes to the tune of over four minutes by the time they reached the Tourmalet. 'Something terrible is happening to me... I want to disappear, to throw myself into the void with my bike,' he bawled, having come to a standstill on the Tourmalet. Fortunately, Lapébie recovered and went on to win the Tour.

The heat of battle

The Peyresourde went on serving as a kind of antechamber to the real theatres of Pyrenean drama. In 1960, the Italian 'divebomber' of the descents, Gastone Nencini, leeched both time and confidence from the Frenchman Roger Rivière with a virtuoso slalom down the eastern side of the Peyresourde and into Luchon – but it wasn't until stage 14 and the Cévennes that Rivière's nerve cracked and with it his spine in a ruinous crash on the descent of the Col de Perjuret. Two years later, Britain's Tommy Simpson took the yellow jersey in Luchon thanks to a brilliant west–east ascent of the Peyresourde, only to capitulate the following day on the stage to Superbagnères.

From recent Tours, fans may have clear memories of Jan Ullrich's slapstick tumble into a (fortunately well-padded) Pyrenean ravine and of a gripping duel between Alberto Contador and the not-long-later-to-be-disgraced Michael Rasmussen, and a hazier recollection of both episodes occurring on the Peyresourde. Such, though, seems to be this mountain's lot: that of a beautiful, in some respects even quintessential, Pyrenean pass, but one rarely afforded its due consideration or respect.

LEFT: Even on a grim day, of which there are many in the Pyrenees, it's not hard to see what former Tour de France director Jean-Marie Leblanc meant by the Peyresourde's 'moss carpet'. Leblanc said, 'It makes you want to lie down on the grass next to the sheep and the cows.'

For amateur cyclists, the Peyresourde remains a joy and not one that should be taken lightly. As is often the case in the Pyrenees, the gradient is irregular and the wind gusts, particularly in the open sections after Garin on the eastern side. The lack of shelter, exacerbated by the relatively low altitude, can turn the Peyresourde into a furnace. In a blisteringly hot 1921 Tour and in particular the stage from Bayonne to Luchon, Pierre Carrey wrote in his book *Légendes du Tour de France – 100 ans de Pyrénées*, the priority was no longer 'pacing oneself on the climbs and taking charge on the Peyresourde at the latest, but simply wasting less time than one's rivals in the fresh waters of the brooks and streams along the route'. While *maillot jaune* Léon Scieur even soaked his sandwiches in an effort to keep cool, one rider, Charles Cento, perhaps dangled his toes for a little too long. Cento's deficit from stage winner Hector Heusghem that day? A mere eight-and-a-quarter hours.

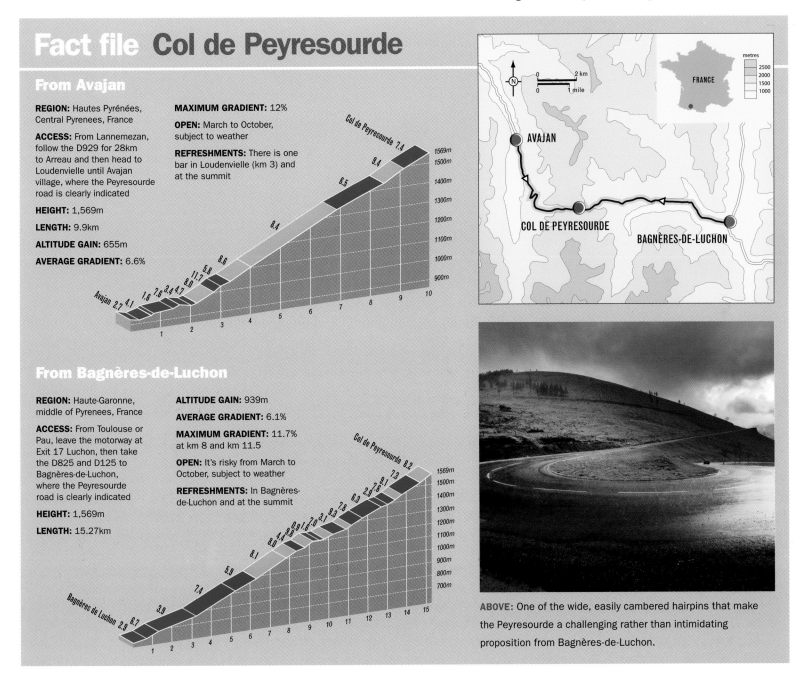

Fact file Col de Peyresourde

From Avajan

REGION: Hautes Pyrénées, Central Pyrenees, France

ACCESS: From Lannemezan, follow the D929 for 28km to Arreau and then head to Loudenvielle until Avajan village, where the Peyresourde road is clearly indicated

HEIGHT: 1,569m

LENGTH: 9.9km

ALTITUDE GAIN: 655m

AVERAGE GRADIENT: 6.6%

MAXIMUM GRADIENT: 12%

OPEN: March to October, subject to weather

REFRESHMENTS: There is one bar in Loudenvielle (km 3) and at the summit

From Bagnères-de-Luchon

REGION: Haute-Garonne, middle of Pyrenees, France

ACCESS: From Toulouse or Pau, leave the motorway at Exit 17 Luchon, then take the D825 and D125 to Bagnères-de-Luchon, where the Peyresourde road is clearly indicated

HEIGHT: 1,569m

LENGTH: 15.27km

ALTITUDE GAIN: 939m

AVERAGE GRADIENT: 6.1%

MAXIMUM GRADIENT: 11.7% at km 8 and km 11.5

OPEN: It's risky from March to October, subject to weather

REFRESHMENTS: In Bagnères-de-Luchon and at the summit

ABOVE: One of the wide, easily cambered hairpins that make the Peyresourde a challenging rather than intimidating proposition from Bagnères-de-Luchon.

Alto del Angliru
1,573m
Spain

❛ WHAT'S THE POINT OF RIDING UP A MOUNTAIN that it'd be quicker to go up by foot? ❜

Marzio Bruseghin

The English mountaineer George Mallory once argued that he had attempted Everest 'because it was there'; Miguel Prieto's reasoning to Bruseghin and his colleagues about the Angliru would have been similar. In 1996, Prieto was the communications director of the Spanish charity for the blind, ONCE, which also happened to sponsor one of the best, if not the best, professional cycling team on the planet. That year Prieto, himself partially sighted but always on the look-out for new summits to spike his passion for the mountains, headed up the Angliru armed with his altimeter and a magnifying glass.

When he reached the top, Prieto couldn't enjoy the vistas of the Atlantic, the Alto de Naranco or Oviedo, but he did glimpse the future of Spain's national tour, the Vuelta a España.

It took the 'blind visionary', as one newspaper would later dub him, a while, but on September 23, 1997 Prieto finally jotted down his thoughts in a letter to then-Vuelta race director Enrique Franco and his right-hand man Alberto Gadea. Taking Franco's interview on the *El Larguero* Vuelta review programme and questions about the race director's 'dream courses' as his cue, Prieto made several suggestions, including this one about the Angliru:

'There exists in Asturias, in the middle of the Sierra del Aramo, in the municipality of Riosa, around 15 kilometres from Oviedo, a mountain whose road is barely marked on maps because it is a cattle road which was only recently paved. This mountain is known as La Gamonal and its altitude is 1,570 [sic] metres. The climb is 12 kilometres long and ascends just over 1,200 metres in altitude, which gives it an average gradient slightly above ten per cent, higher than the well-known Higa de Monreal. Please note in fact that the last seven kilometres of the climb have an average gradient above 13 per cent, dotted with multiple ramps at 20, 18, 17 and even 23.5 per cent. This ascent, whose profile I am pleased to attach, is analyzed in the February 1996 issue of *Ciclismo a Fondo* magazine and, if ever used, is guaranteed to leave unforgettable memories burnt into the retinas of the viewers. Just as people have said the Lagos de Covadonga will become the Spanish Alpe d'Huez, so the Gamonal could equal and, no exaggeration, eclipse the Italian Mortirolo.'

Franco and Gadea were fast to act. They met Prieto, visited the climb, and, in mid-October 1998, *La Nueva España* newspaper published the scoop: the following year's Vuelta would scale a mystery mountain in Asturias harder than anything the race had ever seen.

Thirteen days later, at the official race presentation in Madrid, Franco confirmed the news and the name – the Vuelta would call it the Angliru. Predictably, not everyone was thrilled. One of the world's leading climbers, the Italian Leonardo Piepoli, recced the Angliru before the Vuelta and called it 'impossible', particularly the section known as Cueña les Cabres two-and-a-half kilometres from the finish, with its ramps nudging 24 per cent. Critics said this was a lame attempt to revive the Vuelta, and indeed cycling in Spain, with silly gimmickry. 'What do they want? Blood? They ask us to stay clean and avoid doping and then they make the riders tackle this kind of barbarity,' spat the Kelme team manager, Vicente Belda – perhaps getting his excuses in early for the doping scandal that would envelop his team a few years later.

The long-awaited stage of the Vuelta came and was won by the madcap Spanish climber José Maria Jiménez. In his post-race press conference, Jiménez dedicated the win to his friend Marco Pantani, at the time in self-imposed exile after his ejection from that year's Giro d'Italia. Just a few months apart, in the winter of 2003–2004, both Pantani and Jiménez, the two most gifted climbers of their generation, would die of cocaine overdoses. The *ABC* newspaper entitled its obituary to Jiménez, 'The first man on the moon (or at least the Angliru).'

The perfect climb

More important than Jiménez's victory, in the immediate aftermath, was that the Angliru had lived up to expectations. Or, if you like, justified the outrage of people like Belda. The race returned in 2000 and again inspired one of the world's best climbers, Gilberto Simoni, to success. The fans loved it, and by now other races and their organizers were envious. The Giro d'Italia bosses seemed desperate to reclaim the title of cycling's hardest climb that the Angliru had wrestled from the Mortirolo, unveiling the Monte Zoncolan in 2003 and the easier but equally dramatic Colle delle Finestre two years later.

In the meantime, the Angliru continued, and continues, to divide opinion. Most assumed that David Millar stopped on the finish line and tore off his race number in protest at the difficulty of the 2002 Vuelta stage won by Roberto Heras, but in fact Millar's gripe was with the descent off the Cordal climb that preceded it. 'This is inhuman. We're not animals,' Millar seethed. It was easy to see where the confusion had arisen.

For every rider like the former French pro Patrice Halgand who complained, 'On the Angliru the guys go too pitifully for the climb to have any sporting interest. Even the winner goes up in slow motion. There's no attacking' – there has been a Charly Mottet, an ex-Tour de France star-turned-race-course inspector, who said, 'I think it's good for cycling. I am in favour of these extraordinary difficulties, these extreme gradients. The steepness doesn't shock me because there is always a solution in choosing the right gears.'

While the best climbers on the Vuelta's last visit generally favoured a 36x28 or 34x27 as their smallest gear, other less gifted riders continue to rely on a different kind of assistance – they gratefully accept pushes off the fans at the roadside.

What is rarely emphasized, but ought to be, is the Angliru's smouldering, emerald beauty. While the former Swiss pro Tony Rominger rather cryptically said that 'climbing the Angliru is like looking out of the window of a plane', the Spanish Tour de France star Samuel Sanchez could gaze out of another window, that of his house in Oviedo, and see the dark green saddle of the Angliru itself. Sanchez described it in 2011 as 'the perfect climb.'

'It's extremely beautiful,' Sanchez said. 'I think that the view that the fans get up there is very good, and it also stands out because it's very green. There's lots of woodland up there, a lot of trees. I think it's perfect. I've not ridden up the Zoncolan or the Mortirolo, but I can assure you that even though the Angliru might not be the toughest climb in the world, it is certainly one of them.'

Up here in the Sierra del Aramo, the superlatives are exhausted as quickly as the legs – yet it remains to be seen whether and how well the Angliru stands the test of time. Mountains outlive any bike rider or race, but the trend for ever steeper routes to their summits can go in only one of two directions – onward and upward to even more savage peaks that will outstrip the Angliru, or to boredom with the whole phenomenon. Put another way, whether the Angliru will still be included alongside the Ventoux, Galibier or Alpe d'Huez in a compilation of legendary climbs in 50 years' time, may depend on factors beyond almost anyone's control.

We do know already that Miguel Prieto, 'the blind visionary', has left Spanish cycling a monumental legacy. Whatever happens next, Prieto was right – the Angliru and its images are burnt into our retinas, not to mention a few brave men's calves and thighs.

Fact file Alto del Angliru

La Vega or 'Riosa'

REGION: Asturias, northern Spain

ACCESS: From the N-630 from Oviedo to Mieres, turn right onto the AS-231 to Las Mazas and La Vega (Riosa). From the latter follow signs to the Sierra del Aramo and Grandiella

HEIGHT: 1,573m

LENGTH: 12.5km

ALTITUDE GAIN: 1,266m

AVERAGE GRADIENT: 10.13%

MAXIMUM GRADIENT: 23.5% (at the Cueña les Cabres, km 11)

OPEN: April to October

REFRESHMENTS: At the bottom

ALTERNATIVE ROUTES: Road from Santa Eulalia joins La Vega route close to Via Pará (17.7km at 7.93%)

Alto del Angliru 5.8
13.6
Cueña les Cabres 17.5
14.0
12.1
11.9
13.7
Via Pará 2.1
7.3
9.1
8.4
8.1
La Vega 5.2

1573m
1250m
1000m
750m
500m
250m

1 2 3 4 5 6 7 8 9 10 11 12

metres
1500
1250
1000
750
500

SPAIN

ALTO DEL ANGLIRU

LA VEGA (RIOSA)

0   2 km
0   1 mile

Hautacam
1,653m France

The profile of the road to Hautacam could be mistaken for a wedge of cheese, forming a near-perfect triangle. But, not altogether unusually, the graphic depiction is misleading on two counts.

First, there is the erratic nature of the gradient – 'schizophrenic' is one description – with the eight per cent average hardly doing justice to a climb that steepens to 12 per cent in one section.

Then there is the zigzagging road, slashing its way up the mountainside, initially rising steeply and narrowly from Argelès-Gazost, then emerging in open, verdant Pyrenean meadowlands, before eventually, after 13 kilometres and at 1,653 metres, reaching the resort that gives the climb its name: Hautacam ski station.

It is ironic, perhaps, that the winter sport on offer at the summit is relatively tame, with the ski centre described in tourist brochures as 'a small family resort' – for the name Hautacam has come to have entirely different, and far less benign, connotations in a cycling context.

It is tempting, in fact, to call Hautacam 'the cursed climb', even if this might be considered a second irony, given that the town in the valley below is better known for its miracles of spiritual and physical healing. Yet little of the Lourdes magic appears to have rubbed off on the steep slopes of the mysterious, intriguingly named Hautacam, whose three most recent visits by the Tour de France amount to dark tales, not written at the time but shortly thereafter, of scandal and tragedy.

Hautacam is almost certainly most famous for the second of four appearances in the world's biggest race, in 1996. The mountain's Tour debut, in 1994, passed off fairly routinely at the mist and fog-enshrouded summit as Luc Leblanc won and, behind him, Miguel Indurain calmly defended yellow, en route to the fourth of his five consecutive victories.

Performance enhancing

Two years later, it was here, this time on a crystal-clear, baking hot day, that Bjarne Riis, the Dane, stamped his authority on the Tour in a manner rarely displayed even by the greatest of champions, never mind a 32-year-old rider whose career had followed the strangest of trajectories. Riis had been discarded by his French team as a young professional before reinventing himself as a powerful *domestique*, and then undergoing a second re-invention, emerging this time, more startlingly, as a team leader and Grand Tour contender.

It was, as Riis would eventually admit, a drug-fuelled transformation. But surprise at his revelation was tempered by years of suspicion – suspicion that was stoked on the slopes of Hautacam more than anywhere else. Indeed, Riis's performance on the climb to Hautacam in 1996 arguably still stands as the most vivid illustration of the transformative powers of EPO, the drug that defined an era.

As a large group of around 15 riders tackled the slopes of the climb, Riis, riding second in line behind his Telekom team-mate Jan Ullrich, abruptly stood on the pedals, turned around

and then removed himself from the thin line of riders, swinging to the side of the road like a team pursuiter swinging up the banking of a velodrome.

Was he tired? Did he have a mechanical problem? The confusion was compounded by Riis's next move: he drifted down the line, glancing across at his rivals' faces as he did so, though Riis himself remained impassive and expressionless. And what happened next was extraordinary. Once he reached the end, he accelerated back up the outside as if turbo-charged; and just like that he was gone,

ABOVE: One kilometre from the summit, facing back down the road towards Argelès-Gazost.

❛ IT IS TEMPTING, IN FACT, TO CALL HAUTACAM 'THE CURSED CLIMB', even if this might be considered a second irony, given that the town in the valley below is better known for its miracles of spiritual and physical healing. ❜

taking one or two of the hairpin bends so quickly that he almost overshot them. At the finish Riis won, kissing the tips of his fingers in celebration. It was almost 11 years later that he admitted that, between 1993 and 1998, he used a cocktail of EPO, human growth hormone and cortisone.

Perhaps Riis's performance, before the suspicions were confirmed, also established Hautacam as a mountain on which the Tour could be won – which was effectively what happened in 1996. Four years later, it provided the first summit finish of the 2000 Tour, presenting the defending champion, Lance Armstrong, with an opportunity to silence the sceptics who claimed he'd only won the previous year thanks to the absence of Marco Pantani and Jan Ullrich.

Armstrong had several points to prove as he and his overall rivals began a climb that, on that narrow road, ramps up so steeply at the bottom and enters the smattering of buildings that make up the village of Ayros-Arbouix. Up ahead, the day's early break was disintegrating with one rider, Spaniard Javier Otxoa, emerging at the front. The day was gloomy, as though night was closing in, and the rain fell remorselessly, becoming heavier towards the summit, turning the road into an ink-black strip of glistening tarmac.

A Hautacam hex

While Otxoa laboured, having started the climb nine minutes before Armstrong's group, the American flew, cutting through the remnants of the breakaway like a blade. Pantani held on to Armstrong for as long as he could, then ran up the white flag and dropped back. Only

LEFT: The Hautacam climb starts gently before serving up its first difficult stretches above the 500-metre altitude mark, here around Ayros-Arbouix.

another specialist climber, José María Jiménez, seemed able to ride with Armstrong, who ate into Otxoa's advantage with machine-like intensity, closing the gap to less than a minute as the shattered Otxoa crossed the line for his first professional win, and the biggest of a career cut cruelly short.

The fates of the main players on that day – Armstrong excepted – make for sobering, or traumatic, reading. Pantani and Jiménez would both die of cocaine addiction within four years. And just seven months after his victory at Hautacam, 26-year-old Otxoa, while training in Malaga with his twin brother Ricardo, would be involved in a horrific collision with a car. Ricardo, who also rode for the Kelme team, was killed in the accident. Javier was taken to hospital in a critical condition.

As he lay in a coma with serious head and chest injuries, not to mention a shattered leg, Otxoa came to be referred to as the Hero of Hautacam. For ten weeks he remained in a coma. His parents, already grieving one son, were advised to turn off the life-support machines. They refused, and then Javier awakened. As he returned home, several months later, his Kelme *directeur sportif* said he provided 'living proof that there are miracles'.

The miracle didn't end there, for although the Hero of Hautacam – or is it significant that the 2000 stage finish was listed as 'Lourdes-Hautacam'? – did not return to the professional peloton, he did race again, competing at the 2004 Paralympics in Athens, winning a gold medal in the road event and silver in the pursuit.

With such a poignant postscript to the 2000 visit, the Tour's fourth and most recent visit to Hautacam in 2008 witnessed a return to ignominy. The veteran Italian Leonardo Piepoli led his Saunier Duval teammate Juan José Cobo over the line, but later failed a drugs test for EPO. It means that against the stage to Hautacam in 2008 there is no name, just an asterisk. Otxoa, perhaps fittingly, remains the last 'winner' at the summit of Hautacam.

Fact file Hautacam

From Argelès-Gazost

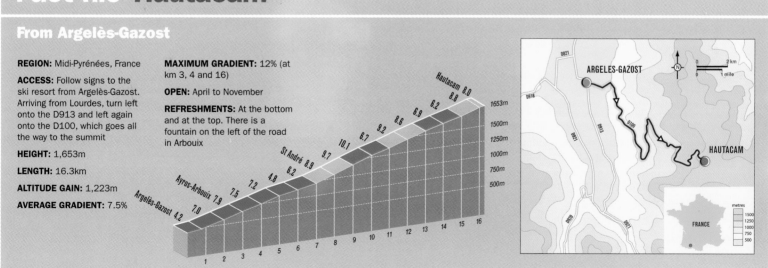

REGION: Midi-Pyrénées, France

ACCESS: Follow signs to the ski resort from Argelès-Gazost. Arriving from Lourdes, turn left onto the D913 and left again onto the D100, which goes all the way to the summit

HEIGHT: 1,653m

LENGTH: 16.3km

ALTITUDE GAIN: 1,223m

AVERAGE GRADIENT: 7.5%

MAXIMUM GRADIENT: 12% (at km 3, 4 and 16)

OPEN: April to November

REFRESHMENTS: At the bottom and at the top. There is a fountain on the left of the road in Arbouix

Col de Joux Plane
1,691m
France

' FOR EVERY TEN OR HUNDRED BACKSTEDTS OR LAURENT FIGNONS WHO 'HATED THE BLASTED COL DE JOUX PLANE... its tight hairpins and steep gradients', there is, it's true, a Richard Virenque or a Floyd Landis who thrived there. **'**

Is the Col de Joux Plane *the* hardest climb ever to feature in the Tour de France? The theory isn't one you'll find in most traditional Tour literature, but it is increasingly fashionable with those who have ridden into Morzine via this steep and sinuous pass. The American rider Chris Horner called the Joux Plane 'epic'. Horner reckoned the 11.6-kilometre road over the top from Samöens to Morzine was more like a 'bike path' with a gradient of 'like, 20 per cent all the way up'. Far from invalidating his assessment, the exaggeration only served to emphasize that the Joux Plane is not only very hard, but also very much harder from the road than it seems from any kind of numerical breakdown.

As to the question of whether it is the hardest mountain pass ever to appear on a Tour de France route, the debate would be long-winded and subjective. It is surely not the 'nastiest climb in the Alps', as the Dutchman Peter Winnen claimed in one book on Europe's great mountain roads. Winnen, who crossed the Joux Plane first on his way to a stage win in Morzine in the 1982 Tour, said in 2005 that he'd only ever returned in his car, and that 'it seemed even harder than it was before'. Like Horner, the Dutchman was either guilty of embellishment or a victim of the same optical illusion that is the Joux Plane's defining trait.

Trompe l'oeil

Statistically at least, which Alpine climbs are tougher? Well, the choice is endless and incorporates Italy, Switzerland, Austria and even France itself. Proceeding in order, and to name but a small selection, Italy's Mortirolo and the Colle delle Finestre are nastier by any gauge; the Grindel Alp from Zweilütschinen and the Alpe del Gesero from Arbedo are among a host of more evil Swiss climbs; the Kitzbüheler Horn and Rettenbachferner feature on an even lengthier list in Austria; and, in France, within a few valleys' range of the Joux Plane, Le Mont du Chat from Le Bourget du Lac and Lachat from Feissons sur l'Isère are longer and, for substantial sections, far more severe.

The Joux Plane's great merit, then, is as the epitome of the *trompe l'oeil* effect that experienced climbers of mountain passes know only too well. It's hard to know whether it was this characteristic of the Joux Plane that caused Lance Armstrong's only true collapse in the mountains in his seven-year Tour de France reign, or whether that was simply the regulation *fringale* or 'hunger knock' that everyone supposed. Either way, the moment halfway up the climb in stage 16 of the 2000 race when Jan Ullrich and Richard Virenque pulled away from Armstrong, left a deep impression on the American. 'That was without any doubt my worst day on a bike. I could have lost the Tour,' he admitted, having limited his deficit from Ullrich to just over a minute and a half. Armstrong never returned to the Joux Plane in a Tour stage, but made a point of exorcizing old ghosts whenever he was in the area, whether in training or racing; in 2002, he crossed the summit first en route to victory in a stage of the Dauphiné Libéré and spoke of his satisfaction at having 'conquered the guy [the Joux Plane] that almost killed me before'; in the 2005 Dauphiné, he again excelled on the Joux Plane, without managing or needing to win; and during his final Tour, in 2010, he climbed the Joux Plane on the first rest day.

While Armstrong was struggling to avert disaster in 2000, back down the road, the Swedish rider Magnus Bäckstedt fought his own solitary battle – to avoid the time cut and elimination from the Tour. He succeeded, just, but not without finding out exactly why the Joux Plane elicited such fear.

'I think I've suppressed the memory of that day,' Bäckstedt joked 11 years later. 'It's very true though, that you only get a vague idea of a climb's difficulty from its profile. In general, seven, seven-and-a-half per cent is the threshold above which you know it's a serious climb, but the layout of the road and various other factors dictate how hard it really is. Alpe d'Huez, for example, is never that bad, because you're constantly winding around the hairpins and getting a kick out of them. On the Joux Plane, you don't get any of that. The Col du Galibier is, in my opinion, one of the hardest climbs in the world for the same reason: it basically just heads straight up into the sky, plus you're always exposed to the elements. Conversely, the Mont Ventoux is another one which both other people and the stats say is stupidly hard, but which never posed me too many problems. So, yeah, it's a very complex set of factors – including the weather and where the climb occurs in a race – that determine how hard a climb proves on the road.'

Dark footnotes

For every ten or hundred Bäckstedts or Laurent Fignons who 'hated the blasted Col de Joux Plane… its tight hairpins and steep gradients', there is, it's true, a Richard Virenque or a Floyd Landis who thrived there. Virenque won two Tour stages in Morzine, the first on the day of Armstrong and Bäckstedt's troubles, owing largely to his breakaway companion Roberto Heras's slapstick tumble on the descent off the Joux Plane and into town. In 2006, Landis rounded off what at the time was hailed as one of the greatest individual performances ever to recoup seven minutes on the Spaniard Oscar Pereiro and set up overall Tour victory. Alas, two days after his enthronement in Paris, Landis learned that he had failed a doping test and would be disqualified.

This dark footnote to the history of the pass was hence added to the tragic deaths of Thierry Claveyrolat and Marco Pantani, respectively first over the pass and stage winners in Morzine in the 1991 and 1997 Tours. Having retired in 1994, five years later Claveyrolat shot himself dead within weeks of allegedly killing a child in a car accident. Pantani passed away in 2004 at the age of 34, the cause of his death a cocaine overdose.

Such morbid connotations seem out of place on the Joux Plane, for all that its slopes are lethally erratic. In every other respect this is a joy of an Alpine climb, wending merrily through silent and deserted pastures, and offering vistas of Mont Blanc to rival the Col de la Faucille's above the 1,000-metre mark. After a short descent at the top, the road then rises again to the Col du Ranfolly before a technical and thrilling test of descending into Morzine.

Up to 2011, the Joux Plane had featured in the Tour de France just 11 times and always as the final obstacle on stages to Morzine. Already it had repelled Lance Armstrong and pressed home the point that climbs can be classified by their vital statistics no more than books should be judged by their covers. The Tour's or the Alps' toughest climb it may not be, but a master, a mountain of deception, the Joux Plane certainly is.

ABOVE: The view of the Mont Blanc massif from the Joux Plane lake at the summit. Better, more spectacular, than the vista from the Col de la Faucille?

LEFT: The road arcs over the summit, around the crater formed by the 1,826-metre Tête du Vuargne and continues past the Joux Plane lake and, finally, the Col de Ranfolly before descending to Morzine.

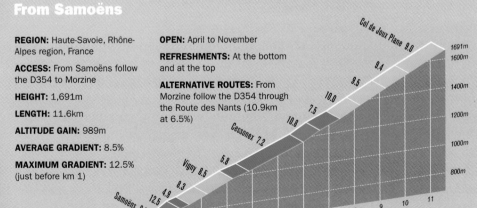

Fact file Col de Joux Plane

From Samoëns

REGION: Haute-Savoie, Rhône-Alpes region, France

ACCESS: From Samoëns follow the D354 to Morzine

HEIGHT: 1,691m

LENGTH: 11.6km

ALTITUDE GAIN: 989m

AVERAGE GRADIENT: 8.5%

MAXIMUM GRADIENT: 12.5% (just before km 1)

OPEN: April to November

REFRESHMENTS: At the bottom and at the top

ALTERNATIVE ROUTES: From Morzine follow the D354 through the Route des Nants (10.9km at 6.5%)

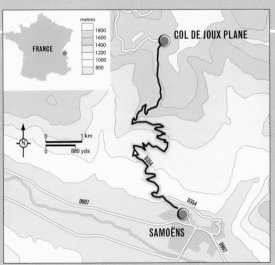

Col d'Aubisque
1,709m
France

ABOVE: The Aubisque in typically truculent mood, here looking back towards the Gourette ski resort in the commune of Eaux-Bonnes, where the Aubisque turns decidedly uncharitable on the Laruns side.

So often in the literal and metaphorical shadow of its neighbour the Col du Tourmalet, the Col d'Aubisque seems, you'd still think, an incongruous candidate for the title of the Tour de France's 'forgotten mountain'.

Surpassed only by the Tourmalet in number of Tour appearances, the Aubisque is, on paper at least, one of the Tour's mountain cornerstones. Last in the terrible concatenation of cols on the Grande Boucle's second day in the Pyrenees in 1910, it had a fierce name, deceptive slopes and, judging by the drawings of cartoonist Pellos, a sinister disposition. The first Tour de France director Henri Desgrange saw its sudden mood swing and steepening gradient after Eaux-Bonnes on the western side (from the village to the summit there are only 11 hairpins and the average gradient is close to eight per cent, with some sections at 13 per cent 2.5 kilometres from Eaux-Bonnes) as proof that 'there's nothing in the world more hypocritical than the Aubisque'. 'It's nasty, tortuous, often mucky – that's when it's not a gravelly dust-bowl,' Desgrange shuddered.

So imposing was the pass's reputation that Desgrange and journalists reporting on early Tours were even prone to attributing to it merits and incidents that weren't strictly the Aubisque's. The east–west ascent of the Aubisque is in fact only a paltry eight kilometres long, beginning as it does at 1,403 metres above sea level, two kilometres beyond the summit of the 1,473-metre Col du Soulor. Once upon a time, from the Soulor, the peloton would squeeze in another pass, the treacherously beautiful and now disused 1,650-metre Col de Tortes, before hooking back towards and finally cresting the Aubisque. Swashbuckling attacks and terrible collapses in reality provoked by its two support acts, the Soulor and the Tortes, were thus commonly documented as the work of the Aubisque. If, as Philippe Bouvet wrote in his *Cols Mythiques du Tour de France*, 'The Aubisque often wears a frown, perhaps because not quite reaching the 2,000-metre barrier has given it a complex', Desgrange seemed determined to massage its bruised ego – even if that meant pretending the Aubisque was three mountains in one. According to Pierre Carrey's *Légendes du Tour de France – 100 ans de Pyrénées*,

'Desgrange wanted to turn the Soulor-Tortes-Aubisque trio into a single climb, the equal of the nearby Tourmalet.'

Eleven years on from Desgrange's death and the Col de Tortes' definitive abandonment, the Aubisque marked the collective memory in 1951 by nearly killing the Tour's surprise leader, Wim Van Est. A total novice in the mountains (but for one previous journey over the St. Gotthardpass in Switzerland... by car), Van Est descended the Aubisque like a kamikaze, eventually overshooting a bend and plunging 70 metres into a ravine. By some miracle, he survived; more famously still, Van Est had to be winched back up to the road with a makeshift safety rope fashioned from plaited tyres. He went on to front an advertising campaign for the watch company Pontiac with the slogan 'I fell 70 metres deep into a ravine. My heart stopped beating but Pontiac was still working.' A monument now marks the spot where he fell, reminding us, 'Here on 17 July 1951 the cyclist Wim Van Est fell 70 metres. He survived but lost the yellow jersey' – but neglecting to point out than Van Est was also forced to abandon the Tour.

There have been further dramas, many of them. Some are etched on the memory, others not. The notion of the Aubisque as the forgotten mountain of the Tour, though, took on new significance when Bernard Thévenet was one of four riders to fall while descending from the summit and off the Soulor in the 1972 Tour. Apparently unhurt but for minor road-rash, the Frenchman reached for his bike and immediately set off towards Pau. Thévenet felt fine, if a little groggy, but for a strange and unnerving sensation: 'I couldn't remember where I was,' he recalled later. 'It was as though, instead of waking up in my bed in the morning, I'd woken up on my bike.'

The accents of the fans at the roadside told him he was in France. The cold and grey conditions, typical of Aubisque, suggested a race in March or February. Still, he couldn't be sure. 'I thought I was going to look like a right idiot, but I had to go and ask someone what we were doing there'. The first suitable candidate was his Peugeot *directeur sportif* Gaston Plaud, who Thévenet saw approaching in his team car. 'Where are we?' he enquired. 'In the Tour,' came Plaud's reply.

Limestone amphitheatre

Slowly, as the kilometres ticked by, and Thévenet studied the stage map he'd found stuffed into his jersey pocket, it was all coming back. All... except the Aubisque, which the Frenchman was convinced had vanished from the route. 'It's a good job we never had to climb the Aubisque. I would have struggled to finish...' he told race doctor Brossard that night. Not wanting to add to Thévenet's disorientation, Brossard nodded.

Thirty-five years later, there was more amnesia on the Aubisque during the 2007 Tour. Prior to stage 16 and the summit finish at Gourette on the Aubisque's western side, that year's race had been dominated by two intense battles – the Dane Michael Rasmussen's with the press over the allegations that he had evaded out-of-competition drug tests, and Rasmussen's daily skirmishes with Alberto Contador in the Pyrenees. Having pulled away from the Spaniard 900 metres from Gourette and seemingly sewn up the overall Tour title, in the press room next to the finish line, Rasmussen faced his umpteenth barrage from the media about his sieve-like powers of recollection when it came to dope controls. Three or four hours later, under mounting pressure, Rasmussen's Rabobank team would call time on his lies and announce his sacking. Late that night, while one group of journalists besieged the Dane's hotel in Pau, another could be found frantically typing their stories in a pair of bus shelters on the road into Argelès-Gazost.

Rasmussen's downfall was a shame if only because it had been a long time since any truly Tour-defining action on the Aubisque. Either eclipsed by the Tourmalet or an uneventful prelude to summit finishes at Luz Ardiden or Hautacam, its impact is often real but unseen. Exposed, uneven in slope and so quintessentially Pyrenean, the Aubisque is the jab preparing for more strategically placed climbs' sucker punch.

In itself, the Col d'Aubisque is and always has been an impressive onslaught on nature, in this case the vast limestone amphitheatre of the Cirque du Litor. 'The pass,' wrote Paul Wilstach in his 1925 *Along the Pyrenees*, 'is on one of the many short massive mountain spurs, so characteristic of the topography of the north slope of the Pyrenees, which reach high up and at right angles to the flank of the main range, supporting it like giant buttresses on a fabulous cathedral. The way is weird and wild, and the white road lifts its girdle around the hills at some dizzy altitudes.'

Even from Wilstach, though, it took 'real heroism' not to spoil his fellow travellers' enjoyment by comparing it unfavourably to the Tourmalet, or by pointing out that the 1,920-metre Col du Puymorens pipped it to second place in the ranking of the highest Pyrenean climbs. This even for someone who knew nothing of the Tour de France, and who nonetheless acknowledged that the Aubisque '[revealed] nature in one of its most heroic expressions' or that 'the engineer's art here expressed itself close to the limit'.

Certainly, looking southwest from the summit of the Soulor towards the unmistakable pyramid of the Pic du Midi d'Ossau, it's easy to conclude that there can be few finer spots anywhere in the Pyrenees. Or that, while the Aubisque has occasionally been forgotten, it can't or at least shouldn't ever be considered forgettable.

OPPOSITE: A dramatic stretch of road, seven kilometres from the pass on the eastern side looking down toward the Col du Soulor.

ABOVE: Dark and dreary: looking down from the summit.

ABOVE: Lower and less fêted than the Tourmalet, is the Aubisque not also more spectacular?

Fact file Col d'Aubisque

From Laruns

REGION: Hautes-Pyrénées, France

ACCESS: From Pau (at 38km from Laruns), follow the D934 via Louvie-Juzon. From Laruns, follow the D918 in the direction of Argelès-Gazost

HEIGHT: 1,709m

LENGTH: 16.6km

ALTITUDE GAIN: 1,190m

AVERAGE GRADIENT: 7.2%

MAXIMUM GRADIENT: 13% just before km 7

OPEN: May to November

REFRESHMENTS: Bars at the bottom, in Eaux-Bonnes (km 4), Gourette (km 12) and at the top of Col d'Aubisque

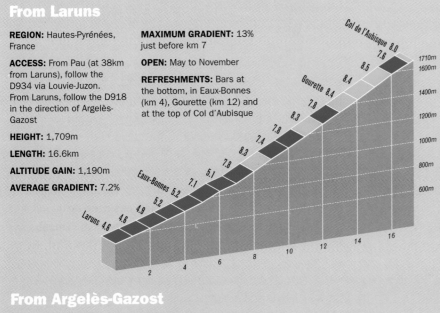

From Argelès-Gazost

REGION: Hautes-Pyrénées and Pyrénées–Atlantiques, France

ACCESS: In Argelès-Gazost town centre, turn right following the D918 over the Col du Soulor

HEIGHT: 1,709m

LENGTH: 30.1km

ALTITUDE GAIN: 1,247m

AVERAGE GRADIENT: 4.1%

MAXIMUM GRADIENT: 12% at km 15

OPEN: May to November

REFRESHMENTS: Bars at the bottom, in Aucun (km 9), Arrens (km 12), at the top of the Col du Soulor (km 20) and top of the Col d'Aubisque

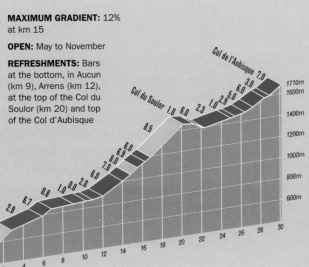

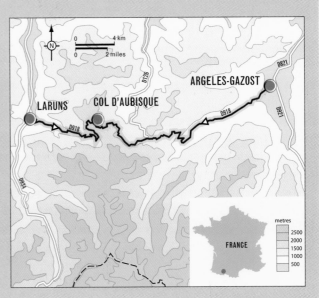

Monte Zoncolan
1,730m
Italy

Before its inclusion on the route of the 2003 Giro d'Italia, Monte Zoncolan was but one obscure peak among many in its vicinity, a rock face in an anonymous crowd of limestone giants. The least wealthy, least explored and least chronicled of the northern Italian regions, it stood to reason that Friuli should be home to some of Italy's most mysterious and unloved mountains, as well as to its own indecipherable language. With their unusual names, such as Fleons and Crostis, the Alps of the Carnic sub-range were also opposite in character to the docile Celts who settled and eventually submitted to Roman rule there. They were inhospitable in climate and in gradient.

The latter of these characteristics made them irresistible to cycling thrill-seekers. Altitude junkies had been whispering about Monte Zoncolan for years, even if they never made it to the summit. Internet forums and blogs named the ascent of the Zoncolan from Ovaro as the hardest paved climb in Italy – or at least rated it tougher than even the infamous Passo del Mortirolo. The women's professional Giro d'Italia got to within three kilometres of the summit in 1997 – but 'only' via Sutrio and the significantly easier eastern side, on a road that gains elevation at a 'modest' average of seven per cent for 11 kilometres up to that point.

Pink dragon

A year later, in 1998, Francesco Guidolin was a former professional footballer now managing the team based in the Friulan capital Udine, Udinese Calcio. Guidolin was also an avid cyclist and summit 'collector'. One afternoon at the Udinese's summer training camp in Arta Terme, he set out on his bike with an old riding buddy. The friend whispered that he was about to let Guidolin in on a secret: it was 15 kilometres away and it was called the Monte Zoncolan. It was also, Guidolin's friend assured him, like nothing else he'd ever seen, let alone climbed.

A regular visitor to Italy's biggest races, Guidolin spread the word to his friends, the TV commentators Auro Bulbarelli and Davide Cassani, and to *La Gazzetta dello Sport* journalist Angelo Zomegnan. They in turn mentioned the Zoncolan to Giro d'Italia boss Carmine Castellano. In 2000, the Vuelta a España had unveiled maybe the hardest climb ever tackled by a professional race, the 12.55-kilometre, 9.9 per cent Alto del Angliru, leaving Castellano scrambling for a riposte. The Zoncolan could be *his* Angliru. Or so he had hoped. Yet after his first recce, in 2001, the Giro chief was unconvinced. Sure it was steep, but it was also 'little more than a donkey track'.

He was right in one sense. In 1939, around 400 men and a peloton of mules had begun trudging up the mountain every day with bags of cement, oblivious to the upturned inferno they were about to create. Within 18 months their work was done. Five years later, on March 2, 1945, they probably rued their efforts when Cossack troops piled into Ovaro via the new road and killed 22 civilians.

The Giro's less tragic version of a massacre occurred in May 2003. Castellano had finally agreed to the 'safe' option of attacking the Zoncolan from Sutrio, perhaps reasoning that, in any case, only the aficionados knew the difference. Still, the favourites for that 2003 edition all visited the Zoncolan in the months leading up to the race and chorused their stupefaction. Gilberto Simoni test-rode the last three kilometres with a 39x27 gear and 'almost had to get off and walk'; his team-mate Leonardo Bertagnolli, riding with a 39x25, didn't even manage that – he turned back. On the morning of the race, *La Gazzetta* christened the Zoncolan 'The Pink Dragon' and exaggerated that 'half of Europe' had been camped on the mountain for three days, such was the 'incredible anticipation, decorated with dreams'. Having attacked on the steepest pitches to win alone, Simoni called the final kilometre 'the hardest I've ever encountered', while the sprinter Mario Cipollini's use of a mountain bike for the same stretch was part-protest, part-publicity stunt.

The following day's *Gazzetta* duly applauded the Zoncolan for 'living up to its "Monster" billing'. And yet the real brute, of course, lay on the western side. Zomegnan, who succeeded Castellano as the Giro director in 2005, knew it, and he and local politician Enzo Cainero were soon conniving to unleash the beast in 2007. Locals who had once hacked down pine trees to create grazing lands were now dispatched to do the same job so that the road and the riders could be filmed from

PREVIOUS PAGE: Two kilometres from the summit. a slither of the Ovaro road appears from out of the pines which coat the Zoncolan's western side.

FAR LEFT: Evidence of the tree-felling which took place before the Giro d'Italia's first trip up the Ovaro road in 2007, to facilitate filming from overhead.

LEFT: Looking back at the campanile Ovaro, low down on the western side. This was the route taken by Cossack troops in 1945 when they stormed Ovaro and killed 22 civilians.

helicopters overhead. The cull cost the Zoncolan 300 trees – a small price for sporting notoriety that would span decades and the 170-odd countries to which the Giro was now broadcast.

In the months leading up to the race, the Giro riders again came, saw and swooned in amazement. The consensus among them was that the Zoncolan tackled from Ovaro was the 'hardest climb in Europe' and 'much harder than the Mortirolo'. After the first two relatively 'normal' kilometres to Liariis, the road narrowed and scarcely kinked for five kilometres; the average gradient in this section was 15.3 per cent, the maximum well over 20. Simoni said it was like a slow, steady execution. 'Mortifying' was the adjective he used.

No matter: he triumphed again and in the process became 'Signor Zoncolan'. This time Simoni used a 34x27 and glorified his success with the verdict: 'The easiest part of this climb is harder than the most difficult you ever get at the Tour de France.'

But the real star was, of course, the Zoncolan. Maybe most importantly, unlike other recent Giro discoveries, it seemed extreme but not gimmicky, and gave the impression of having lain dormant and undiscovered for centuries, in contrast to the equally steep but artificial Plan de Corones, another Zomegnan invention. The Zoncolan also had a distinctive visual identity; the narrow, almost entirely tree-lined road, three tunnels in the final two kilometres and the extraordinary natural grandstand at the summit, embedded the mountain immediately into the Italian national psyche. It wouldn't be long before the Zoncolan had also infiltrated their colloquial language, like the Mortirolo before it. Politicians needing to overturn a heavy deficit in opinion polls now had 'a Zoncolan to climb'. Any kind of struggle against nature or the odds, be it on the sports field, in love or at the workplace, was now 'as tough as the Zoncolan'.

The 'Monster's' other, immediate, legacy was to accelerate the arms race in which Europe's mountain roads had always been unwitting participants. The Tour de France had climbed its first mountain pass, the Col du Pin-Bouchain, in its inaugural 1903 edition, and six years later the first ever Giro d'Italia took its riders over the 684-metre-high, 3.5-kilometre long, 7.5 per cent steep Valico del Macerone in the southern Molise region. Easy by modern standards, the Macerone appalled many of the riders, including eventual Giro winner Luigi Ganna. He punctured four times on its cinder surface and was reduced to tears.

The 1911 edition had seen the first ascent to over 2,000 metres, at Sestriere; the 1937 Giro made a first foray into the Dolomites, via the Passo Rolle; 1953 witnessed the maiden journey up the Stelvio; and 1990 saw the discovery of the Mortirolo.

With doping often rampant, some believed that cycling had already taken the Olympic imperative of 'faster, higher, stronger' too literally, and that the Zoncolan had upped the ante even further. No sooner had Simoni mopped his brow at the top and swung around to admire a shimmering panorama of the Carnic Alps than the search for the next behemoth began literally under his nose. There was, murmured the experts, a third, even *harder* way up the Zoncolan, starting a kilometre to the south of Sutrio in Priola and joining the Sutrio road just where it became brutal, at the Rifugio Moro. This road had been tarmacked in 2006 and sure enough it was, with an average gradient of 12.9 per cent over 8.9 kilometres, harder than the Ovaro side. Those in the know had dubbed it the 'Zar' (Italian for Czar) of the three approaches.

Games without frontiers

The truth of course was that the Zoncolan was never the 'hardest climb in Europe'. It was just the hardest one deemed easy enough for professional road cyclists on conventional bikes. There was a road near Trento, the 7.5-kilometre, 17.6 per cent Via Scanuppia, which made even the 'Zar' look like child's play. That briefly excited the masochists until someone piped up that there was a climb even tougher than the Scanuppia, the road to Pozza San Glisente (8.2 kilometres at an average of 17.7 per cent above Esine), not far from Brescia and the Lago d'Iseo. And no doubt another one somewhere else, that no one had either the folly or strength to mount or measure.

For the moment, the Zoncolan could at least bask in its status as Europe's most infamous cycling climb, and, thanks to that (dis)honour, as perhaps Friuli's best-known mountain. It was no longer just one obscure peak among many. The Monster, The Pink Dragon, the Zoncolan was above all a mountain whose awesome reputation now negated the need for silly sobriquets. The Zoncolan was, quite simply, 'as tough as the Zoncolan'.

Fact file Monte Zoncolan

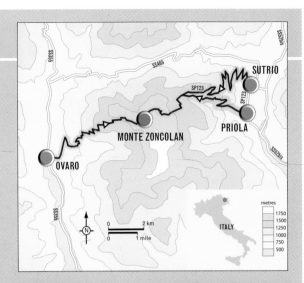

From Ovaro

REGION: Friuli-Venezia Giulia, Italy

ACCESS: From Raveo go to Ovaro on the Via Pedrada (SS-355) until the crossroads with Via Lanjagnas, go right on Via Ex Ferrovia, do a U-turn and follow Via Barc, Via delle Scuole, Via Lenzone and Via Liariis

HEIGHT: 1,730m

LENGTH: 10.1km

ALTITUDE GAIN: 1,203m

AVERAGE GRADIENT: 11.9%

MAXIMUM GRADIENT: 22% (km 3.5)

OPEN: Depending on weather

REFRESHMENTS: Bars in Ovaro and at the top

From Sutrio

REGION: Friuli-Venezia Giulia, Italy

ACCESS: From Tolmezzo, head towards Ovaro following the Via Nazionale/Roma (SS-52bis) until the crossroads with Viale dei Martiri (SS-465). Take Via dei Martiri (SS-465), turn right then left to take Via Monte Sutrio to the top

HEIGHT: 1,730m

LENGTH: 13.5km (climb begins 700 metres from centre of Sutrio)

ALTITUDE GAIN: 1,196m

AVERAGE GRADIENT: 8.9%

MAXIMUM GRADIENT: 22% (at 0.7km to the top)

OPEN: Depending on weather

REFRESHMENTS: Bars in Sutrio and at the top. The Rifugio Moro is 3km from the summit.

From Priola

REGION: Friuli-Venezia Giulia, Italy

ACCESS: From Tolmezzo head towards Ovaro following the Via Nazionale/Roma (SS-52bis) until the crossroads with Via 25 Aprile. Take left Via 25 Aprile and follow the same road to go to Priola. Then turn left to head to the summit

HEIGHT: 1,730m

LENGTH: 8.9km

ALTITUDE GAIN: 1,140m

AVERAGE GRADIENT: 13%

MAXIMUM GRADIENT: 22% (at 7km to the top)

OPEN: Depending on weather

REFRESHMENTS: Bars at the top. The Rifugio Moro is 3km from the summit.

ABOVE: The bronze Monumento al Ciclista Scalatore or 'Monument to the Climber' unveiled in 2007, vandalized later, but now fully repaired and restored.

ABOVE: High on the most infamous of the Zoncolan's three climbs, the Ovaro side – at least until the thrill-seekers discovered the 'even harder' ascent from Priola.

Monte Grappa
1,745m
Italy

BELOW: The giant ossuary on the summit of Monte Grappa is the symbol of a mountain that is itself, in many ways, the talisman of an entire region. The remains of 23,000 soldiers are stored in the mausoleum.

Monte Grappa glares out over the Veneto plains much in the same way that Mont Ventoux keeps solemn guard over the Rhone Valley. Extending 30 kilometres from the banks of the Piave river – almost to the Brenta – Il Grappa dominates the skyline from Venice to Vicenza, its features as dark and inscrutable as its history, its moods as fickle as its weather.

For cyclists, the mountain has also become a magnet. Every weekend, at least in summer, it morphs into an anthill, swarming with fanatical local cyclists on each of its nine ascents. For the many professionals who have lived in the cycling hotbeds around Vicenza, Verona and Padova, it is also a private gymnasium like no other in Italy or perhaps indeed Europe. 'The Grappa has absolutely everything,' Filippo Pozzato, one of the area's leading pros, once said. 'Between them, its nine climbs offer absolutely every challenge imaginable.'

Of those nine, it is purely incidental that the most famous and most popular, the Strada Cadorna, happens to be the easiest. Heading out of Bassano del Grappa – home of the eponymous after-dinner liqueur, Palladio's Ponte degli Alpini (Bridge of the Alpini) and, for a period in the First World War, Ernest Hemingway – the *strada provinciale* 57 runs northwest for two kilometres to Romano d'Ezzelino and the foot of this most classic route up the Grappa.

After a sharp left-hander and several hundred metres at ten per cent, the road soon concertinas into a sequence of gentler hairpins for the next seven kilometres before Costalunga. From there, the Grappa eases into what is barely more than false flat for the next seven kilometres, lilting between landscapes, from craggy awnings and raking views towards the Adriatic to more hairpins, and then, finally, the delightful final section among misty pastures and grazing herds after Ponte San Lorenzo. Only here, 18 kilometres into a sensory crescendo more than an aerobic ordeal, do the slopes stiffen once more to around seven per cent. A sign points right to Campo Croce two kilometres from the summit, then a final shimmy through the rocks and a last westward ramp leading to the Rifugio Bassano complete one of the longest and most visually varied climbs anywhere in Italy.

It was this northbound ascent that Giro d'Italia organizer Vincenzo Torriani chose for the race's first assault on the Grappa in 1968. By then, the mountain already occupied a sombre and significant place in Italian history thanks to its role in the First and Second World Wars. In three horrific battles spread over a year between 1917 and 1918, Italian troops fought heroically on the Grappa to repel the advance of their German and Austro-Hungarian counterparts. Their efforts earned the mountain the nickname 'Italy's Thermopylae' after the battle fought in 480BC between the Greek city-states and the Persian Empire at the pass of Thermopylae. The fighting would also scar the Grappa with trenches of the kind seen in Verdun in France after an even fiercer conflict, and litter its ridges with the remains of 23,000 troops, now stored on the summit in the vast white-stone ossuary. Its other, remarkable, legacy was the Italian army's Galleria Vittorio Emmanuele III: five kilometres of underground fortress now accessible to the public via the Caserma Milano, a few hundred metres short of the summit on the southern side.

The Grappa was again the scene of bloodshed and a brave partisan uprising in the Second World War. This prompted *La Stampa*'s Giro correspondent to lyricize about 'a mountain which can't not be dear for sentimental reasons' in 1968 – before confessing his surprise at the ease of the climb from Romano d'Ezzelino. The media and fans expected a clash of the titans and a winner of the calibre of Eddy Merckx or Felice Gimondi; instead, they saw a freak breakaway win for the journeyman Emilio Casalini while the warlords of the peloton stood on ceremony.

'Patriotism doesn't preclude us from declaring that [...] Monte Grappa was a big bluff – a climb almost 27 kilometres long but with very few truly hard sections and a mostly gentle gradient, interrupted what's more by false flats and a few kilometres of downhill,' *La Stampa* grumbled. 'Monte Grappa fooled the aces of the Giro pack, who continued to mark each other all the way to the top, curve after curve, while the *domestique* Casalini, who had never won a pro race until yesterday, slipped away to a clamorous victory.'

If he'd wanted drama, Torriani would have been better served by one of the Grappa's other angles of attack. He had tried in 1974, opting for the still relatively straightforward route from Caupo, with Merckx triumphing in Bassano to give the Grappa its first truly worthy winner. Eight years later another Giro legend, Giuseppe Saronni, left with more mitigated memories of the same, northern side of the mountain; descending on what was then still a dirt road into Caupo en route to the stage finish in San Martino di Castrozza, Saronni

ABOVE: The lush, wooded slopes of the Grappa's northern side serve up two lovely and varied climbs starting just a few hundred metres apart, this one from Caupo and the other from Seren del Grappa.

punctured six times. 'I remember it well,' Saronni said in 2011. 'After the first three punctures, there were no more spare wheels in my team car so I had to call the neutral service car. Problem was, their wheels and tyres were even less robust than mine and I had three more flats before the bottom of the descent. Amazingly, I was still able to rejoin the main group five kilometres before the stage finish in San Martino.'

Nine types of torture

The Giro returned after a 28-year hiatus in 2010 – Vincenzo Nibali ascending from Semonzo then bombing down the Strada Cadorna to a stage victory in Asolo – but the Grappa retains an allure that exists and flourishes mostly outside the confines of professional cycling. Every year, in August, it plays host to one of the most prestigious races on the Italian amateur calendar, the Bassano–Monte Grappa. Non-competitive riders can also satisfy or cultivate a fixation with the Grappa at any time of year by 'collecting' all nine ascents of the mountain and the *Brevetto del Grappa*. A *brevetto* (licence) logbook is purchased from the Non-Profit Center in Romano d'Ezzelino, then stamped at authorized bars and cafés at the foot of all nine routes and again at the Rifugio Bassano after every successful ascent.

As Pozzato and others have remarked, the beauty and singularity of the Grappa lies in the vastly different character of all nine climbs. The evil incline up to Bocca di Forca from Possagno, home of Antonio Canova's stunning neo-classic temple, is one of the hardest climbs in Italy and Europe; moving anticlockwise around the mountain's base, the routes from Cavaso del Tomba, Pederobba and Alano di Piave, up to the intermediary summit of Monte Tomba, are also narrow, rough and nasty; the two north–south routes from Caupo and Seren del Grappa are parallels only in direction – the former a breeze and

the latter a brute, particularly in its middle section; and finally, back on the southern slope, are the best-known and busiest routes from Romano d'Ezzelino and Semonzo – but also the Grappa-phile's most recent discovery, the redoubtable Salto della Capra or Goat's Leap from Valle San Liberale to La Vedetta.

Variety, though, needn't be the spice of every cyclist's life. Who says? A local entrepreneur by the name of Ginesio Ballan. He climbs the Grappa almost every day, and only ever via Romano d'Ezzelino and the Strada Cadorna.

'Why does he do it? I don't know,' says Giancarlo Andolfatti, director of the Non-Profit Center in Romano d'Ezzelino and inventor of the *Brevetto*. 'I see him on the way up early in the morning, often in the dark. I think he likes people to know he's doing it but not why. He's not too keen to talk about it if you ask him. He's a very shy gentleman. But he's being doing it for decades!

'As for me, well I'm not really a cyclist, and I also take the Grappa for granted a bit, having lived here all my life. That said, one day a few years ago I got off the train in Venice and it suddenly hit me, why people are so drawn to the Grappa; it was a perfect, clear day and the sky was this amazing cobalt blue. You could see the whole pre-Alpine chain from the Grappa to Trieste. At that moment, I felt the attraction, the magnetism of the mountain.'

BELOW: An ascent of the Grappa via the Bocca di Forca could be considered extreme sport, such is the severity of the gradient and the texture of the road.

Fact file Monte Grappa

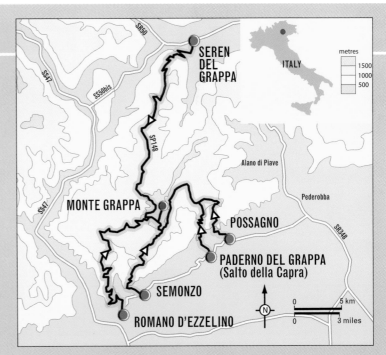

From Possagno

REGION: Veneto, Italy

ACCESS: From Possagno, follow signs to Massiere, then Cima Grappa. After 22km, the road connects with the Semonzo road

HEIGHT: 1,745m

LENGTH: 23.8km

ALTITUDE GAIN: 1,472m

AVERAGE GRADIENT: 6.2%

MAXIMUM GRADIENT: 21% (km 10)

OPEN: All year, subject to weather

REFRESHMENTS: In Possagno and at the summit

ALTERNATIVE ROUTES: From Pederobba via Monte Tomba (24.5km at 6.2%) and from Alano di Piave via Monte Tomba (21.93km at 6.6%)

From Romano d'Ezzelino

REGION: Veneto, Italy

ACCESS: Take the SP148, turn left on Via Molinetto after 1.1km, then proceed on SS47

HEIGHT: 1,745m

LENGTH: 25.13km

ALTITUDE GAIN: 1,558m

AVERAGE GRADIENT: 6.2%

MAXIMUM GRADIENT: 11% (km 1)

OPEN: All year, subject to weather

REFRESHMENTS: In Romano d'Ezzelino, Ponte San Lorenzo and at summit. Numerous fountains

From Semonzo

REGION: Veneto, Italy

ACCESS: From Semonzo, go through Spezzamonte and take the SP140 to the Cime Grappa

HEIGHT: 1,745m

LENGTH: 18.6km

ALTITUDE GAIN: 1,530m

AVERAGE GRADIENT: 8.3%

MAXIMUM GRADIENT: 12.2% (km 12 and km 14)

OPEN: All year, subject to weather

REFRESHMENTS: In Paderno del Grappa and at summit

From Paderno del Grappa (Salto della Capra)

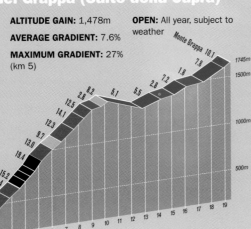

REGION: Veneto, Italy

ACCESS: From Crespano del Grappa, head towards Possagno to the Fiette crossroads in Paderno del Grappa, turn left in the centre of the village and take the Valle San Liberale road

HEIGHT: 1,745m

LENGTH: 19.4km

ALTITUDE GAIN: 1,478m

AVERAGE GRADIENT: 7.6%

MAXIMUM GRADIENT: 27% (km 5)

OPEN: All year, subject to weather

From Seren del Grappa

REGION: Veneto, Italy

ACCESS: Follow signs to Stalle, Chiesa Nuova and Monte Grappa from Seren del Grappa

HEIGHT: 1,745m

LENGTH: 21.1km

ALTITUDE GAIN: 1,335m

AVERAGE GRADIENT: 6.3%

MAXIMUM GRADIENT: 20% (km 7)

OPEN: All year, subject to weather

REFRESHMENTS: In Seren and at summit

ALTERNATIVE ROUTE: From Caupo (28.9km at 4.9%)

Sierra de la Pandera
1,779m
Spain

ABOVE: The Sierra de la Pandera in all its glory, behind the Valdepeñas de Jaén's brilliant white townscape and to the left of this shot.

❝ THOSE GREEN GATES ARE THE LID TO
A PANDORA'S BOX, the Pandera, and within
500 metres, between rocks and yellow broom,
the road is rising for almost a kilometre between
ten and 15 per cent. ❞

There are certain climbs that prove harder to locate than they are to ascend. While the adage may not apply to the Sierra de la Pandera, Andalucia's 'Angliru of the south', mainly because the mountain in question is an absolute brute, woe betide anyone who heads to this desolate, sun-baked outcrop without pinpoint directions as well as tiny gears and twinkling toes. Not for nothing did the Vuelta a España only discover what instantly became one of its favourite, most feared high-altitude haunts in the race's 57th edition, in 2002. Even then it took a letter from a local woman to Vuelta chief Victor Cordero, extolling the Pandera's virtues, to rouse it from obscurity.

No fanfare, no warning and certainly no signpost heralds the entrance to the Pandera proper. Technically, the two routes to its summit begin 21 kilometres apart on the A6060 linking Alcalá la Real and Jaén, in Valdepeñas de Jaén and Los Villares, but in practice the two approaches converge in a pincer movement to the foot of an 8.3-kilometre cul-de-sac then shared all the way to the top. Finding the point of their intersection is, alas, just one of many challenges on the Pandera. Leaving Los Villares, don't be duped by wishful thinking into turning left towards the Meson de la Pandera just before the road doglegs right and over a bridge five kilometres out of town. Chance would be a fine thing; the real mineshaft begins after five-and-a-half more kilometres of sinuous climbing followed by five more of false flat on the A6060, with the Pandera summit and its aerial masts looming high above your head and to the left. To be precise, it kicks off and up just over four kilometres after the JA-3301 joins from the right, or, if you're arriving from Valdepeñas de Jaén, after five kilometres of climbing and a 300-metre descent as the A6060 swings to the left. So no signs, no warning; just a rusty green gate, a dusty four-metre-wide strip of untended tarmac and, above the quarry straight ahead, a glimpse of the rugged Pandera plateau.

Angliru of the south

Your first thought at this point might be how or why on earth a professional bike race ever ended up here. Cognoscenti of rare and difficult summits may see similarities with the forest road or Trou du Rat up the Côte de Vidauque in southeast France, while noting that was only ever tackled from the opposite, more sanitized side in the Critérium International pro race. Too narrow, too steep and too restricted in capacity for the circus that accompanies events like the Tour de France or Vuelta a España, roads like these more often become the preserve of the 'weekend warrior', relics of an age when men were men and roads just ribbons of gravel.

La Pandera was one of the rare exceptions to the rule. Faced with increasing competition and falling television audiences, having unsheathed the Alto del Angliru in 1999, three years later Vuelta boss Cordero premiered his 'Angliru of the south', La Pandera. Jutting suddenly, solitarily out of the olive groves that have earned Jaén the distinction of World Capital of Olive Oil, the mountain was as intimidating in appearance as it promised to be in gradient, particularly when viewed from Valdepeñas de Jaén. Spanish newspaper *ABC* said the antennae at the summit 'give it the look of a top-secret military base'. The same source, however, also regretted in January 2002 that 'the mountain they called an Angliru in miniature, with colossal ramps and incredible views of Jaén – part-mountain, part-bone-crusher' had failed to live up to Spanish climber José Maria Jiménez's expectations on a pre-Vuelta recce. 'It's not the Angliru,' Jiménez sniffed. 'There are sections at 15 per cent but also flatter parts where you can recover.'

He was right… up to a point. Nine months later, that September, Roberto Heras's accelerations were perhaps more responsible than either temperatures in the high 30s or the slopes for turning the Pandera into an inferno. The Vuelta has since returned four times and on each occasion the Pandera has left its protagonists gasping. Andrei Kashechkin and his Kazakh compatriot Alexandre Vinokourov, in particular, suffocated the opposition in 2006 with a fiendish onslaught, albeit one that took on a new light when they both failed dope tests the following year. Of the four riders to win here, indeed, only the Italian Damiano Cunego's victory in 2009 hasn't subsequently been overshadowed by a doping scandal. Heras, 2003 winner Alejandro Valverde and Kashechkin all defeated the Pandera before losing their credibility.

No longer a top secret climb

Mere mortals, of course, are unlikely to be as underwhelmed as Jiménez was in 2002. Those green gates are the lid to a Pandora's box, the Pandera, and within 500 metres, between rocks and yellow broom, the road is rising for almost a kilometre between ten and 15 per cent. From there it loops to the left towards Jaén and flattens, but by now breath is short and a two kilometre let-up will seem equally brief. With the mountainside almost bare but for a stubbly moquette of thyme and wild rosemary, a triangular road sign forewarns of 15 per cent gradients that promptly unfurl around a vicious right-hand bend. From here, it's bad news for the next four

kilometres save for some sublime glimpses of the Sierra Nevada to the south and, as the road curls around the back of the mountain and past the first of the antennae, of Jaén and its 13th-century Castillo de Santa Catalina. Slowly, the rosemary has given way to rocky patios on one side and a terrifying precipice disappearing beneath your ankles and towards Jaén on the other. Here, the wind can howl but the gradient also abates on the approach to a second gate through which lie 300 metres of false flat and impending relief: another sign showing 15 per cent this time refers to a 500-metre descent permitting speeds of 60km/h and effectively cancelling out half of the last, 11-per-cent wall to the military base and the end of La Pandera.

BELOW: The sharp right-hander five kilometres from the summit signalling the advent of the steepest gradients – the 15 per cent pitches that inspired the Pandera's 'Angliru of the south' moniker.

From here, all that remains is to gaze towards the Sierra Nevada in the southeast or turn to face Jaén and the Sierra de la Grana in the northwest. The chances of a clear view are good; not for nothing do the Spanish Army still use the antennae here for infrared surveillance and the adjacent watchtower to scour the plains for forest fires.

Thanks to the Vuelta, it may no longer be the top-secret climb known only to Andalusians, but La Pandera retains a privacy and tranquillity that you may only find on the Muro di Sormano of the other climbs featured in this book. Like the Muro, the Pandera is closed to motorized traffic, this only enhancing its standing as one of cycling's new must-climb mountains. Before the Angliru, and particularly up

until 1995, when the Vuelta moved from April to September, many of Spain's most famous climbs owed their prominence to races other than their national tour. The Basque Country's Urkiola, the Jaizkibel and the Lagunas de Neila in Burgos were all good examples. With the Angliru and the Pandera came a new breed of Vuelta superclimb, joined in subsequent races by the likes of Xorret de Catí, the Bola del Mundo, Calar Alto and La Covatilla.

As Spanish journalist José Carlos Carabias put it in 2002, Spanish climbs can be divided into two categories: the Angliru and everything else. La Pandera perhaps won't alter that – but it does continue to make a strong and painful case for the honour of best of the rest.

Fact file Sierra de la Pandera

From Valdepeñas de Jaén

REGION: Province of Jaén, Andalucia, southern Spain

ACCESS: From Valdepeñas de Jaén, take A6060 north towards Jaén and, after 5km and a 300m descent, turn into unmarked road to right, through green gate

HEIGHT: 1,779m

LENGTH: 15km

ALTITUDE GAIN: 931m

AVERAGE GRADIENT: 6.2%

MAXIMUM GRADIENT: Multiple ramps at 15%

OPEN: Open all year, subject to weather

REFRESHMENTS: Numerous bars and shops in Valdepeñas de Jaén. No refreshments on or at the top of climb itself

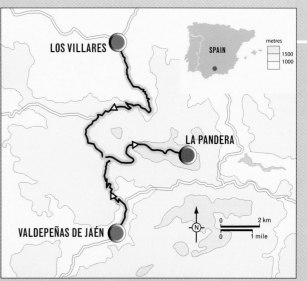

From Los Villares

REGION: Province of Jaén, Andalucia, southern Spain

ACCESS: From Los Villares, take A6060 south towards Valdepeñas de Jaén and, after 14km, turn into unmarked road to left, through green gate

HEIGHT: 1,779m

LENGTH: 24km

ALTITUDE GAIN: 1,237m

AVERAGE GRADIENT: 5.2%

MAXIMUM GRADIENT: Multiple ramps at 15%

OPEN: Open all year, subject to weather

REFRESHMENTS: Numerous bars and shops in Los Villares. No refreshments on or at the top of climb itself

ABOVE: Remnants from the Vuelta a España's 2009 visit to the Pandera – graffitied support for the Xacobeo Galicia team.

Alpe d'Huez
1,803m
France

As far as the Tour de France was concerned, its first date with Alpe d'Huez in 1952 was neither an immediate success nor, literally, a roaring one. Photos and film reel of the day show just a smattering of supporters, a mere *soupçon* of excitement. In a lone Fausto Coppi, the Italian *campionissimo*, the Alpe couldn't have wished for a more glamorous baptist, yet even the Tour's unofficial mouthpiece, *L'Equipe* newspaper, was unimpressed. Their chief cycling correspondent Claude Tillet complained that what ought to have been an epic 266-kilometre stage in the best Alpine tradition had been reduced to a 13.1-kilometre-long uphill time trial. Tour chief Jacques Goddet admitted that Coppi had been 'too strong' and the peloton in general too intimidated to wage real war before Le Bourg d'Oisans and the foot of the Alpe. Goddet's closing assessment of the stage sounded like the Alpe's death knell: '[The stage] offered no reason to lobby for more stage finishes at altitude'.

With five or six summit finishes *de rigueur* on modern grand tour routes, it's easy to underestimate just how radical the idea of finishing on top of a mountain seemed in the early 1950s. High-rise endings were, in short, considered an unsatisfying, made-for-TV contrivance that put an end to the Homeric breakaways of the old days, when the best climbers would make their move on the first pass of the stage and spend the rest of the day trying to safeguard or extend their advantage. The new vogue had shifted, if not reversed, a paradigm: now the big hitters could doze for the majority of a stage and count on the final obstacle to eliminate the weak. This was what the Alpe had done in 1952 and what mountain-top finishes would continue to do – only, increasingly, with riders so hardwired to wait for the grand, uphill dénouement that they forgot there were other ways to race in the mountains.

This made no odds to the people over the border running the Giro d'Italia. They simply resolved to snuff out ever more difficult and dramatic high-altitude arenas to win over the critics. Their counterparts in Paris, though, and especially Jacques Goddet, wouldn't forget the anti-climax of that 1952 visit to the Alpe in a hurry.

RIGHT: The view across the Oisans valley, with possibly the most famous mountain road corkscrewing towards the lens and the summit.

And it had all promised so well. A local painter who knew the Tour's chief *commissaire*, Jean Barbaglia, had got together with the owner of a hotel on the Alpe, Georges Rajon, and managed to raise the 2,000 pounds sterling required to host the race. Until then, the Alpe had been known for one sport only – Alpine skiing, its first ski-lifts having opened in 1935. Earlier still, for centuries, the mountain had been home to chamois, marmots, a few farmers and, of all things, a silver mine. These days, its transient population on the day of a Tour de France is usually estimated at around half a million.

Goddet and the Tour wouldn't chance a return to the Alpe until 1976. In the 20 years since its first and last appearance on the route, summit finishes had gone from being a fad to a fact of racing, and one that even Goddet and his new wingman Félix Lévitan had slowly embraced. The 1975 Tour featured no fewer than five stages to ski resorts, three of them back to back, plus a mountain time trial. It was high time for the Tour to try again at the Alpe, not that anyone would have foreseen the wildly successful results. That 1976 visit was also a double reprieve: originally due to finish in Grenoble, stage nine was rerouted to the Alpe when the Isère regional authorities had second thoughts about hosting the Tour in their capital. Lévitan had promptly put the call in to his old pal Rajan; not only would the Alpe gladly step in as Lévitan's plan B, Rajan said, but this would finally give him the chance to show off his latest innovation – the numbered hairpins he had copied from the Vršič Pass in Slovenia, where he'd holidayed in 1964.

A sea of fans

The Alpe's other great blessing in the years following its reinstatement was its remarkable effect on one group of cyclists: the Dutch. Riders from the Netherlands would win eight of the next 13 stages to the Alpe, which was now an almost annual fixture. The sequence would gave the climb a nickname, The Dutch Mountain, and, in part, its unique atmosphere. The Americans had Woodstock, the British Glastonbury, and the Dutch… Alpe d'Huez. Road trips there became a rite of passage for Dutch teenagers and 20-somethings. Then as now, up to a week before the Tour's arrival, they would colonize the bend between hairpins six and seven (they count down from the top) which hence became the Dutch Corner and, for

a few evenings each summer, the party capital of Europe. By day, they would paint the road with the names of their heroes – 1977 and 1978 winner Hennie Kuiper, another Alpe d'Huez two-timer Joop Zoetemelk, or perennial bridesmaid Michael Boogerd; by night, the same strip of tarmac turned into a dancefloor, with the strains of 'Boogie is de Best', their ode to Boogerd, or other dubious 'classics', resonating across the Oisans valley.

The people truly made the place – not least because the road itself was practically invisible on race day. As *L'Equipe* journalist Philippe Brunel recalled, Marco Pantani's victorious ascent in 1995 was unprecedented as much for his record time as for the fact that Pantani didn't see the road 'unless you meant that thin ribbon of burning asphalt, covered in graffiti, between two deafening walls of spectators, which threaded beneath his wheels'. Pantani confirmed at the time that he 'was climbing blind, in the middle of this sea of people opening in front of me'.

The fans on the Alpe had the effect of a giant human vacuum cleaner, sucking the riders towards the summit. French rider Jacky Durand lived close to the Alpe for years, and soon noticed the difference between climbing it in training and racing; the Alpe was invariably awarded *hors catégorie* or 'special category' status in the Tour's King of the Mountains competition, but Durand reckoned it was the only 'easy' climb in that upper tier. One key reason was the fans, another those famous 21 hairpins, each of which is now dedicated to one or more riders who have won on the Alpe. 'The hairpins are practically flat – if you want to take a breather, you just take them on the outside,' Durand explained in *Procycling* magazine. The only real difficulty on the Alpe, the Frenchman believed, was the brusqueness of the first two kilometres, also by some distance its steepest. With an average gradient between 10.4 and 10.6 per cent, this rude introduction made Durand 'want to hit my head against the rock walls at the side of the road'.

All joking aside, it seems incredible that the supporters' jubilation – or inebriation – hasn't overspilled more often on the Alpe, causing more accidents. More than one rider has admitted to feeling afraid as well as exhilarated on the Alpe. Prior to stage 18, the 1986 Tour had been dominated by one story: the rivalry between the young American Greg LeMond and his team-mate, the five-time Tour

Fact file Alpe d'Huez

From Le Bourg d'Oisans

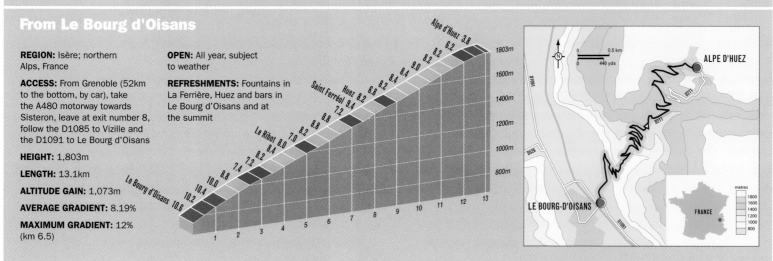

REGION: Isère; northern Alps, France

ACCESS: From Grenoble (52km to the bottom, by car), take the A480 motorway towards Sisteron, leave at exit number 8, follow the D1085 to Vizille and the D1091 to Le Bourg d'Oisans

HEIGHT: 1,803m

LENGTH: 13.1km

ALTITUDE GAIN: 1,073m

AVERAGE GRADIENT: 8.19%

MAXIMUM GRADIENT: 12% (km 6.5)

OPEN: All year, subject to weather

REFRESHMENTS: Fountains in La Ferrière, Huez and bars in Le Bourg d'Oisans and at the summit

OPPOSITE: A feature of the Alpe that can't be appreciated during televised stages of the Tour de France – the view, in this case towards the Ecrins massif. In the foreground, a sign tells us that we are three hairpins from the top, and that this one is dedicated to the Italian climber Marco Pantani.

LEFT: The streets of Bourg d'Oisans – now a magnet for cyclists thanks to the climb of the Alpe.

champion Bernard Hinault. On stage 18 the pair romped clear on the Col de la Croix de Fer and arrived in Le Bourg d'Oisans with LeMond in the yellow jersey and their La Vie Claire manager Bernard Tapie urging him to gift Hinault the stage victory. But when they crossed the line hand in hand, there was, LeMond revealed, another reason why he hadn't pressed home his supremacy: 'I was worried, thinking about how Eddy Merckx had been punched by a spectator [on the Puy de Dôme in 1975] and that there could be someone else like that out there. There was such strong feeling, because I was racing against France's best known athlete. It was getting frenzied.'

The Hollywood climb

Two years earlier, on the Tour's rest day at the Alpe, Tapie and Hinault had dispatched a striking brunette clad from head to toe in black leather to fetch LeMond on a motorbike and bring him to their hotel. There they had promised to make him professional cycling's first millionaire if he joined their new La Vie Claire team. After LeMond's victory in the '86 Tour, secured on the Alpe, it sounded as though Hinault for one regretted the decision: 'I could have had the American's skin on the Alpe,' the Badger wrote in his autobiography, his bluster equal only to his self-delusion.

Once, infamously, the audience participation for which the Alpe is renowned did almost produce catastrophic results: 900 metres from the finish line in the 1999 Tour, the Italian Giuseppe Guerini was riding towards a certain victory when a young German fan stepped into the middle of the road to take a photo. They collided, Guerini tumbled and his dream with him. Or so it seemed: aided by a push from his mortified assailant, he recovered just in time to keep his lead and give the Italians their seventh victory in eight visits to the Alpe in the 1990s.

The defining performances of the next decade on the Alpe were Armstrong's in 2001 and 2004 – although the American had to endure jeers, boos and considerably worse on his way to victory in

the first mountain time trial ever staged on the Alpe in 2004. Worse was to come two years later, when 12 months into a retirement that would turn into a sabbatical, Armstrong dropped in on the Tour at the Alpe and was greeted with the following front page headline in *France Soir* newspaper: *Bienvenu en France, trou-du-cul*, or, translated, *Welcome to France, a**hole.*

Principally a reference to ill-judged remarks about the French that Armstrong had made at an awards ceremony earlier that year, the slur also betrayed an ill-feeling towards the American partly, perversely, nourished on the Alpe. Although respectively 25 seconds and one second slower than Pantani's 1997 record, Armstrong's 2001 and 2004 rides were cited by some physiologists as evidence that he must be using performance-enhancing drugs. Hinault and LeMond, they pointed out, had taken ten minutes longer to complete the 13.1 kilometres in 1986, before the advent of the peloton's new poison *du choix*, EPO. The first sub-40-minute time, Gianni Bugno's in 1991, indeed coincided with what many believed was the new wonder drug's cascade into the mainstream.

Not that any rider, suspicion or scandal could transcend the Alpe by now. Proof of that comes from the 300 or so amateur cyclists who climb the Alpe on any average day, buying and stamping a punch-card at the bottom, then again at the top, to compare their times to those of Coppi (45 minutes, 22 seconds), Pantani and Armstrong. The more masochistic of them return every July for one of the most demanding cyclosportive events anywhere in the world, the Marmotte, which crawls to the Alpe via the cols of the Croix de Fer, Télégraphe and Galibier.

Some purists will continue to pooh-pooh it as a *nouveau venu* among classic climbs, tacky and artificial like its eponymous ski resort (which, nonetheless, does boast the world's longest single piste – the 16-kilometre Sarenne black run), but thousands of people at the roadside, and millions more on TV, can't all be wrong. As Jacques Augendre, the Tour's official historian put it: 'The Tourmalet, Galibier and Izoard used to be the race's three mythical climbs, but these three passes have been surpassed in notoriety by Alpe d'Huez. It's become the summit of the modern era... No other stage has such presence. With its 21 bends, steep ramps and massive crowds, it has become the Hollywood climb.'

Passo del Mortirolo
Italy

1,852m

'ON THE HARDEST PARTS, I WAS HURTING, REALLY HURTING. The Mortirolo is the hardest climb I've ever ridden. '

Lance Armstrong

There are cognoscenti of cycling climbs whose noses turn up at roughly the same angle as the Mortirolo at the mere mention of this 12.5-kilometre, 10.5 per cent leg-breaker. The Mortirolo is not particularly pretty nor historically important, and neither is it dotted with interesting artefacts or landmarks. What it is, is hard. Very, excruciatingly hard and unpleasant.

In one sense, it is also a purer cycling climb than many more fabled ascents such as the Stelvio or the Gavia, both of which lie within an hour's ride to the north. While they and others have a heritage and attraction that far transcend and predate cycling, the Mortirolo has practically nothing. True, its murderous name does relate the mass cull of pagan insurgents by Charles the Great's army in 773, but that's about all. Anything else significant that has happened on these slopes has occurred since 1990 – when professional cycling and the Giro d'Italia discovered what has been called the first of the über-climbs.

The road linking Mazzo di Valtellina with Monno and the Val Camonica began life as a goat track and today it retains roughly the same dimensions, only with a much smoother surface. Almost entirely submerged in dense woods, noodling tortuously through 39 hairpins past barely a house or a soul, the Mortirolo offers as little in the way of views as it does in respite. The section between San Matè at kilometre three and just beyond Piaz de l'Acqua at kilometre eight, in particular, is a thankless, airless grind with a gradient constantly above ten per cent. Only at the end of this stairway to hell does the forest give way to the first decent views of the Valtellina. It is also here that the crowds have usually been thickest during the Giro d'Italia.

At Piaz, another ghastly left-hander brings the cyclist face to face with one of the more modern and curious monuments to be found on European passes. Completed in 2006, two years after Marco Pantani's death, a sculpture set high on a walled embankment depicts the Italian climber in full flight on a steep shard of mountain road – the mountain road, this one to be precise, where his legend was truly born in a stage of the 1994 Giro d'Italia.

'When we saw that wall, the only one of the climb, we didn't have any doubt about where to put the monument,' said Michele Biz, one of the sculpture's designers. 'Because this climb is a wall. And so, the wall itself became part of the monument.'

Such is Pantani's connection with the climb that a special award, the Cima Pantani or Pantani Summit prize is now awarded to the first rider over the Mortirolo whenever it features in the Giro.

Pantani's consecration, Cavendish's nightmare

Maybe wisely, the *Corsa Rosa* had first become acquainted with the Mortirolo via the easiest of its three ascents in 1990 (the third and least well known, from Grosio, is 14.8 kilometres long at an average of 8.3 per cent). The climb from Monno (17.2 kilometres long at an average of 6.7 per cent) barely even counts as a low-cal Mortirolo, and that year the Venezuelan Leonardo Sierra positively skipped across the summit in first place. Here Sierra's problems began: the Venezuelan was an awful descender and this was an awful descent. Despite crashing, Sierra still won in Aprica – and above all he set Giro chief Carmine Castellano thinking: wouldn't that drainpipe down to Mazzo be even more spectacular (not to mention safer) if tackled in the opposite direction?

Sure enough, the following year, Castellano unshackled the monster. While some riders complained, naturally, the Italian *tifosi* rejoiced as Franco Chioccioli attacked six kilometres from the pass and embarked on a 52-kilometre escape to victory. Already one minute and ten seconds clear on the Mortirolo, Chioccioli cemented his advantage on the Santa Cristina climb and triumphed easily at Aprica. A week later, Chioccioli was the Giro champion.

In 1994 the climb did more than just decide the Giro – it left a legacy for the Italian sporting public to cherish. On stage 14 of the Giro, a waifish, balding rookie from the Adriatic coast, Marco Pantani, stunned the Giro peloton and the watching public by winning on the longest and most mountainous day of the race so far in Merano. Beginner's luck, muttered the experts – until the next day, when with almost balletic grace, Pantani shimmered away from champion-elect Evgeny Berzin and Tour de France king Miguel Indurain on the Mortirolo. Pantani duly won his second straight stage in Aprica, sending the fans and TV commentators into raptures.

Hindsight and subsequent revelations about rampant doping in the early 1990s haven't been kind to Pantani or any of his contemporaries, and indeed it's hard to say whether one anecdote from that day in 1994 heightens our admiration or distaste. Famously dismissive of any pro rider who used a 25-tooth sprocket, with the Mortirolo in mind, Pantani had allowed his Carrera team mechanics to fit a 24. As the road kicked up out of Mazzo and Pantani twiddled at his gear lever, though, his chain fell like a Freudian slip onto the 22. Pantani tried again and again and again… until, gleefully, he stopped twiddling and just kicked harder. 'Sensational,' said his Carrera *directeur sportif* Giuseppe Martinelli years later. Others would call climbing the

Mortirolo in a 22-tooth sprocket an act of folly – or a testament to the performance-enhancing properties of the banned drug EPO.

Pantani's compatriot Ivan Gotti's performances on the Mortirolo have faced similar scrutiny. The nuggety climber's record of 42 minutes and 40 seconds for the ascent from Mazzo, set on the penultimate stage of the 1996 Giro, still stands today. Coincidentally or not, the following year cycling's governing body introduced blood tests in the hope of at least containing EPO abuse, and on the Mortirolo Gotti went 30 seconds slower. He also faced the taunts of his Russian rival Pavel Tonkov for his choice of gear – but had the last laugh when he stuck with Tonkov all the way to the top to effectively seal Giro victory.

Tens of thousands converged on the mountain in 1999 in the expectation of seeing Pantani do the same, only to learn that *il Pirata*'s destiny and the Mortirolo were bound by a fickle karma; instead of 'trouser-pressing' the Mortirolo, as the *Gazzetta* had described it in 1994, the Italian was leaving the Giro in disgrace after a failed blood test that morning. Roberto Heras's stage win in Aprica – and Gotti's second overall Giro title in Milan the next day – were comprehensively eclipsed.

Gotti's controversial coach, Michele Ferrari, also provided Lance Armstrong with training advice and allegedly much more besides for much of his career, and it was on one of his trips to see Ferrari just over the Swiss border in St. Moritz that Armstrong trained on the Mortirolo for the first time in 2004. 'It's a terrible climb,' was the American's

FROM LEFT TO RIGHT: Looking back towards Mazzo, the Valtellina and the Adda river, low down on the Mortirolo; A rare opening on the mostly tree-lined road up the Mortirolo; Trees blocking the view on both sides, gradients bordering on unreasonable – this is all familiar territory on the Mortirolo; The Mortirolo and professional cycling became acquainted long after Fausto Coppi's time, but this hasn't stopped one fan paying homage to *il campionissimo* one kilometre from the summit.

PREVIOUS PAGE: The summit of the Mortirolo – one of the hardest to reach and hence one of the most rewarding in cycling.

conclusion. 'It's perfect for a mountain bike. On the hardest parts, I was riding in a 39x27 and I was hurting, really hurting. The Mortirolo is the hardest climb I've ever ridden.'

Three years later, the British rider Mark Cavendish echoed Armstrong's assessment. Noted for his prowess on the flat but not uphill, Mark Cavendish had unsurprisingly struggled on the Mortirolo in the 2008 Giro d'Italia. 'It's the hardest climb I've ever done,' said the Manxman, a winner of 15 Tour de France stages between 2008 and 2010. 'It's savage, f**king savage – unbelievably steep and it just goes on and on. If you asked me for two words to sum it up I'd say "steep" and "long". Actually, make that three words: "long", "steep" and "sick".'

Fact file Passo del Mortirolo

From Mazzo di Valtellina

REGION: Lombardy, Italy

ACCESS: Take the road towards Mazzo di Valtellina off the Strada Statale 38 dello Stelvio, 9.5km from Tirano in the south and 30km from Bormio in the north

HEIGHT: 1,852m

LENGTH: 12.5km

ALTITUDE GAIN: 1,300m

AVERAGE GRADIENT: 10.5%

MAXIMUM GRADIENT: 18%

OPEN: From April to October

REFRESHMENTS: At the Agriturismo al Castagneto after 2km of climbing. The municipality of Mazzo has plans to build a refuge at the summit, probably to be called the Malga Mortirolo and likely to open in 2012

ALTERNATIVE ROUTES: From Grosio (14.8km at 8.3%) and Monno (17.2km at 6.7%)

Mont Ventoux
1,912m

France

PREVIOUS PAGE: The weather station on the Ventoux's summit, still several suffocating kilometres away across the moonscape that characterizes the final six kilometres of the Bédoin ascent.

RIGHT: The Chalet Reynard: a humble bar that became one of cycling's sacred landmarks. Here two climbs end, from Bédoin and Sault, and another very different one begins to the Ventoux's summit.

The 'witches' cauldron' described by former *L'Equipe* correspondent Antoine Blondin; 'a sloping desert, the Sahara of stones' in the eyes and words of former Tour de France director Jacques Goddet; the 'God of Evil demanding sacrifice' portrayed by French philosopher Roland Barthes, 'a veritable Moloch, the despot of cyclists… it never forgives the weak and charges an unjust tariff of sufferance'; the 'evil beast' about which Felice Gimondi warned his protégé Marco Pantani in 2000; or, most basic and best of the lot, this from Raphael Geminiani to his team-mate Ferdi Kübler, moments before their date with the Giant of Provence in the 1955 Tour: 'Attention, Ferdi – the Ventoux isn't a climb like any other'.

A climb like no other. Geminiani might just as well have said 'mountain'. For while cycling has played a major role in the myth, Mont Ventoux has always been much more than just a road, more even than the altar to sporting deities described by Barthes. It stands alone, literally – a 'geographical heresy', as French journalist Philippe Brunel called it – closer in kilometres to the Alps than the Pyrenees, but in nature nothing like either.

Visible from 100 kilometres away in all directions, its bare upper slopes appear permanently snow-capped – and the optical illusion once applied to the whole mountain. By the beginning of the 19th century, the deforestation and wood-burning that began in the Middle Ages had stripped the Ventoux from head to toe, whereupon the locals drew up a plan of action to restore the mountain's evergreen cloak – or at least a corset. They planted oaks, Austrian pines, cedars and larches. Soon, the villages around the base of the mountain had a new saying – that on the Ventoux, you went 'from Saharan Africa to Greenland'. Not long later, in 1882, the mountain acquired a meteorological observatory and, more importantly, a road accessing it from the village of Bédoin on the southern side.

By now, of course, the Ventoux was already famous. In Italy, long before it was associated with the chrome-domed climber Pantani, the *Mont Chauve* or 'Bald Mountain' was known as the site of the great poet Francesco Petrarch's expedition of April 1336, which Petrarch chronicled in a letter to his old friend Francesco Dionigi di Borgo San Sepulcro from a hostelry in Malaucène the same evening. Defying the warnings of a shepherd he met on the way who claimed to have climbed the Ventoux 50 years earlier, Petrarch, his brother and two servants had completed an audacious and spiritual journey, with the poet's thoughts drifting ever more insistently towards his lost love Laura, back in Italy. At the summit, he stood 'like dazed' by the view of the Alps, 'rugged and snow-capped' to the east, and the realization that 'what I had read of Athos and Olympus seemed less incredible as I myself witnessed the same things from a mountain of less fame'. Soon, he was also castigating himself for 'admiring earthly things, [I] who might long ago have learned from even the pagan philosophers that nothing is wonderful but the soul, which, when great itself, finds nothing great outside itself.'

Modern analysts might argue that Petrarch's greatest crime – or achievement – on the Ventoux was one of deception: many scholars are in fact quite certain that his ascent of the Ventoux never took place. They say that his account was a fictional one written not the same night but in the 1350s, an allegory capturing his inner torment, a state of limbo between earthly pleasures and soulful and religious callings on the 'summit of beautitude' – the Ventoux.

Death on the mountain

Mystery, of course, has always swirled in the fierce Mistral winds that batter the Ventoux's turret 130 days a year, and that gave the mountain its name – literally 'The Windy Mountain'. Meteorologists say that the Mistral has reached speeds of 320km/h here, not that locals feel the need to check; the owner of the Chalet Liotard, 1,432 metres high on the northern side, says simply that 'When the chalet walls start to move, then I know it's blowing hard.'

The weather is a part of the legend, a phenomenon more paranormal than meteorological. As Roland Barthes said, 'Its climate (it is much more an essence of climate than a geographic place) makes it a damned terrain, a testing place for heroes, something like a higher hell.'

Everyone knows about the heat and the Mistral, but the image of the Ventoux as a kind of climatic chameleon, a slice of the Sahara and Greenland transplanted to Provence, is highly apt. When Leslie Stephen wrote in his *Playground of Europe* in 1871 that 'nothing can be less like a mountain at one time than the same mountain at another', he could well have been referring to the Ventoux. The French Office National des Forêts reports that cases of hypothermia here are common. Of the

RIGHT: A south–north view through the vineyards of the Côtes du Ventoux appellation to the Giant of Provence, the mountain from which they take their name.

BOTTOM RIGHT: A typical vista into the Drôme region from high on the Malaucène side of the Ventoux.

dozens who have lost their lives on the mountain over the decades and centuries, many have perished in blizzards.

The notion that death, like mystery, lurks all around, is anything but a cliché on the Ventoux. Antoine Blondin concluded grimly that 'not many happy memories are linked to this witches' cauldron' – and he wasn't only talking about cycling. Petrarch's darkening mood as he went up from Malaucène, even if only in his imagination, may have been prophetic. On one day in 1970, the wind blew so hard that one of the *lauzes* – the flagstones that give the Ventoux its off-white gloss above Chalet Reynard on the south side – flew up into a woman's face and killed her. When the Tour de France visited in 1994, a lightening bolt did the same thing to a spectator. In 2007, an 80-year-old woman died on a walk in the woods and police were bamboozled when it took them four days to find her body in a spot they'd already scoured thoroughly. And three years later, two tourists crashed a jet plane into the mountainside and died in the wreckage.

The most famous calamity in the Ventoux's history, though, came in the Tour de France. Cyclists had first raced up the Giant in the 1935 Circuit du Mont Ventoux, and 16 years later, for the first time, the Tour peloton swept through the sepia streets of Bédoin to the sound of cicadas and expectant applause. That day in 1951, it was the legendary Fausto Coppi who climbed the Ventoux with a heavy heart, his brother Serse having died three weeks earlier in the Giro del Piemonte in Italy; while Lucien Lazarides was first across the summit and Louison Bobet the first across the finish line in Avignon, Coppi's toils were the harbingers of future struggles on the same slopes – troubles that, like Petrarch's, smouldered as much in the mind as in the legs and lungs.

Geminiani had said it to Ferdi Kübler on the Tour's second visit in 1955: 'Careful. The Ventoux isn't a climb like any other.' Kübler hadn't listened and reached Malaucène at the end of the descent in a state of delirium. His pitstop for a beer in Le Pontet, mixed with whatever else he'd ingested, can't have improved matters; when a spectator tried to stop him setting off in the wrong direction, the Swiss became enraged. 'Get out of the way, leave me, Ferdi's going crazy, Ferdi's going to explode!' he raved. Kübler's otherwise illustrious career lasted one more day – which was nearly one more than the Breton rider Jean Malléjac's life. With the temperature

ABOVE: One of few kinks in the road in the forest that cloaks the Ventoux after Saint Estève on the Bédoin side. These are some of the toughest pitches anywhere on the Ventoux.

edging 40°C in the forest, three kilometres before Chalet Reynard on the north side, Malléjac had zigzagged dementedly across the road before finally collapsing in the gutter. 'He was no longer of the material world, never mind the Tour de France,' wrote Jacques Augendre in *L'Equipe* the next day. Malléjac, second in the 1953 Tour and fifth in 1954, would never challenge again and retired in 1959.

Malléjac had been saved on the Ventoux by the Tour's official doctor, Pierre Dumas. Dumas said at the time that he was ready to 'report for attempted murder' whoever had plied Malléjac with amphetamines, and the doctor was under no illusions about the risks some riders were still taking when the Tour returned to the Ventoux 12 years later. 'The heat will be terrible today,' he said to *L'Equipe* journalist Pierre Chaney as he looked out of his hotel room window in Marseille on the morning of stage 13. 'If the guys get stuck in to the drugs, we're in danger of having a death on our hands.'

If Dumas knew all about the Ventoux and its perils, so did the 1965 world champion, Tom Simpson. On his first time up there, the Englishman said he sweated so much that his shorts nearly fell down. According to the French rider Roger Pingeon, while amphetamine use was almost *de rigueur* in the peloton, Simpson also 'had a tendency to go over the top'. And everyone, none more so than Dumas, had seen how dangerous that could be on the Ventoux in 1955.

Weird and diabolical

Today, still no one can say for certain whether a cocktail of drugs and the stiffener Simpson had knocked back in Bédoin caused or even contributed to his death two kilometres from the Ventoux's summit. What they do know, thanks to recent investigation, is just that – contrary to what the Tour organizers perhaps wanted to imply, he had died *on* the Ventoux and not in the helicopter taking him to a hospital in nearby Avignon. His legacy was the sadness and foreboding with

which the Tour and even other races such as the Dauphiné Libéré would approach the Ventoux on every ascent thereafter; that, his charisma and achievements, plus a monument where he fell bearing the tribute (in French):

> In memory of Tom Simpson, Olympic medallist,
> World Champion, British Sporting Ambassador.
> Died 13th July, Tour de France 1967

Some believe the Ventoux has been haunted ever since. Others such as Geminiani suggest that 'with the Ventoux, people always exaggerate', and argue that the climb is simply hot and hard, no more than that. Whatever it is, the Ventoux went on casting its weird and diabolical spell right from the Tour's next visit in 1970. The only high-profile rider to attend Simpson's funeral, Eddy Merckx paid his old friend a fitting tribute that day by winning alone, but not before also paying the 'unjust tariff of sufferance' spoken of by Barthes. Merckx returned to his team hotel that night in an ambulance. He had broken off his post-race interviews complaining that he had 'fire in his stomach'.

Lance Armstrong maintained that the Ventoux disliked him and not the other way around, but he also rightly identified the lack of oxygen and vegetation at the top as two key reasons why the climb from Bédoin is one of the hardest in cycling. Kinking hard left in the village of Saint Estève after five-and-a-half kilometres of climbing is like entering a gas chamber, as the road judders straight then barely deviates for the next ten kilometres up to Chalet Reynard. There a different climb begins, tacking northwest across the lunar landscape where Simpson withered, often into the Mistral. Almost throughout these final six kilometres, the end is in sight – but much further away than it ever appears.

From Malaucène the incline is steadier, less schizophrenic and less fabled. It is also, inexplicably, three metres higher than from Bédoin, How, if they both finish in the same place? At this point locals put fingers on lips. '*C'est comme ça*' – 'It just is', they say.

One mystery among many on the Ventoux – if not cycling's greatest or hardest climb, surely its most beguiling mountain.

RIGHT: Switchbacks such as this one before Chalet Reynard are few and far between on Mont Ventoux's marginally tougher southern ascent.

FAR RIGHT: Looking back down in the direction of the Mediterranean from close to the Simpson monument on the Bédoin side.

Fact file Mont Ventoux

From Bédoin

REGION: Vaucluse, Provence-Alpes-Côte d'Azur region, France

ACCESS: From Bédoin follow the D974

HEIGHT: 1,912m (or 1,909m, depending on who you ask!)

LENGTH: 21.5km

ALTITUDE GAIN: 1,552m

AVERAGE GRADIENT: 7.22%

MAXIMUM GRADIENT: 12% (ramps in km 7 and 21)

OPEN: April to October

REFRESHMENTS: At the bottom, in Sainte Colombe (km 4), Saint Estève (km 6), Chalet Reynard (km 15) and at the top

ALTERNATIVE ROUTE: From Sault (joins Bédoin route at Chalet Reynard): 25.7km at 4.5%

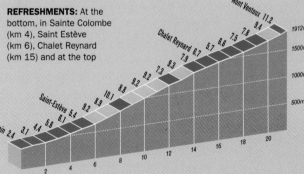

From Malaucène

REGION: Vaucluse, Provence-Alpes-Côte d'Azur region, France

ACCESS: From Malaucène town centre follow the D974

HEIGHT: 1,912m

LENGTH: 21.2km

ALTITUDE GAIN: 1,515m

AVERAGE GRADIENT: 7.15%

MAXIMUM GRADIENT: 10.9% (from km 12 to km 13)

OPEN: April to October

REFRESHMENTS: At the bottom and at the top

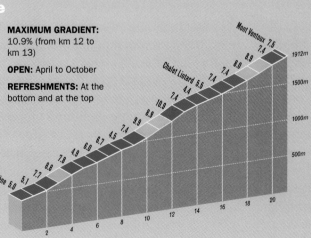

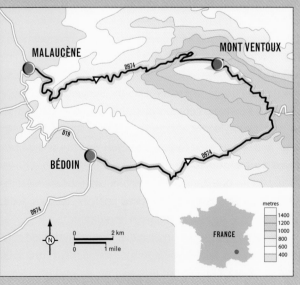

Kitzbüheler Horn
1,970m   Austria

If ever a climb could drive a man to perversion, never mind insanity, it was the Kitzbüheler Horn – and this had nothing to do with the name. In 1877, long before the current road to the summit had been built and before cyclists had ever had the misfortune to climb it, the Austrian journalist Daniel Spitzler had regarded the Horn from Kitzbühel in the valley and been reminded of the, ahem, twin peaks of a female's décolletage. 'When viewed from the city, [they] form two round hills that pretty closely resemble a woman's bosoms,' he observed.

Spitzer was half right: the Kitzbüheler Horn looked and still looks like one bosom. Where he got the other one, it's hard to tell... unless he'd looked at the small ridge beneath the summit and seen the portent of a botched silicone implant. You could certainly argue that the construction of the 10.2-kilometre, 12.53 per cent road to the summit was a terrible mistake or at least some sick joke. 'The hardest cycling climb in Austria' as the local tourist board describes it – and that's some billing considering that Austria has more horrors than anywhere else in Europe – the Horn may also be the toughest in this book. More challenging than any of Monte Zoncolan's three routes, steeper than the Fedaia, or than anything on Monte Grappa, the Angliru or the Mortirolo.

The best climber in the world

Authorities on the matter all have their own convoluted formulae to calculate the difficulty of a climb, accounting for steepness, length and a host of other factors, and they all agree: the Kitzbüheler Horn is harder than any of the better-known 'über-climbs' hyped as Europe's or even the world's most brutal. There are also the subjective testimonies of people well placed to make comparisons: the American rider Ted King rode the Horn in the Tour of Austria and called it 'the hardest climb I've ever done' and 'a wall'; the Swiss Beat Breu won the annual race to the top, of which more later, every year between 1981 and 1990, yet still said of his first success, 'The suffering was depraved. Countless times I asked myself why I do this s**t'; the same year, the German pro Erich Jagsch called the final section of the Horn 'murderous'.

The severity of the slope isn't all that makes the Horn exceptional. One of Austria's leading pros in the early years of the 21st century, Bernhard Eisel, pointed out that this is just one of its many challenges: 'It's open almost the whole way up,' Eisel, who twice took on the climb in the Tour of Austria, observed in 2011. 'There is no shade or shelter whatsoever. It's just a killer. It starts off bad and then gets worse and worse all the way up. The Großglockner is still the climb for Austrians, but the Kitzbüheler Horn is way tougher and steeper. For one thing, on the Großglockner you can rest a bit on the hairpins, but not on the Kitzbüheler Horn. It's bloody horrible.'

Another leading Austrian rider, Georg Totschnig, may indeed have been underestimating the Kitzbüheler Horn when he called it Austria's Alpe d'Huez. True, the Horn has seven more hairpins than the Alpe's 21, but Eisel's observation – that here they offer no succour – was equally valid. When seven-time Tour de France champion Lance Armstrong opened a bike shop and café in his native Austin, Texas, it was with good reason that the strongest blend of coffee for sale was named Kitz after... you guessed it, the Kitzbüheler Horn.

Since its inauguration in 1971, the annual race from the town of Kitzbühel up to the Alpenhaus, eight kilometres from the foot of the climb, has reaffirmed the Horn's credentials, almost unbeknownst to the international media. That first race in 1971 saw the emergence of the first *König* or king of the Horn, Wolfgang Steinmayr, who went on to win the first four editions of the main race to the Alpenhaus – and in 1974 also the previous day's two-and-a-half kilometre individual time trial from the Alpenhaus to the bottom of the 102-metre Austrian state TV tower at the summit. The previous year he'd nearly won the time trial, despite having derailed his chain and fallen off on one of the steepest bends. This had prompted the Austrian press to speculate that a rider who remained almost unknown abroad might be the 'best climber in the world'. The Swiss legend Ferdi Kübler called him 'a phenomenon'.

Two years later the cyclist who truly was the sport's finest on mountainous terrain, Lucien Van Impe, was enticed to Kitzbühel by a 30,000 schilling appearance fee and the prospect of a clash of the Titans. Or make that the clash of three titans: Van Impe, who just two weeks earlier had been crowned King of the Mountains at the Tour de France for the third time, the local hero Steinmayr, and the ogre itself – the Horn.

OPPOSITE: The horribly steep ascent of the Kitzbüheler Horn alternates shaded sections like this with long, unsheltered stretches.

Steinmayr had never felt more ready: riding a 7.4 kilo superbike built specially for the occasion, in his final training session he had bettered his record of the previous year, 31 minutes and 17 seconds, by seven seconds. He reckoned he had 'two more minutes in me'. His choice of gear was an ambitious, some would say audacious 39x22, but why shouldn't he be bold? Was he not after all about to prove himself as the best climber in the world, cycling's real monarch of the mountains?

The short answer is that no, he wasn't. Exhausted by Van Impe's continuous attacks, after six kilometres, with the Belgian still visible but only just, Steinmayr did the unthinkable and got off his bike to catch his breath. That gargantuan gear – at least for slopes as steep as the Horn's – had demolished him. 'On the first corner, I could tell his gear was unsustainable,' Van Impe said later, having won by over seven minutes and lowered Steinmayr's record to 30 minutes and three seconds. Van Impe added that only the greatest rider, never mind climber on earth, the Belgian Eddy Merckx, climbed with gears like the ones Steinmayr had used. Van Impe then underlined his superiority by trouncing Steinmayr by over a minute in the time trial to the summit.

Sporting mecca

The Steinmayr era ended with his final victory in 1976, after which Breu's began, reaching its apogee with his 28-minute, 53-second ride in 1986. Only since the Tour of Austria began hosting a stage finishing at the Alpenhaus in 2000 has that been bettered, with the Austrian pro Thomas Rohregger setting a new mark of 28 minutes and 24 seconds in 2007.

The International Kitzbüheler Horn Mountain Race continues to take place and thrive every summer, welcoming both elite riders and recreational cyclists. Another race, this one for runners and taking place at the end of August, sets out from the centre of Kitzbühel and heads up the Panoramastraße all the way to the summit. The New Zealander Jonathan Wyatt held the record at the time of writing with what the organizers described as an 'unbelievable' 55 minutes and 58 seconds.

The two events, plus the Tour of Austria's now-regular visits, have merely added to the Kitzbüheler Horn's standing as a hive of high-class sport. The tradition began way back in 1892, when a local gentleman, Franz Reisch, read the Norwegian polar explorer Fridtjof Nansen's *On Skis through Greenland* and was so inspired that he headed up the Horn with a pair of homemade skis. Reisch's journey down the mountain was the first ever Alpine descent in Austria.

Although now commonly described as a snowboarder's paradise, Kitzbühel remains most famous for Alpine skiing on the formidable Hahnenkamm, the mountain directly south of the town and the Horn. The Streif downhill course on the Hahnenkamm is widely regarded as the most extreme and challenging on the World Cup circuit, infamous for its reverse bank turns and poor visibility.

Kitzbühel is rightly proud: there aren't too many places on earth that can legitimately lay claim to the two most notorious locations in two different sports… or for that matter to a mountain that resembles a woman's breast.

" MORE CHALLENGING THAN ANY OF MONTE ZONCOLAN'S THREE ROUTES, steeper than the Fedaia, or than anything on Monte Grappa, the Angliru or the Mortirolo. **"**

LEFT: Kitzbühel takes its status as an international sporting mecca very seriously – and you always know where you are on the Kitzbüheler Horn.

Fact file Kitzbüheler Horn

From St. Johann in Tyrol

REGION: Alps, Tyrol, Austria

ACCESS: From Kitzbühel town centre, follow the Johanner Straße (B-161) to the crossroads with the Himmelreich and the Walsenbachweg. Take the Walsenbachweg, then the Ried Riesberg and the Kitzbüheler Panoramastraße

HEIGHT: 1,970m

LENGTH: 10.2km

ALTITUDE GAIN: 1,278m

AVERAGE GRADIENT: 12.53%

MAXIMUM GRADIENT: 22.3% (in the final kilometre, before the Goinger Alm)

OPEN: May to November

REFRESHMENTS: Bars in Kitzbühel, at the Alpenhaus after 7.5km of climbing and in the *Gipfelhaus* at the top

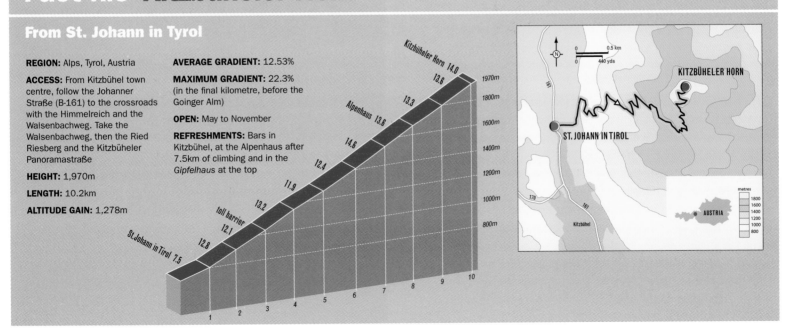

Col de la Madeleine
1,993m
France

It isn't merely for alliterative reasons that this mountain is so often prefixed by the word 'majestic'. It owes it, too, to its scale, its beauty, its grace; in short, its majesty.

Yet to some cyclists the Col de la Madeleine represents something less than majestic and more like monstrous. In terms of size it is, certainly, one of the monsters of the Alps. And it is one of those climbs that seems to involve a proper journey, transporting the cyclist from deep, lush valleys to the roof of the world. Or so it feels, with its views from the summit of Mont Blanc and the Lauzière massifs.

The only road linking the valleys of the Maurienne and Tarentaise, and one of only two roads, along with the faraway Col d'Iseran, to cross the Vanoise Alps, the Madeleine soars to a giddy 1,993 metres. Then there's the length of the climb by road. From Aigueblanche, in the north, the road from foot to summit measures 28.3 kilometres: that's a long way from the sign that marks the start of the climb, and includes an altitude gain of 1,533 metres.

An average gradient of 5.4 per cent is deceiving since it includes, after an intitial 13 kilometres of meandering ascent on a smooth road that passes through pretty villages and over small stone bridges – features that appear and disappear like ghostly apparitions when the fog and mist descend – a three-kilometre section that is predominantly downhill. Then comes the real test: 12 kilometres at 7.4 per cent, and up to ten per cent in places. Even here it is, in places, only gently rising – it is an erratic climb on which the distance is, for many, the killer.

From La Chambre, in the south, the climb is shorter, 'just' 19.3 kilometres, but steeper, at eight per cent, rising to 11 per cent in places. It makes for a long, technical descent, with the road switchbacking through Alpine meadows as it plunges down towards La Chambre.

It was on this descent that David Millar, the Scottish rider, salvaged his hopes of remaining in the Tour de France in 2010. It was the Tour's 23rd visit to the Madeleine, and while up ahead the climb caused carnage, with the yellow jersey Cadel Evans losing his place among the leaders and his hold on that jersey, behind, Millar fought the kind of lonely battle that occurs daily in the mountains of the Tour, out of sight of most, often never known. Millar arrived in Aigueblanche alone, the last man on the road, 35 minutes behind the leaders. Ahead of him the Madeleine loomed like an impassable obstacle.

IT'S SUCH A LONG CLIMB THAT NO MATTER HOW GOOD YOU'RE FEELING, you know you're going to be spending a long time working your way up its slopes. "

David Millar

BELOW: The final twists and turns on the Aigueblanche side of the Madeleine are among the hardest on one of the hardest and most historic Alpine passes.

Millar had bitter memories of the Col de la Madeleine even before July 13, 2010. In his 2011 autobiography, *Racing Through the Dark*, Millar admits: 'I don't like the Madeleine. It holds very bad memories for me, of a different life, of a summer's day in 2001 when I got into a Cofidis team car and gave up my dreams, a time I tried to forget.'

The Madeleine came to symbolize the dividing line between the young, idealistic Millar – who, the previous year, won the stage one time trial to claim the first yellow jersey of the 2000 Tour – and the pragmatic professional who reached the conclusion that he needed to dope to fulfil his 'responsibilities' as the leader of his team; because it was upon abandoning the 2001 Tour, on a Madeleine stage won by Laurent Roux, that Millar decided to start using EPO.

Nine years later, having admitted his drug use, served a two-year ban and returned to the sport as an advocate for clean cycling, Millar once again faced his nemesis: the Madeleine. But he was in bad shape: he was coughing and he had a broken rib from an earlier crash. And, upon checking with the last cars in the convoy, he learned that his deficit to the leaders was a monstrous 35 minutes. It was too much; he was convinced that he'd be eliminated at the finish in Saint Jean de Maurienne, where stage nine would finish after plummeting from the summit of the huge climb in front of him.

'It's such a long climb that no matter how good you're feeling you know you're going to be spending a long time working your way up its slopes,' Millar wrote in his book. 'I couldn't cope with the thought of 25 kilometres of climbing, so I broke it up into five-kilometre sections, working through them one by one. I found a rhythm of sorts and could feel myself strengthening, physically and spiritually. Even though it was a long shot, I started believing I could do it...'

Millar, with a lone motorcycle-mounted *gendarme* in front of him, slowly climbed the mountain. He was astonished by the response of the crowds who were still there. Initially he felt guilty that they had to wait for him, then he realized they were not standing by the roadside because they had to, or out of a sense of charity. They understood his predicament. They clapped and cheered and yelled encouragement. Millar began to feel quite emotional.

'The last few kilometres of the climb came quickly,' wrote Millar. 'I looked up towards the summit, at the thousands of people dwarfed by the monumental landscape, at the flags and banners outlining the ribbon of road all the way to the wonderful peak.

'I wasn't weakening. I rode over the top and zipped up my jersey, knowing that if I was to stay in the Tour I had to throw myself down the mountainside. The descent of the Madeleine is steep and technical, which makes it ideal for a lone rider. During the whole day, my constant companion had been a *gendarme* motorbike outrider, opening the road ahead of me...'

'Now something unspoken between us surfaced. He understood me, understood my desperation. He read my intentions and for that wild, crazed descent off the Madeleine, we had the most exciting ride. From the first corners he knew what I needed, lifting his pace to match mine and carving a line through the bends ahead of me. I put myself in his hands and followed his line. It was exhilarating. I've rarely felt so alive.'

Millar arrived in Saint Jean de Maurienne in 181st place, 42 minutes and 45 seconds behind the winner, Sandy Casar (the tenth French winner on a Madeleine stage). But he had, to some extent, exorcized his Madeleine demons, and he had survived – just.

Others have fonder memories. Bobby Julich, the American rider, even named his daughter Olivia Madeleine Julich, after the climb on which he consolidated his third-place overall finish in the 1998 Tour.

BELOW: Two kilometres from the summit on the La Chambre side, the valley and the Saint François Longchamp ski resort recede slowly out of sight.

Perhaps the best endorsement of the Madeleine's credentials as a 'climbers' climb' is the fact that the two most prolific winners of the King of the Mountains title have both won a hat trick of stages that have featured ascents. Richard Virenque, the seven-time mountains winner, is one. And Lucien Van Impe, the Belgian super-climber of the 1970s and early '80s, and 1976 Tour winner, is the other.

While Virenque's achievements were tarnished after his involvement in the Festina scandal and eventual confession of doping, Van Impe remains, for many, the archetypal mountain goat; a pure climber whose scrawny frame, and ability to dance on the steepest of ascents with balletic grace, made him much imitated, seldom copied.

As well as its place in cycling history, the Madeleine is a mountain whose reputation is said to date back to Roman times. It was familiar to the monks of Tamie Abbey in the 12th century, and in the 18th the pass was made by General Kellerman and his troops in the conquest of Savoie.

A stone road was constructed by Spanish refugees in 1938, with work on the current pass beginning in 1949. The Tour de France marked the road's completion in 1969 by featuring the new climb; the Spaniard Andrés Gandarias was the winner that year. Its strategic location, linking the Maurienne and Tarentaise valleys, partly explains its regular inclusion on the Tour route since then.

Fact file Col de la Madeleine

From La Chambre on the D213

REGION: Savoie, France

ACCESS: Take the D213 from La Chambre, following signs for the Col

HEIGHT: 1,993m

LENGTH: 19.3km

ALTITUDE GAIN: 1,522m

AVERAGE GRADIENT: 8%

MAXIMUM GRADIENT: 11% (km 11)

OPEN: May to September

REFRESHMENTS: Bars in La Chambre, at Saint François Longchamp. The Banquise 2000 at the Col serves meals

ALTERNATIVE ROUTE: Col de la Madeleine from La Chambre on the D76 (19.8km at 7.7%)

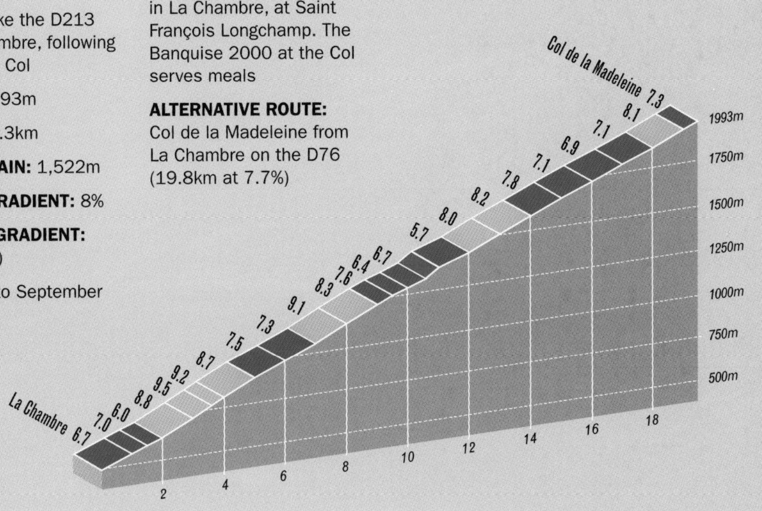

ABOVE: One peloton very much at home on the long and difficult ascent to the Madeleine summit.

From Aigueblanche

REGION: Savoie, France

ACCESS: Take the D990 from Aigueblanche, proceed through La Léchère and turn left onto the D213, following signs to the Madeleine before Feissons-sur-Isère

HEIGHT: 1,993m

LENGTH: 28.3km

ALTITUDE GAIN: 1,533m

AVERAGE GRADIENT: 5.4%

MAXIMUM GRADIENT: 10.4% (km 21)

OPEN: May to September

REFRESHMENTS: Bars in Aigueblanche and La Léchère. The Banquise 2000 at the Col serves meals

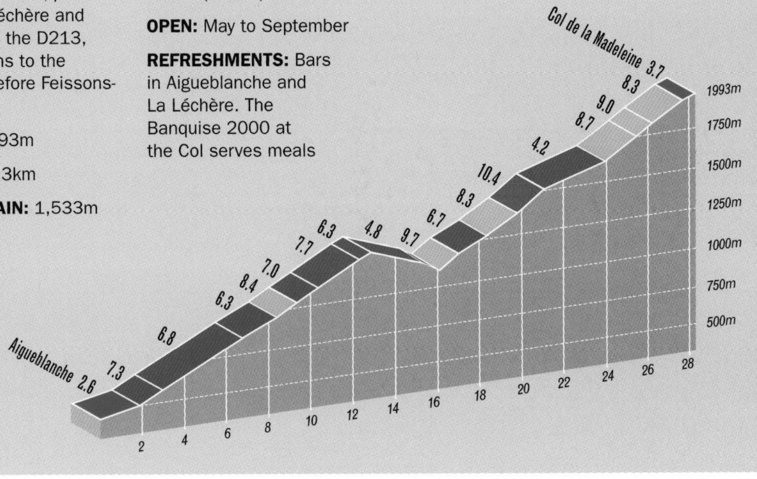

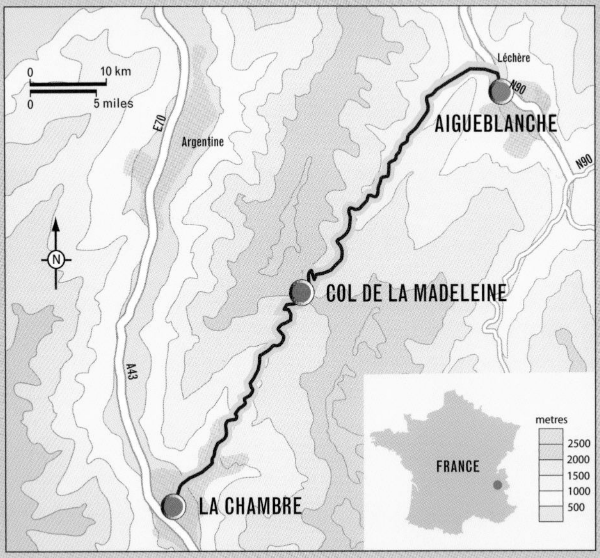

2,000m +

Passo Fedaia
2,057m   Italy

If there is such a thing as the ugly duckling of Dolomite passes, then it is the Fedaia – not that this brute can be likened to anything as remotely small or docile. Intimidating even in name, mostly unlovely in appearance and repellently steep in gradient, this is the mountain that generations of cyclists have loved to hate, or hated to love.

Put another way, the Fedaia is compelling in the same way as a horror movie from which it's somehow hard to avert the eyes.

One portion of the climb from Caprile has become infamous. Variously dubbed the graveyard of champions, the valley of death or the corridor of fear, the unbending, unending three-kilometre shaft beginning just before Malga Ciapela, five-and-a-half kilometres from the summit, is one of the most feared stretches of any Italian ascent. Shorter but even steeper and straighter than the notorious segment between Saint Estève and Chalet Reynard on the southern side of Mont Ventoux, it is one of those cycling meccas elevated to that status purely by virtue of its brutality.

With a road tucked so close beneath the Marmolada that the climb often goes simply by that name, you'd expect the Fedaia to elicit hyperbole. But here, for a cyclist, the views of the highest mountain in its range, the so-called Queen of the Dolomites, are incidental and indeed disappointing. 'You see, it is true, the whole of the Marmolata [its Tyrolese name],' noted Reginald Farrer in his 1913 book *The Dolomites*, 'but you see her from a stone's throw, and from just underneath; beauty and dignity are lost in mere enormousness, seen in too intimate and foreshortened detail to do more than squash you into stupid acquiescence.'

On the Fedaia, and particularly between Malga Ciapela and where a different kind of hairpinned hell begins at the Capanna Bill *rifugio*, it is the slopes themselves that inspire awe. Rising to 18 per cent at its most severe, the gradient never dips below 12 per cent for three kilometres. 'Climbing by foot, your shins even hurt,' said Angelo Zomegnan, who became race director of the Giro d'Italia in 2005. Two-time Giro champion Gilberto Simoni believed the section made the Fedaia 'probably the hardest climb in Italy'. And the 1988 winner Andy Hampsten reckoned it was 'definitely one of the hardest climbs [in professional cycling] – it's like someone's horribly steep driveway.'

When does the Marmolada start?

The Russian Pavel Tonkov used to have nightmares about Malga Ciapela. He frazzled there in the 1996 Giro d'Italia, barely holding on to win that year's race. *La Gazzetta dello Sport*'s Claudio Gregori summed up Tonkov's trepidation on the eve of the '98 Giro's return visit to the Fedaia thus: 'Tonight, there was the suspicion of splendid drama. A name was scarcely whispered, like the central point on a map of treasure: Malga Ciapela. The memory of the stage two years ago sends shivers down Tonkov's spine.'

The 'splendid drama' duly arrived. At Malga Ciapela, Tonkov foolishly goaded Marco Pantani with a limp acceleration, Pantani's cue to blow the Russian away. Meanwhile, race leader Alex Zülle was in the process of losing his 'pink jersey and his underpants', in the words of the Italian TV pundit Franco Cribori. A few hundred metres before his lethal counter-attack, Pantani, riding the Fedaia for the first time, had turned to his faithful *domestique* Roberto Conti and asked: 'So when does the Marmolada start?' Conti had nearly fallen off his bike.

Pantani, who died of a cocaine overdose in 2004, will be remembered as one of the greatest climbers of all time. It's fair to say that he may also have been the only cyclist in history to relish the Fedaia. Years later, *La Gazzetta* remarked that Malga Ciapela was where the trophy-eared Italian graduated from one nickname and persona – *Elefantino* – to the more menacing *il Pirata*. It was also where he laid the groundwork for overall victory in that '98 Giro.

The Corsa Rosa had been due to take on the Fedaia for the first time in 1969. But race organizer Vincenzo Torriani's experiment was to end in tears, quite literally, as bad weather forced the cancellation of a stage scheduled to finish at Malga Ciapela; one rider, Silvano Schiavon, wept when he heard the announcement, so excited had he been about seeing the Marmolada. Ignorance was clearly bliss.

The following year Torriani tried again. This time the day dawned warm and clear and Michele Dancelli stole away from a group containing the great Eddy Merckx to win at Malga Ciapela. Now it was Italo Zilioli who cried, his epic breakaway having ended four kilometres from the line. Five years later, the entire peloton could have been forgiven for reacting in similar fashion on discovering during stage 20 from Pordenone to Alleghe that the 'real' Marmolada only began at Malga Ciapela.

ABOVE: The Serrai di Sottoguda gorge dazes you with its beauty before the road emerges near Malga Ciapela to face three of the most terrifying kilometres in international cycling. British travel writer Reginald Farrar rated the Sottoguda canyon one of the most beautiful in Europe.

RIGHT: The Lago di Fedaia, on the plateau just beyond the pass. To the left are the lower portions of the Marmolada glacier.

Sinuous and sinful

But there is also a danger of neglecting what lies either side of the Fedaia's murderous midriff. After three undemanding kilometres from the climb's starting point in Caprile comes the village of Rocca Pietore, once reckoned to be the world's smallest republic, nestling as it did between the autonomous regions of Venice and the Tyrol. The real treat, though, awaits two kilometres later, at Sottoguda. Here, a road now closed to motorized vehicles leaves the SS641 to the right, enters Sottoguda and slithers parallel to the Pettorina stream and into a towering gorge. After two more kilometres, on exiting the gully, you'll know exactly why the Serrai di Sottoguda is sometimes referred to as the *gola* or 'throat' of Sottoguda. And what prompted Reginald Farrer to poeticize in 1913: 'I have seen many of the big Alpine canons [sic], the Gorge Trient, the Aareschlucht, the Gorner; never have I seen anything more surprisingly impressive than the Serrai di Sottoguda. It is a ravine deep down between walls of limestone some hundreds of feet high, and so close together that daylight only filters dimly through the slit above you…'

Visually less striking but far more demanding for the cyclist, the final three kilometres from Capanna Bill clamber in sinuous knots towards the pass. Again, like at Malga Ciapela, neither the metal guardrail nor adjacent ski slopes do anything for the aesthetics, and it's the physical ordeal that is most memorable. The summit itself is also unremarkable; relief, a dose of pride and hearty sustenance from the *Rifugio Fedaia* are the cyclist's consolation.

Beyond the saddle, the Lago di Fedaia glistens like blue topaz under the Marmolada's alabaster snows. The descent to Canazei is a further scenic improvement and a pleasant enough climb in the opposite direction (13.9 kilometres at 4.4 per cent), but one completely upstaged by the uglier yet more famous route from Caprile. The Passo Fedaia on this side is but a 'normal' climb.

The Marmolada itself was first scaled in 1864 by the Austrian Paul Grohmann, a prolific collector of Dolomite peaks. The Englishman and president of the Alpine Club, John Ball, had unsuccessfully attempted the same ascent four years earlier. Today, just about anyone can reach the glacier that cloaks the north side via a cable car departing from the pass.

The same, unfortunately, cannot be said of the bike ride up the Fedaia from Caprile. Love to hate it or hate to love it, this is one climb that will stick in the memory as well as the legs… whether you make it over the top or not.

BELOW: Malga Ciapela – the graveyard of champions that has given the Fedaia its formidable reputation. In this three-kilometre section, the gradient never dips below 12 per cent and the road hardly deviates from a ramrod-straight trajectory.

OPPOSITE: Evidence of the strong Germanic influences in these parts is visible on roadsigns and restaurant menus. We are in the heart of the Dolomites.

Fact file Passo Fedaia

From Caprile

REGION: On the border of the Trentino-Alto Adige and Veneto regions in northeast Italy

ACCESS: Take the Strada Statale 641 del Passo Fedaia from Caprile. Be sure to bear right towards the Serrai di Sottoguda, 2km beyond Rocca Pietore

HEIGHT: 2,057m

LENGTH: 14.1km (15km from centre of Caprile)

ALTITUDE GAIN: 1,059m

AVERAGE GRADIENT: 7.5%

MAXIMUM GRADIENT: 18% at Malga Ciapela

OPEN: May to October, depending on snowfall

REFRESHMENTS: Bars in Caprile, Rocca Pietore and at Malga Ciapela. Two *rifugi*, the Rifugio Capanna Bill and the Rifugio Fedaia at the pass itself serve drinks, snacks and complete meals

ALTERNATIVE ROUTE: From Canazei (13.9km at 4.4%)

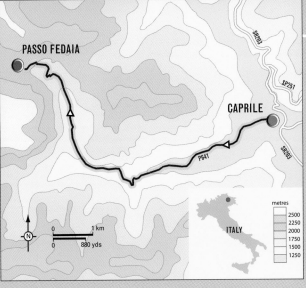

Col du Glandon/Croix de Fer
2,067m

France

❝ **THE GLANDON FROM THIS SIDE IS A LONG AND GRUELLING CRESCENDO.** In the last two kilometres, the gradient remains constantly above ten per cent. ❞

Just three kilometres apart, both in the shadow of the magnificent 60-kilometre expanse of the Chaîne de Belledone, the Cols of the Croix de Fer and Glandon are, depending on your viewpoint, either the Siamese twins or the snarling two-headed dog, the Orthrus, of the great Alpine passes.

The two cols are or at least can be, put more simply, the interchangeable point of arrival for four separate climbs. Arriving from the east, turn right after 2.5 kilometres of descending off the Croix de Fer and the cyclist finds himself almost immediately cresting the summit of the Glandon. Conversely, hit the Glandon from the north and turn left 500 metres beyond the summit and the Croix de Fer is just 2.5 uphill kilometres away. Or, the third and fourth options, whether coming from west or east, never deviate from the D296 and one can bypass the Glandon altogether; similarly, a truncated combination of D926 and D927 means missing the Croix de Fer.

If the permutations sound complicated, making a case for the inclusion of these passes in a list of legendary highways is less tricky. Untypically *staccato* by Alpine standards, for all its 13 per cent ramps and two downhill interludes, the climb from the Barrage du Verney reservoir is also a procession of spectacular scenery. In the second half of the climb, waterfalls crash theatrically to the valley floor on the right while the Aiguilles de l'Argentière (not to be confused with the Aiguille de l'Argentière first, famously, scaled by Edward Whymper in 1864) soar to the left. From the opposite direction and Saint Jean de Maurienne, the journey towards the summit is a similar assortment of landscapes and gradients; of forest and grassland; of shelter and exposure; wondrous vistas of the three-pronged Aiguilles d'Arves in the first half, and of the Chaîne de Belledone in the second.

Armstrong's best day

Reaching the Glandon before the Croix de Fer means ascending from La Chambre, where another Alpine sibling, the Col de la Madeleine, also begins. Consistently rated one of the hardest passes to regularly feature in the Tour de France, the Glandon from this side is a long and gruelling crescendo. In the last two kilometres, the gradient remains constantly above ten per cent.

It was on this tough, final section of the Glandon that one of the most mythologized episodes of modern Tours de France played out in 2001. First scaled in a Tour de France in 1947 by the Pole Edouard Klabinski, who weeks earlier had won the first ever edition of the Dauphiné Libéré, by the turn of the millennium the Glandon had become a regular haunt for the Grande Boucle. The great Belgian climber Lucien Van Impe had led the Tour over the summit on three occasions. The man who considered himself to be Van Impe's successor, Richard Virenque, then emulated him twice, in 1994 and 1997.

In '94, another young rider, Lance Armstrong, had already abandoned the Tour by the time the peloton reached the foot of the Glandon. Seven years later, he was a cancer survivor, a *miraculé* as they said in France, a two-time Tour winner – and also a man with a double dilemma: two days earlier, a freak breakaway in the Jura mountains had plunged Armstrong to 25th position on the Tour's general classification and now, in the Alps, his team-mates were already flagging. The abridged, popularized (by the Armstrong camp) version of what happened next is that he 'bluffed' – pretended that he was also suffering, thereby fooling his rival Jan Ullrich. He then went on to humiliate the German on the final climb of the day to Alpe d'Huez. That, as we said, has been always Armstrong's version. Ullrich and others have begged to differ.

The bare facts, agreed upon by everyone, are these: on the climb preceding the Glandon, the Madeleine, Armstrong dropped back to his team car to consult his *directeur sportif* Johan Bruyneel; on the Glandon, as Ullrich's Telekom team-mates set an increasingly furious tempo, Armstrong languished at the back of the group of favourites, seemingly on the brink of collapse; on the climb to Alpe d'Huez, finally, with 11 of 13.1 kilometres to the summit remaining, Armstrong surged ahead of Ullrich, turned around momentarily to fix him with his gaze, then stomped on his pedals and rode away – minutes away – to victory.

So far away, in fact, that speaking years later, Armstrong called it his 'best day' in his seven-year reign as the Tour champion.

Armstrong claimed in the second instalment of his memoirs, *Every Second Counts*, that the plan was hatched by, or at least with, Bruyneel on the Madeleine. His long-time team-mate, the Spaniard Chechu Rubeira, contradicted him slightly, crediting Armstrong and not Bruyneel with the ruse, but still corroborating the idea that Ullrich

and his team-mates had been duped. 'Lance himself decided to act like he was bad, going in the back of the group all day long and even on the climbs in the switchbacks,' Rubeira remembered in 2010. 'He changed his face like he was suffering when the guys from Telekom looked back – we were having fun seeing them talking to each other and on the radio with the director, and some of them excited because they thought that it was for real!'

Ullrich's own goal

Meanwhile, another rider belonging to neither Ullrich's nor Armstrong's team, the Briton David Millar, had abandoned the race on the Madeleine, but knew exactly what the American had in store. 'Good luck for today,' had been Millar's parting message. 'Don't need luck,' Armstrong had smiled back. 'It's a pity you're not going to see it – I'm going to destroy it.'

There's no doubt that Ullrich, his Telekom cohorts and managers had seen Armstrong puffing. The question is whether it was this that led them to impose such a furious and foolhardy rhythm on the Glandon, or whether, as Ullrich suggested in his autobiography, they were simply concerned about their leader's lowly 26th position on general classification and wanted to eliminate riders – any riders – ahead of him. 'Armstrong said that we fell for his bluff and had set a crazy tempo because of his masquerade. That's nonsense,' Ullrich wrote in his own autobiography. 'We wanted to eliminate a whole load of rivals – Armstrong was just one among many.'

ABOVE: An orientation table on the Croix de Fer points to the snow-capped twin peaks of the Aiguilles de l'Argentière, the signature mountain of the climb from the Barrage du Verney.

According to Ullrich, his team-mates simply got carried away. He said that they had 'lacked discipline'. At one point, when his team-mate Alexandre Vinokourov went back to the team car to fetch drinks, two more Telekom riders, Kevin Livingston and Andreas Klöden, were hammering so hard at the front that Vinokourov almost lost contact altogether. He finally clawed his way back having thrown away the six water bottles he'd just collected and sprinted to bridge the gap.

The upshot was that Ullrich looked rather silly when Armstrong cruised to the front on the Alpe and, in Ullrich's words, 'turned around and looked at us as if to say farewell'. How silly depended on whether you believed, as Ullrich would later claim, that he and his team manager Rudy Pevenage had rumbled Armstrong and Bruyneel's ruse long before the Alpe. It had, they said, taken not brilliant intuition but a slice of good fortune: while fiddling with his intercom radio in the team car early on the stage, Pevenage had found the frequency being used by Armstrong and Bruyneel, thus enabling him to eavesdrop on their mid-race conversations. Ullrich said that Pevenage had even informed his riders on the Glandon that 'Lance is pretending to be weak… but as long as you haven't got rid of him, you mustn't assume that he's having a bad day.'

The bad day that never was just happened to be Armstrong's best in Tours de France. Not to mention, in all likelihood, the Glandon's.

Fact file Col de la Croix de Fer

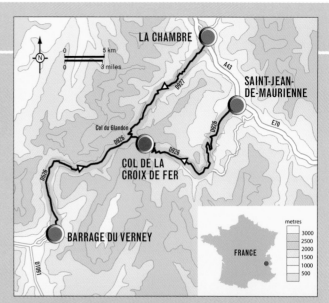

From Barrage du Verney

REGION: Isère, Rhône-Alpes, France

ACCESS: Follow the D199 from Bourg d'Oisans to Rochetaillée. Turn right and follow the D526/D44 to the Barrage du Verney and to the top

HEIGHT: 2,067m

LENGTH: 27.53km

ALTITUDE GAIN: 1,292m

AVERAGE GRADIENT: 4.7%

MAXIMUM GRADIENT: 11.1% (short section between km 12 and 13.1)

OPEN: June to October

REFRESHMENTS: Bars at the bottom, at Odalys Residence Les Sybelles (km 25) and at the top

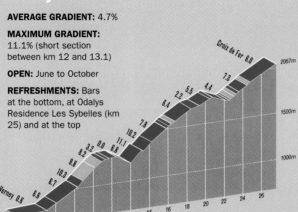

From Saint Jean de Maurienne

REGION: Savoie, Rhône-Alpes, France

ACCESS: Follow the A43-E70 and take the highway exit just before Saint Jean de Maurienne. Follow the D906 to Saint Jean de Maurienne. Then follow D926 to the top

HEIGHT: 2,067m

LENGTH: 30km

ALTITUDE GAIN: 1,521m

AVERAGE GRADIENT: 5.07%

MAXIMUM GRADIENT: 11.5% (short section at km 6.5)

OPEN: June to October

REFRESHMENTS: Bars at the bottom, at Les Chambons (km 19), at Saint Sorlin d'Arves (km 22) and at the top

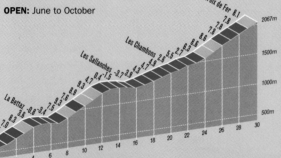

Col du Glandon (1,924m)

From La Chambre

REGION: Savoie, Rhône-Alpes, France

ACCESS: Follow the A43 (Autoroute de la Maurienne) and take highway exit number 26, nearly La Chambre. Then follow the D927 to the top

HEIGHT: 1,924m

LENGTH: 21.8km

ALTITUDE GAIN: 1,474m

AVERAGE GRADIENT: 6.76%

MAXIMUM GRADIENT: 15% (short section at km 20.5)

OPEN: June to October

REFRESHMENTS: Bars at the bottom, at Saint Étienne de Cuines (km 1), at Saint Alban (km 4.5), at Saint Colomban des Villards (km 11), at Le Châtelet (km 12.5) and Odalys Residence Les Sybelles near the top

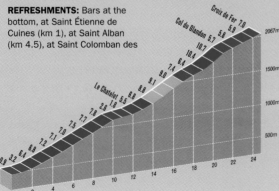

ABOVE: The steep upper reaches of the Glandon – scene of Jan Ullrich's self-sabotage in 2001.

St. Gotthardpass
2,106m
Switzerland

Better known to motorists than it is to cyclists, the St. Gotthardpass nowadays is either a whimsical detour or where car-bound passengers end up after a wrong turning before the 16.9-kilometre tunnel of the same name. One of three engineering marvels facilitating access over or through the Gotthard massif – the others being the pass and one of Europe's most spectacular sections of railway – the tunnel was constructed in 1980 and has its own colourful and tragic history. In 2001, it was closed for two months after a fire killing 11 people – a solemn echo of a more serious disaster in the shorter Mont Blanc tunnel in 1999. Today, on summer weekends, it is a horrendous bottleneck due to its location on a motorway that effectively heads in a straight line for kilometres from Hamburg in Germany to the end of Italy's 'toe' in Reggio Calabria.

Built to relieve traffic on the pass, the tunnel accomplished its mission much in the same way as its railway equivalent a century earlier. Not that the latter has ever been considered an unqualified success, having accumulated a death toll worthy of a small military campaign during its construction. The number of victims differs depending on the source you read, varying from 177 to 500, and certainly including the man who drew up and soon became totally absorbed by the project, Louis Favre. Accounts of working conditions throughout make the mind boggle: according to one report, a double bed in one dorm was occupied in succession by 24 different labourers in 24 hours.

Favre's posthumous reward ought to have been unstinting praise for what Douglas Ashby described in his 1928 travelogue, *Things Seen in Switzerland in Summer*, as 'that marvellous hole in the

hills, the St. Gotthardpass tunnel'. Many were, and indeed still are, staggered by the architect's achievement. Rather than a single channel from one side of the mountain to the other, the tunnel is in fact a series of burrows strewn up and through its flanks, until finally it emerges fully in the south. 'And again the train plunges into a tunnel, like a huge black beast going into its den; and each time it emerges the landscape is different, either softer or more stern,' Victor Tissot wrote of the view from the road pass in his book *La Suisse Inconnue* in 1888. Tissot, like other earlier travellers, seemed thrilled by the railway but concerned about its impact on what was previously the only way over the Gotthard, the pass. 'We enter the valley of the Reuss, and follow the line of the old Gotthard road, poor forsaken thing, towards which the locomotive seems to send a mocking whistle as it goes.' Charles Freeston's 1910 *High Roads of*

the Alps was less sympathetic; in Freeston's mind the Gotthard road was getting what it deserved. 'From the strictly motoring point of view it is possible to rate the St. Gotthardpass too highly,' Freeston wrote, before adding, 'As a railway route it is quite without a rival, neither the Mt Cenis nor the Simplon line being at all comparable with it in interest or picturesqueness.'

Not for the first or last time, the oldest and most attractive of any way over the Gotthard was somehow being treated as the mongrel of the litter. And yet its history was not only long but captivating and illustrious – more so than that of almost any other climb in this compilation. With such rich heritage, of course,

ABOVE: Looking back up the Val Tremola – the Gotthard's signature ascent and one of Europe's most unusual.

came inconsistency. Many historians would have it that the Gotthard was first made accessible for pack mules by Emperor Charlemagne, dating it between the late 760s and his death in 814, but the first reliable documentation can't be traced until 1230, when the Holy Roman Emperor upgraded what was by then a vital access route to his territories in the land today known as Italy. Six centuries later, in 1832, the Gotthard became the carriage road now referred to as the *ancienne route* or 'old road' over the pass.

A long and mysterious past

In the intervening centuries, the Gotthard's strategic position between the Germanic and Latin halves of Europe placed it at the fulcrum of wars and epic journeys. Midway through the 13th century, it was included in the *Annales Stradenses*, the seminal reference for pilgrims from northern Europe heading for Rome. In 1403, the Gotthard was at the centre of a bitter and bloody power struggle between Milan in the south and the canton of Uri in the north; also in the 15th century, Pope Pius II added his name to the many luminaries who have crossed the Gotthard.

Too many to mention have made the same voyage since then, but Charles Greville, the first person across the summit in a wheeled carriage in 1775, and Hans Christian Andersen, who came and bickered with a chauffeur over a taxi fare in 1852, perhaps deserve special citation.

Evidence of the pass's long and mysterious past lies all around on the Gotthard, whether climbed from Airolo in the canton of Ticino, on the Italian-speaking south side, or from the north. Perhaps most famous of all of its artefacts, and what truly distinguishes the Gotthard from any other legendary mountain pass, is the old cobbled road or Tremolastrasse through the Val Tremola or Trembling Valley from Airolo. An extraordinary noodle of 38 tightly bunched hairpins, this is the only

route permitted for cyclists on the southern side – not that anyone in their right mind would favour the main road. Charles Freeston called the Tremola 'grim rather than grand' but went on to compare its windings to those of the Stelvio from Trafoi. Hugh Merrick was of the same view, calling the Val Tremola a 'marvel of engineering and a driving thrill'. In both cases, on the Gotthard and Stelvio, there can be no higher commendation than to say the road itself perhaps even eclipses the natural beauty of the surrounding summits.

The glamour of the Gotthard

The Gotthard's own crest will not, it's true, win any beauty contests. With a museum, three lakes and a monument to Adrien Guex, a Swiss airman who crashed his plane and died at the top in 1928, there is at least plenty to see. 'The scene is not beautiful but it is impressive,' said Merrick. While that may be true, numerous writers and travellers have noted the wonderful sense of transition when crossing the pass in the opposite direction, from north to south, from the last Germanic valley to a land of Italian speakers, Switzerland's canton of Ticino. 'We shall be unimaginative indeed if we do not feel the warm breath of the south come up to meet us,' cooed Douglas Ashby. Victor Tissot more or less echoed him: 'The delight of people from the north may be imagined when they thus find themselves suddenly transported into a kind of promised land, into the midst of a sunny, blooming scene, with the freshness of an oasis, fragrant as a garden under a soft blue sky in which light clouds rise and disappear like a distant flight of wild birds.'

There is less to inspire the cyclist further down the wide, smooth and sterile road to the summit from Hospental. Although the Tour of Switzerland has climbed the Gotthard more than any other mountain (35 times up to 2010), and often from this side, those visits have spawned considerably fewer legends than, say, the Devil's Bridge across the Schöllenen Gorge in Göschenen, on the approach to Hospental. A meandering tale goes that a local herdsman hoodwinked the devil into building the bridge and, on realizing, the devil reached for a rock with the intention of smashing it. An old woman saw him and promptly drew a cross on the rock, making it impossible to lift. The cross and 220-tonne rock are still there today, as are two bridges, one built during the construction of the main Gotthard pass road in 1830 and now closed and, above it, the main 1955 structure. Look hard and you'll also see the abutments of the first footbridge across the gorge, built in 1595 and destroyed by a storm in 1888.

Perhaps it was to tales like this that Charles Freeston was referring when he talked about the 'glamour' of the Gotthard. If by glamour he also meant history, importance and one of the most unusual stretches of mountain road anywhere in the Alps, he may never have penned a truer word.

LEFT: The monument dedicated to Alexandre Souvorov on the Gotthard summit. The Russian general crossed the Alps with his army in 1799 in the hope of driving the French out of Switzerland.

Fact file St. Gotthardpass

From Andermatt/Hospental

REGION: Canton of Uri, Switzerland

ACCESS: From the centre of Andermatt, follow signs to the Gotthard pass, then in Hospental follow signs marked Zum Sankt Gotthar or Alte Gotthard-Strasse (old St. Gotthard road) and you'll reach the main road for cyclists

HEIGHT: 2,106m

LENGTH: 8.6km (from Hospental)

ALTITUDE GAIN: 610m

AVERAGE GRADIENT: 7.1%

MAXIMUM GRADIENT: 9% (km 6.5)

OPEN: June to October

REFRESHMENTS: Several bars at the bottom, in Mätteli (km 4) and at the top

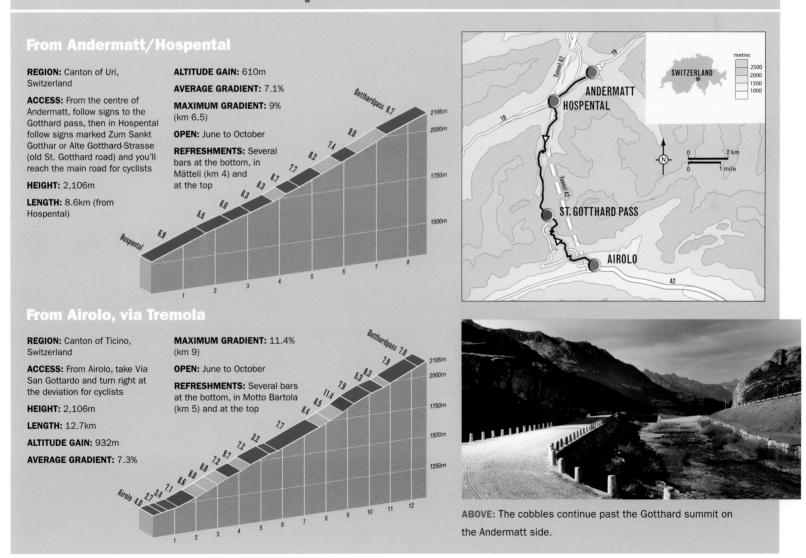

From Airolo, via Tremola

REGION: Canton of Ticino, Switzerland

ACCESS: From Airolo, take Via San Gottardo and turn right at the deviation for cyclists

HEIGHT: 2,106m

LENGTH: 12.7km

ALTITUDE GAIN: 932m

AVERAGE GRADIENT: 7.3%

MAXIMUM GRADIENT: 11.4% (km 9)

OPEN: June to October

REFRESHMENTS: Several bars at the bottom, in Motto Bartola (km 5) and at the top

ABOVE: The cobbles continue past the Gotthard summit on the Andermatt side.

Col du Tourmalet
France
2,115m

> **THE IMAGE OF MERCKX ROMPING CLEAR ALONE AT THE TOP OF THE MOUNTAIN** before a jaw-dropping solo victory in Mourenx is one of the Tour's most impressive and cherished memories. ⁊

If a clue was in the name, the Col du Tourmalet seemed forever destined to become the most visited and most hallowed mountain in the sport of cycling's most famous race. The Tour de France had scaled vertiginous heights before, as early as its third edition in 1905, but the Ballon d'Alsace in the Vosges seemed a mere pimple by comparison with what lay in wait five years later, a few hundred kilometres to the southwest.

So Tourmalet as in 'Tour de France'. Or, literally, Tourmalet as in 'nasty detour', a glowering, grey hulk of a hill straddling the Ardour and Campan valleys. Tour founder Henri Desgrange, who had holidayed in the Pyrenees but preferred the Alps, considered the notion of climbing the Tourmalet pure lunacy. His colleague at *Auto* newspaper, Alphonse Steines, himself a gifted rider, set out for the Pyrenees in late January 1910 on a mission to prove Desgrange wrong. He defied the advice of an innkeeper at the foot of the mountain who told him that the Col was barely passable in July, let alone January, climbed to within three kilometres of the pass, then abandoned his vehicle in the snow. Steines was found by a search party at three o'clock the following morning, dazed, groggy and triumphant: Desgrange was wrong – the Tourmalet was 'perfectly passable' – and a telegram was dispatched to the office of *Auto* the following day to break the astonishing news.

Unsurprisingly, Desgrange remained nervous. Neither his young colleague's travails nor the context of the times helped to allay his fears. As the French author Pierre Carrey remarked in his book, *Légendes du Tour de France - 100 ans de Pyrénées*: 'We're talking about an era when man has only just learned to fly, and the idea of a man on the moon belongs to the realm of science fiction. To ascend is to defy nature, to thumb one's nose at the gods. Most often, magnificent and temerarious men in their flying machines end up earthbound and broken. The mountains are also killers: on the 8th of July, seven mountaineers wound up buried beneath a glacier on the Jungfrau.'

Desgrange's concerns, then, seemed well founded. Nonetheless, two days before their rendezvous with the Tourmalet, the Tour riders tackled their first Pyrenean climbs, the first in the race's history, and only four abandoned. Desgrange thanked the heavens... then said another prayer.

The date is now engraved in Tour folklore: July 21, 1910. Sometime that afternoon, the peloton hurtled down the Col d'Aspin,

swung into Sainte Marie de Campan and prepared to face the 17.2-kilometre ascent of the Tourmalet. Cycling mythology records that, to a man, they were terrorized by the experience; the reality, perhaps disappointingly, is rather different. For while stage winner Octave Lapize's tirades in the direction of Desgrange's cohorts Steines and Victor Breyer are well documented – he told Breyer that they were 'criminals', and Steines that Desgrange was a 'murderer' – the majority of journalists, spectators and riders were quite simply exhilarated. 'As for your Tourmalet, I climbed it and must admit that it was an exploit that I'm proud of,' Gustave Garrigou deigned to inform Desgrange having finished the Tour in third place in Paris.

A legend was now in its infancy. Three years later, the Frenchman Eugène Christophe seemed bound for Tour glory as he followed the Belgian Philippe Thys over the summit of the Tourmalet, only to plough into a pothole and snap his front forks on the descent. Having walked ten kilometres down the mountain to Sainte Marie de Campan, Christophe sought out the local forge and, he thought, salvation. He emerged several hours later, his bike again fully intact, and one of cycling's epic tales of human endeavour already half-written. Alas, a place in Tour history would be Christophe's only consolation: a ten-minute penalty for asking a young boy to work the bellows added insult to the injury of the three-and-a-half hours he had conceded to Thys by the time he crossed the finish line in Luchon. Denied overall victory in 1912 by a nonsensical points system discarded the following year, by the First World War in his peak years, then by broken forks again in 1919 and 1922, Christophe was doomed never to win the Tour. Instead, he became arguably its most fabled and unfortunate tragic figure.

PREVIOUS PAGE: Above La Mongie – a ski resort that won't win any beauty prizes but has become famous in international cycling.

OPPOSITE: High up on the Luz-Saint-Sauveur side of the Tourmalet, the D918 road via Pont de La Gaubie is the more *sauvage* of the two routes to the top.

Canvas for the ridiculous

The Tourmalet, meanwhile, was establishing itself as cycling's greatest natural theatre, the scene of heroism, tragedy and comedy. In 1927, the Belgian Gustaaf Van Slembrouck lurched towards the summit with a cigarette dangling from his lips… then won the following day's stage in Perpignan. In 1969, with overall victory already assured, the great Belgian Eddy Merckx vowed not to attack on the Tourmalet 'unless I find myself in a good position'. Whatever prompted the urge, attack he did, and the image of Merckx romping clear alone at the top of the mountain, still with over 100 kilometres to ride before a jaw-dropping solo victory in Mourenx, is one of the Tour's most impressive and cherished memories.

Having played host to the sublime, a year later the Tourmalet turned canvas for the ridiculous, with Merckx again the central figure. After declaring its intention to become France's premier winter resort, the monstrosity known as La Mongie on the eastern flank of the Col welcomed a stage finish for the first time – and a furious race leader. The source of Merckx's ire? The unripe peaches in the lunch bags or *musettes* handed to the riders at the stage start in Saint Gaudens. 'We anxiously await the day when the champion demands *moules marinières* in Sainte Marie de Campan, or maybe lobster thermador,' sniffed a nonplussed Antoine Blondin in his *L'Equipe* column the following day.

The Tour's favourite mountain

In 2010, the Tour celebrated the hundred-year anniversary of its first visit to the Pyrenees, and to the Tourmalet, with ascents of both the eastern and western flanks, from Luz-Saint-Sauveur and Sainte Marie de Campan respectively. Identical in gradient, at 7.4 per cent, the two climbs are different in character and challenge, with the route from Luz longer by just under two kilometres and gaining 137 metres more in altitude. The western side is also considerably more picturesque, free from the breezeblock eyesores that rise out of La Mongie on the eastern slopes, and more exposed. From Luz, the gradient in the final eight kilometres before the summit never dips beneath 7.5 per cent, and climaxes with a final kilometre above ten per cent. The ascent from Sainte Marie de Campan, by contrast, starts gently amid lush green fields, the summit and indeed entire mountain hidden from

view, only to rear up inexorably towards La Mongie, where the ramps are at their steepest.

There is no higher main road pass in the Pyrenees and none with quite such an aura or heritage. Perhaps only Alpe d'Huez is so inextricably associated with cycling and the Tour de France. Two statues at the Tourmalet's summit cement the 100-year connection – one a memorial to Jacques Goddet, the Tour's director from 1936 to 1987, another immortalizing Octave Lapize, he of the 'murderers' diatribe and also the honour of first rider to reach the summit in 1910, having walked much of the way.

Up to 2011, the Tourmalet had appeared on the Tour route 75 times, more than any other mountain. Its status as a Tour icon therefore seems assured – and will be consolidated should speculation about a stage finish at the Pic du Midi, 250 metres above the pass, ever come to fruition. A tortuously narrow road leading from the Col to the Observatoire des Laquets and the Pic already exists, and has aroused the curiosity of Tour organizers Amaury Sport Organization. By rights, the lack of space for vehicles, television crews and hospitality areas at the Pic ought to make this a forbidden frontier. But then didn't Henri Desgrange have and eventually jettison similar reservations about the Tourmalet in 1910?

The Tourmalet, indeed, is itself nature's tribute to those quintessential Tour de France maxims – nothing is impossible and no mountain is too high. Today, the world's greatest cyclists approach the climb with respect rather than awe, but it remains a totem that far transcends any measure of its dimensions or difficulty. That name – Tourmalet or 'nasty detour' – adorns bikes, clothing and, most of all, dreams. It transcends. Inspires. Intimidates.

In the words of Octave Lapize, Desgrange and Steines were 'murderers', but posterity will remember them as pioneers. Before them, the Tourmalet was just a mountain. Today, it is a monument.

Fact file Col du Tourmalet

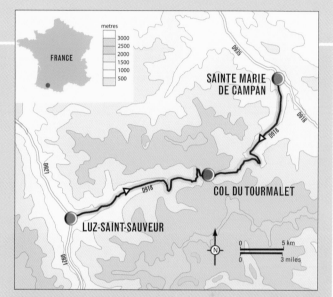

From Sainte Marie de Campan

REGION: Hautes-Pyrénées, Central Pyrenees, France

ACCESS: Follow the D935 from Bagnères de Bigorre to Sainte Marie de Campan and turn right at the main village square, near the church. Follow the D918 to the top

HEIGHT: 2,115m

LENGTH: 17.2km

ALTITUDE GAIN: 1,268m

AVERAGE GRADIENT: 7.4%

MAXIMUM GRADIENT: 13% (km 15 and 16.5)

OPEN: May to October, depending on weather

REFRESHMENTS: Several bars at the bottom, at La Mongie (km 13) and one at the top

From Luz-Saint-Sauveur

REGION: Hautes-Pyrénées, Central Pyrenees, France

ACCESS: From Lourdes, follow the D921 via Argelès-Gazost and Pierrefitte-Nestalas. Then follow the D918 from Luz-Saint-Sauveur

HEIGHT: 2,115m

LENGTH: 18.8km

ALTITUDE GAIN: 1,405m

AVERAGE GRADIENT: 7.4%

MAXIMUM GRADIENT: 13% (km 4 and 8)

OPEN: May to October, depending on weather

REFRESHMENTS: Bars in Barèges (km 7) and one at the top

ABOVE: Looking back down the valley towards Luz-Saint-Sauveur on the upper reaches of the Tourmalet, on the D918 road via Pont de la Gaubie.

Gran Sasso d'Italia
2,130m
Italy

If the Gran Sasso d'Italia, literally The Big Rock of Italy, sounds and looks like a mountain massif with grander and more famous virtues than the challenge it presents to cyclists, first impressions of this vast outcrop of central Italy are entirely correct.

Largely unknown or at least overlooked abroad, the Gran Sasso massif is home to the highest peak, the 2,912-metre Corno Grande, of one of Europe's foremost mountain ranges, the Apennines. The Corno, or literally Horn, was first climbed in 1573 by Francesco De Marchi, a sort of David Blaine or Harry Houdini of the Renaissance period, as adept at deep-sea excavation as he was at climbing mountains. De Marchi claimed to have been yearning to climb the Corno for 30 years before he arrived in Assergi in the summer of 1573 and recruited a chamois hunter, Francesco di Domenico, and two other local gents to be his guides. Their ascent took them five-and-a-quarter hours. 'Looking all around me, it was like being in mid-air,' De Marchi wrote of reaching the summit.

It was from Assergi that some of the world's best cyclists would later make their own assault on the Gran Sasso in four editions of the Giro d'Italia. Before that, though, the same 17-kilometre-long Alpine meadow where those stages would finish had played host to one of the more infamous and significant episodes of the Second World War.

Saving Mussolini

Campo Imperatore. That was the name that Otto Skorzeny's secret agent Herbert Kappler had heard on the Italian airwaves – or at least a coded version. Weeks after Fascist dictator Benito *il Duce* Mussolini's arrest in July 1943, Adolf Hitler had entrusted Skorzeny with the task of locating him, and the SS captain had done just that. Without further ado, the Führer dispatched him and 90 commandos in gliders to the Gran Sasso to rescue the Duce and pull off an outrageous and morale-boosting coup for the fascists.

More intelligence had told them that the only safe way to Campo Imperatore was by cable car. That meant they would have to take to the skies. Before the raid, Skorzeny had completed a recce in his Heinkel He 111, even leaning out of the window in an Arctic 200mph wind to take pictures of potential landing spots. It didn't exactly pay dividends – his pilot made an emergency landing on the edge of a precipice Skorzeny described as 'much like the platform for a ski

jump' – but neither did it seem to matter: soon Skorzeny and his men had breezed past the guards at the Campo Imperatore hotel and seized Mussolini. 'Duce, the Führer has sent me to set you free,' Skorzeny announced, to which Mussolini is said to have replied, 'I knew that my friend would not forsake me!'

Twenty-eight years later, journalists following the Giro d'Italia seemed more excited about visiting Campo Imperatore and the scene of Mussolini's release than they were about reporting on the Corsa Rosa's first visit to the site. Even without the history, there was something enchanting about this vast, verdant swathe backed by sharp, grey pinnacles. One famous Italian mountaineer, Fosco Maraini, said that Campo Imperatore could 'easily be Tibet', and more specifically the plateau of Phari Dzong. As a result, this area of the Gran Sasso is still often referred to as *piccolo Tibet*, or little Tibet.

That 1971 Giro proved the climb from Assergi to be a long but not excessively difficult test. The fact that the winner, Vicente López Carril, had little real pedigree in the mountains confirmed the perception of an ascent that only really became difficult in its last two kilometres, up on the plateau, when the wind and rarified air began to take their toll. In 1985, the Giro again headed for Assergi and the Gran Sasso, but only went as far as Fonte Cerreto, 1,130 metres above sea level. The young Franco Chioccioli's success that day prompted the great Bernard Hinault to tip Chioccioli for future glories that he would partially attain. A further visit by the Giro in 1989, this time to the summit, saw another surprise winner in the Dane John Carlsen.

The Giro's only really famous trip to Campo Imperatore, though, came in 1999. At the route presentation the previous autumn, defending champion and climbing maestro Marco Pantani had looked closely at the profile of the Gran Sasso and frowned. 'I've never climbed the Gran Sasso, never been there, but it looks pretty simple,' Pantani muttered. Meanwhile, a fellow Italian icon much less at home in the hills, Mario Cipollini, was looking up and down the mountainous route with chiselled jaws agape. 'I hope that when they give us our race number they also give us a ski pass,' he said. 'More than a Giro d'Italia, it looks like a tour of Italian ski resorts!'

Cipollini's flippancy turned out to be prophetic, as the peloton rode to Campo Imperatore in polar conditions. It was the end of May, but more to the point, this was central Italy, hundreds of kilometres south of Alpine skyscrapers such as the Gavia or the Stelvio where walls of snow on the upper slopes seemed the logical décor.

Pantani had looked out of his window that morning, seen the weather 'and scared myself to death'. And yet his attack two kilometres from the finish line took him clear on his own and towards an emphatic victory. It was vintage Pantani… except for one thing: it was too cold to take off his bandana, as was his wont before his trademark attacks.

While the fans, or *tifosi*, toasted Pantani, back down the mountain an old friend cursed him. The then Italian national champion Andrea Tafi had bickered with *il Pirata* about the Italian Cycling Federation's new regimen of blood tests, and on the Gran Sasso, Tafi shed icy tears as he faced insults from colleagues who sided with Pantani. 'I hope Pantani's not scared of more tests,' said Tafi's Mapei team-owner, Giorgio Squinzi. Two weeks later Pantani would leave the Giro when in the lead on the penultimate day… having failed a blood test.

Another rider competing that day, the Italian Filippo Simeoni, grew up not far from the Gran Sasso and agrees that it's a 'beautiful climb on a wide and good road, with a descent, some steep ramps and the wind to break up your rhythm.' On April 6, 2009, never mind snow or wind, the Gran Sasso was under attack from much more formidable elements when an earthquake measuring 5.8 on the Richter scale struck near L'Aquila, the regional capital to the southwest of the Gran Sasso. At Assergi, as in many other towns, buildings and streets crumbled. Two years on, throughout the Abruzzo region, some families were still housed in tents, corrugated iron containers and other forms of temporary accommodation.

The disaster revived controversy that began in the early 1980s, with the construction of the first of two road tunnels under the Gran Sasso and also an underground particle physics laboratory. While earthquakes in Italy tend to be less deadly than in other areas of the world, they are frequent, and the ramifications of the 2011 Japanese quake for the Fukushima nuclear power plant have raised fresh concerns about the facility under the Gran Sasso.

The resistance to any proposed alteration or violation of the Gran Sasso's natural environment underlines how dearly the Italians hold their Big Rock. Now a national park, it is also a national treasure – Italy's cherished heart of stone.

PREVIOUS PAGE: The road heads for the plateau known as 'little Tibet', just after the turn-off to Campo Imperatore.

RIGHT: The landscape begins to change as the road nears the left-hand turn to Campo Imperatore.

OPPOSITE: Facing back towards Assergi, a glimpse of Abruzzo and what makes it one of Italy's most appealing yet unheralded regions.

Fact file Gran Sasso d'Italia

From Assergi

REGION: Province of L'Aquila, Region of Abruzzo, Italy

ACCESS: Leave Assergi on the SR17BIS. After 20km, turn left on the SR17BIS DIR C to Campo Imperatore

HEIGHT: 2,130m

LENGTH: 31.1km

ALTITUDE GAIN: 1,263m

AVERAGE GRADIENT: 4.1%

MAXIMUM GRADIENT: 8.2% (ramp near km 16)

OPEN: April to October, subject to weather

REFRESHMENTS: Bars in Assergi and at Campo Imperatore

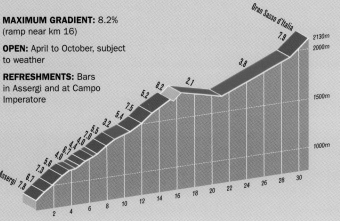

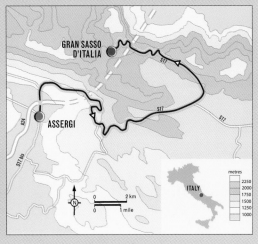

Blockhaus
2,142m
Italy

Green and capricious, windy and wild, the Majella massif in the Abruzzo region of central Italy has inspired many a nickname in the estimated 800,000 years since man first settled there. The Mother Mountain or Father of the Mountains as Pliny the Elder dubbed it, for cyclists this rogue Apennine outcrop has also and above all become synonymous with a climb that has excited and terrorized them for generations: the summit known as Blockhaus.

In her 1908 book *In the Abruzzi*, Anne MacDonell depicted its backdrop as a poor, primitive region obsessed by religion and mythology. On the Majella, she reported, the locals were sure that devils still lurked. According to one legend, they would shovel lingering snows and pelt the surrounding villages with what fell as hail until someone down below rang a church bell and the devils would retreat to hell. The demons were thought to be guardians of buried treasure left by wealthy men, whose souls would only rest when their spirit was exorcized, either by a *scongiuro* (spell) or some gesture of fearlessness. The quantity of buried treasure in the Abruzzo, MacDonell observed, was 'surprising' – although presumably also elusive for those who still took to the mountains to find it 'in secret.'

The Majella today is a very different place. In 1991, it became a national park, one of 24 in Italy and three in Abruzzo along with the Parco Nazionale d'Abruzzo and the Parco Nazionale Gran Sasso e Monti della Laga. The massif's wooded lower escarpments and barren summits are roamed by, among other rare fauna, wild cats, lynxes, brown bears, Appenine wolves, snow voles and the stunning, cream-coated Abruzzo chamois. It remains largely undiscovered by foreigners, but Italians and particularly the Abruzzesi come here to hike, explore or ski at one of the park's five resorts, one of which, the Passo Lanciano, dubiously claims to be the only winter sports destination in Europe with sea views.

Over 800 metres in altitude above the Passo Lanciano and 11 kilometres by road rises a crest whose name, in common with all the great mountain passes, reverberates through cycling's annals like a death knell. Referring to a stone garrison dating from the 1860s and christened by a commander of German origin, the true climb of the Blockhaus begins 1,648 metres above the sea at the Hotel Mamma Rosa. There, the third and hardest access route, from Roccamorice in the north, joins the road arriving from the pass and the final push to the top proceeds for six-and-a-half kilometres along a single, narrow road.

One of the beauties of the Blockhaus lies in the diversity of the three ascents up to this point. From Lettomanoppello, the Giro d'Italia's angle of attack in 2006, the gradient remains constantly between seven and nine per cent almost throughout, the road spearing through rocky scrubland before three gruellingly straight kilometres ending in the woods before the Passo Lanciano. It was on that difficult middle section that Damiano Cunego baited his rival Ivan Basso with a fierce acceleration in the 2006 Giro, only for Basso to catch and pass him a few hundred metres later en route to an emphatic stage victory. Timed by French physiologist Frédéric Portoleau, Basso took 34 minutes and 49 seconds to ascend from an altitude of 276 metres, a kilometre before Lettomanoppello, to the finish line at 1,306 metres above the nearby Adriatic. Portoleau reckoned the Italian's average power output on the climb had been a scarcely credible 450 watts – a figure lent unflattering perspective by subsequent revelations about Basso's 'collaboration' with Spanish doping doctor, Eufemiano Fuentes. Almost a year later, it was Basso's belated admission that defied belief: he had plotted and prepared illegal blood transfusions but never got around to consummating the act.

Three years later, local cyclists rejoiced at the news that the Giro was to venture all the way to the Blockhaus in its centenary edition, only to groan when they learned that it would take the easiest and in many ways least attractive of the three routes, from Fara Filiorum Petri in the east. Their frustration then turned to dismay when, in the days leading up to the race, lingering winter snows at the summit forced Giro chief Angelo Zomegnan to move the finish line down the mountain to the Hotel Mamma Rosa. The result was also, as in 2006, somewhat unsatisfactory, at least in retrospect; it took nearly two years, but stage winner Franco Pellizotti and third-placed rider Danilo di Luca were both eventually disqualified from the stage result and indeed the Giro's final rankings due to doping convictions. This left Stefano Garzelli as the theoretical winner of the Blockbuster that never was – a conclusion as bitter and nebulous as the conditions at the summit when the clouds huddle over the Majella.

The greatest cyclist ever to have lived, Eddy Merckx, knows the Blockhaus's whimsical nature well: he won his first ever Giro stage here in 1967, the climb's first appearance in the Giro, but saw the Spaniard José Manuel Fuente tear Merckx's Molteni team to shreds in calmer conditions five years later. That day, with Fuente's attack and Merckx's heavy deficit of over two minutes, the legend of Blockhaus, the 'severe judge of the Abruzzo' in the words of one national newspaper the next day, was truly born.

That 1972 stage, in particular, proved that any notion of ease is misplaced when discussing the Blockhaus, even undertaken from Fara Filiorum Petri. Di Luca, who hails from nearby Pescara and claimed to have climbed the Blockhaus 'hundreds of times', said of the Fara Filiorum Petri ascent, 'It's a very deceptive climb. It might seem easy but it never lets up and there are some sections which really hurt, even though the gradient doesn't seem to change.' The defining characteristic of this least arduous route to the Passo Lanciano may indeed be the consistency of its gradient, as well as the beech wood that continues for two kilometres beyond the pass, dispersing before the Roccamorice road cuts in from the right close to the Hotel Mamma Rosa. The asphalt all the way from Fara Filiorum Petri to the pass is smooth, the carriageway ample and the traffic often dense, particularly on summer weekends.

By comparison, the Roccamorice road seems rustic, romantic and turbulent – an impression borne out by a profile that shows frequent changes of gradient. Signs of life are scarce, and the final opportunity for any roadside refreshment comes courtesy of a fountain in the village of Roccamorice. With only three genuine hairpins between here and the Mamma Rosa, plus little shelter, this can feel like a trial by asphyxiation.

The suffocating nature of the Blockhaus is indeed just one of several similarities with Mont Ventoux in the south of France. What the Chalet Reynard is to the Ventoux – a watershed before the forest melts away into a windswept, sun-lashed moonscape – the Passo Lanciano or perhaps the Mamma Rosa is to the Blockhaus, heralding as they do the advent of radically different challenges and landscapes from the ones encountered thus far. As the beeches recede, the wind, sun and slope often form an unholy trinity that is the real essence of the Blockhaus. Eleven kilometres after the pass and 6.5 after the junction with Roccamorice, the TV masts at the Rifugio Pomilio signal the beginning of the end, which duly arrives 2,142 metres above sea level as the tarmac runs out alongside a small wooden shrine. The climb's symbol, the Blockhaus itself, or rather its dry-stone foundations, are clearly visible, though hardly imposing, 80 metres higher up. Once upon a time, the ascent to this point would have been referred to simply as La Majella; cycling's greatest inventor, erstwhile Giro boss Vincenzo Torriani, changed that when before the 1967 race he decided that the name Blockhaus was far more evocative and intimidating.

Equally as impressive as the climb's reputation are the summit views of emerald hills making their way in ever-decreasing ripples to the Adriatic, 50 kilometres to the northeast, and of the Apennines' highest peaks, the Corno Grande, to the northwest. That and the knowledge, if you make it this far, that the greatest climb in the Italian peninsula palpitates beneath your feet.

BELOW: These TV masts close to the Rifugio Pomilio lend a sinister air to the final twists and turns below the Blockhaus summit.

Fact file Blockhaus

From Fara Filiorum Petri

REGION: Abruzzo, Italy

ACCESS: Take the SP53 from Fara Filiorum Petri

HEIGHT: 2,142m

LENGTH: 29.6km

ALTITUDE GAIN: 1,932m

AVERAGE GRADIENT: 6.5%

MAXIMUM GRADIENT: 9.4% (km 26)

OPEN: May to October

REFRESHMENTS: Bars in Fara Filiorum Petri, Pretoro, at the Passo Lanciano and Hotel Mamma Rosa, after 23.5km

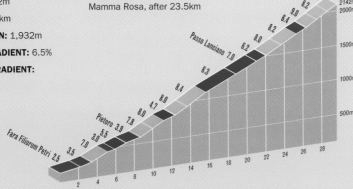

From Roccamorice

REGION: Abruzzo, Italy

ACCESS: Leave Roccamorice southbound on the Via Pagliari, which becomes the SP64

HEIGHT: 2,142m

LENGTH: 31.6km

ALTITUDE GAIN: 1,961m

AVERAGE GRADIENT: 6.2%

MAXIMUM GRADIENT: 10.8% (km 16)

OPEN: May to October

REFRESHMENTS: Bars and a fountain in Roccamorice and Hotel Mamma Rosa, after 25.5km

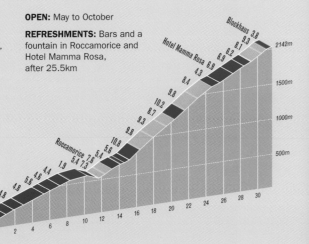

From Lettomanopello

REGION: Abruzzo, Italy

ACCESS: Leave Lettomanopello southbound on the SP60

HEIGHT: 2,142m

LENGTH: 28km

ALTITUDE GAIN: 1,961m

AVERAGE GRADIENT: 7.3%

MAXIMUM GRADIENT: 9.4% (km 23 and 28)

OPEN: May to October

REFRESHMENTS: Bars in Lettomanopello and at the Passo Lanciano and the Hotel Mamma Rosa after 22km

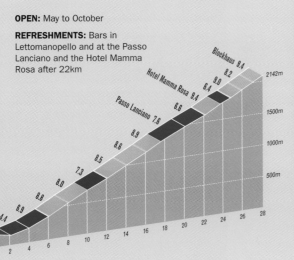

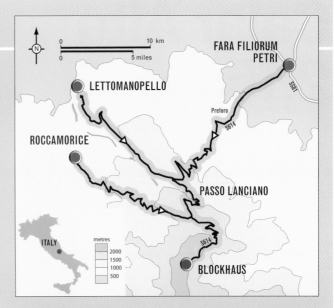

ABOVE: A sunset view of the Corno Grande, way over to the west, above Campo Imperatore. Looking in the other direction, to the east, the Blockhaus offers fine views of the Adriatic Sea.

Calar Alto
2,155m Spain

If ever a place illustrated why climbing mountains in southern Spain and Andalucia in particular is an acquired taste, Calar Alto is it.

Almost extraterrestrial in its desolation, with the fitting exception of one of the world's best astronomical observatories on its summit, Calar Alto overlooks the A-92 autoroute as if from the vantage point of another world or even galaxy. No villages bustle on its pleats, no road forsakes its camouflage amid the scrub and pines, and no branch or bush betrays the Poniente winds that frequently lash the Sierra de Los Filabres from the west. Everything seems lifeless, embalmed in silence and inactivity behind the heat haze that engulfs the immense valley stretching south to the Sierra Nevada for much of the year.

A little further east lies the Desierto de Tabernas, Europe's only true desert and film set *de choix* for many Hollywood westerns. To the west, towards Granada, legions of wind turbines whirr soundlessly, eerily. Devotees of cool, fragrant Alpine passes dotted with bell towers and edelweiss may want to turn back here rather than off the road towards Aulago or Gérgal; in Andalucia and at Calar Alto more than anywhere else, menace is the mountains' only inhabitant.

The Vuelta a España took the back road via Serón en route to Calar Alto and a stage finish at the nearby Alto de Velefique in 2009, having ascended from Gérgal on its previous two visits in 2004 and 2006. On both of those occasions, the finish line was situated at the observatory and the stars of the Vuelta came promptly to the fore. In 2004, having already cracked race leader Floyd Landis, Roberto Heras attacked seven kilometres from the summit to win alone and set up his third overall Vuelta title. Two years later, the Basque climber Igor Antón surged away close to Venta Luisa, just over three kilometres from the summit, to score his first ever Vuelta stage win.

To date, then, the Vuelta has never climbed from Aulago in the west, yet this is easily Calar Alto's most compelling side both on the way up and down. In reality not even skimming Aulago – the village tucked beneath the road and the mountain like a napping cat after six kilometres of climbing – the climb begins in earnest where the AL-4404 from Gérgal and the A-92 *autovia* part ways and signs point towards Aulago Calar Alto. From here, four kilometres of false flat, often into a headwind destined to deteriorate, lead west and into the Sierra's cauldron.

BELOW LEFT: Looking south towards the snow-capped Sierra Nevada, just past the midway point on the climb from Aulago.

BELOW: Beautiful Aulago, tucked underneath the road that climbs to Calar Alto from the west. The climb, at this point, is steady, and the scene idyllically Andalusian.

❝ FOR SOME, THE ESSENCE OF THE MOUNTAINS RESIDES HERE, in the wilderness, while for others the exercise may seem a little too Spartan, soulless even. ❞

Calar Alto | 143

A climb with a kick

The beauty of Calar Alto from this side, like a lot of climbs, lies in its contrasts. While the slopes here are relatively constant, the landscape never stops evolving, particularly in the latter half. Before then the road settles into a relentlessly straight and exposed hike up the mountainside for the first 13 kilometres, followed by the carrot of a short descent and the stick of the brutal ramp that follows. The lack of trees ensures not only exposure to the wind and sun but also to the view of impending agonies; often, the sight of a diagonal roadside barrier a kilometre or two above your head is simply far too much information.

Towards the 20-kilometre mark, the observatory begins to make frequent cameos on the skyline as the road twists to the left and into the prevailing wind. Now, the stubble of scrubland becomes a bristle of low pines. The scene feels vaguely Alpine. To the left, in spring and autumn months, the snow-coated Sierra Nevada glistens. Suddenly it seems to draw closer as smaller ridges fill the foreground.

Twenty-three kilometres from the foot of the climb and the last trace of civilization, a sign to the Refugio Arroyo Veruga points off to the left. Many a cyclist will have made the detour and regretted it later, having found the *refugio* closed or the three-kilometre climb back up to the main road an insult to their ongoing injury.

Much better to carry on and savour views to the north, which now seem to stretch towards infinity – or at least to Madrid. Of course they don't, but the wooded sierras to your left ripple over the horizon like Rockies or Appalachians. The scene ahead of you, with the observatory's white baubles gleaming in the sunshine, mimics the view of La Dôle and its spherical weather station from beneath the Col de la Givrine in the Jura.

If the peaks and passes around La Givrine, and especially Le Col de la Faucille, are said to offer the finest views of Mont Blanc, one could make similar claims about Calar Alto and the Sierra Nevada. Of course, this isn't the only vista for which the mountain is renowned; having signed a collaboration agreement in 1973, the German and Spanish governments chose Calar Alto as the site for their Centro Astronómico Hispano-Alemán on account of the exceptional visibility here. On average, 200 days a year at Calar Alto are considered 'astronomically useful'.

It has to be said that the meteorological conditions are less congenial to cyclists. One reason, but far from the only one, why the climb from Gérgal is less appealing, is that the wind on this side blows both harder and more consistently into your face. After the turning towards Bacares, at the five-kilometre mark, pines border the road all the way to the top, but are far too low and sparse to offer any protection from the sun or wind. At times, those gusts and the foliage, if not the milder gradients, give the ascent from Gérgal a *soupçon* of a Spanish Mont Ventoux. Or at least an inverted one, given that the harder, often hairpinned ramps come in the second half, between the tenth and twentieth kilometres, in contrast with the 'bottom-heavy' Ventoux.

Also unlike the Giant of Provence, what none of the routes to Calar Alto will ever become is either vaguely busy or famous. Of all of summits in this book, it may be the closest of any to a motorway, and yet it would be unusual to meet more than half a dozen cars either outward or homeward bound. Rush hours for observatory employees are the rare exception.

The lack of traffic, lack of life (discounting what must be the most spectacularly and incongruously located five-a-side soccer pitch in the world after 17 kilometres on the Gérgal side, at La Merendera) and the sense of climbing into a void at Calar Alto make this a stark cycling experience. For some, the essence of the mountains resides here, in the wilderness, while for others the exercise may seem a little too Spartan, soulless even. Those in the second category will probably also find no benefit in the fact that, quite unusually, the two main ascents here begin just a few minutes' ride apart; if you wanted to, you could spend an entire day climbing from Aulago and descending to Gérgal or vice versa.

Perhaps more than an acquired taste, then, Calar Alto is a mountain you'll either love or you'll hate. What it won't do is leave you indifferent – or, for that matter, unchallenged.

LEFT: One of the four observatories dotted across the summit. This, the southernmost of the four, is easily visible from the plain and for much of both ascents.

FAR LEFT: One of the rare hairpins on the eastern side. Fierce winds from the west can wreak havoc here.

Fact file Calar Alto

From Aulago

REGION: Andalucia, southern Spain

ACCESS: At roundabout junction of A-92 and AL-3401, take AL-4404 towards Aulago. After 6km, ignore signs to Aulago and continue along AL-4404

HEIGHT: 2,155m

LENGTH: 30.5km

ALTITUDE GAIN: 1,427m

AVERAGE GRADIENT: 4.68%

MAXIMUM GRADIENT: Sections at 10% after Aulago and in km 14

OPEN: All year

REFRESHMENTS: Bars and shops in Aulago, 500m off

the road to your right after 6km of climbing. No refreshments on or at the top of the climb itself

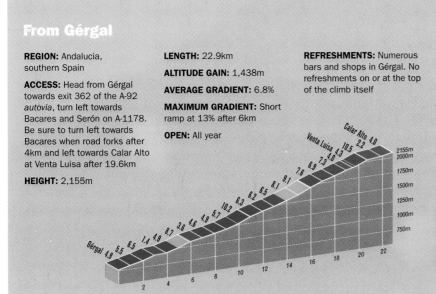

From Gérgal

REGION: Andalucia, southern Spain

ACCESS: Head from Gérgal towards exit 362 of the A-92 *autovia*, turn left towards Bacares and Serón on A-1178. Be sure to turn left towards Bacares when road forks after 4km and left towards Calar Alto at Venta Luisa after 19.6km

HEIGHT: 2,155m

LENGTH: 22.9km

ALTITUDE GAIN: 1,438m

AVERAGE GRADIENT: 6.8%

MAXIMUM GRADIENT: Short ramp at 13% after 6km

OPEN: All year

REFRESHMENTS: Numerous bars and shops in Gérgal. No refreshments on or at the top of the climb itself

ABOVE: Not steep, but windy and mercilessly exposed, the Gérgal climb has thus far been the Vuelta a España's preferred route to Calar Alto.

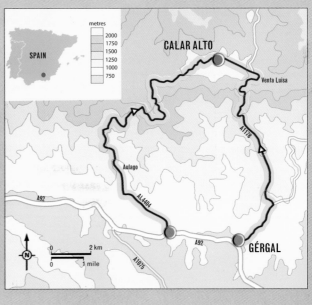

Colle delle Finestre
2,178m
Italy

Some climbs need decades to attain mythical status. Most never do. It took the Colle delle Finestre less than an hour – if you discount the months of anticipation leading up to a stage of the 2005 Giro d'Italia that surpassed every expectation, and the months, years and, yes, decades for which that day will be remembered.

Giro chief Carmine Castellano had first visited the Finestre one Sunday afternoon in 1995. Built somewhat prematurely in 1700 to serve the Forte Fenestrelle, itself first commissioned by Louis XIV of France in 1694 yet only completed in 1849, the road connected the Val di Susa in the north to the Val Chisone in the south. Its backdrop was an upland Eden with stupendous views of the 3,538-metre Rocciamelone, the mountain widely and wrongly considered to be the highest in the Alps for much of the Middle Ages.

In Meana di Susa, Castellano had seen a sign to the Colle delle Finestre and chivvied his friend and driver Alberto Della Torre into an impromptu detour. After 11 kilometres, at the Colletto di Meana, the road had disintegrated into a treacherous flume of mud and rock – 'an impassable goat track' Castellano said later, yet pass they did. At the summit, they abandoned the car and stomped gleefully through the mud. 'Behind them there was an infernal journey,' *La Gazzetta dello Sport* recorded later, while 'before them lay the *finestre sul paradiso*', the windows onto paradise. That and a tantalizing glimpse of what Castellano thought at the time was a forbidden fantasy.

It took him ten years. In 2006, Torino was to hold the Winter Olympics and the president of the Piedmont region, Enzo Ghigi, wanted his fief to be the talk of the sporting world months before the event. What better way than to host the Giro and to take it over the Colle delle Finestre in Castellano's final year as race director? Ghigi liked the idea and set about improving but not entirely resurfacing those beastily beautiful last eight kilometres. It would be the Giro's first taste of unmade mountain road since 2000, when three kilometres of the Passo di Gavia were still untarmacked. It would also be the race's biggest gamble since 1982, when the unpaved descent of the Monte Grappa had caused punctures galore and general uproar.

To Castellano's relief, May 28 dawned warm and sunny. The gamble was on. The race was also exquisitely poised two stages from the end in Milan, with 2002 champion Paolo Savoldelli just over two minutes clear of 2001 and 2003 winner Gilberto Simoni, by far the superior climber, and three minutes ahead of the Venezuelan José Rujano.

The omens were good and what followed was better. Rujano's Selle Italia team attacked *en masse* as the road climbed out of Meana di Susa, through Meana and into the Finestre's narrow labyrinth of oak, acacia and ash. Almost immediately, the group shattered like a vase and Savoldelli trailed in Simoni and Rujano's wake. Aided by Danilo di Luca, that pair emerged from the woods after the Colletto di Meana and seemingly into a bygone era. As the *troika* forged ahead through the dust, and Savoldelli 'lost ten years of my life' watching his deficit expand, Italian broadcaster Rai got so caught up in the mood that it turned its pictures to black and white.

All that seemed predictable at this point was the cascade of hyperbole that duly rained down the next day. The Finestre had 45 hairpins (32 in the forest, paved, including 11 in the seventh kilometre alone, and 13 steeper ones on the *sterrato*) and 45 *finestre* or 'windows onto the world', wrote Marco Pastonesi of *La Gazzetta*. It was an 'intestine of vertical asphalt' with 'alcoholic gradients'. Lined up along the sharp crest, the 'border between heaven and hell' according to the same paper's Claudio Gregori, thousands of waiting fans resembled Aztecs keeping guard over their mountain. With this image, the Finestre's moniker, The Mountain of the Indians, was born.

Overnight legend

The final destiny of the *maglia rosa* (pink jersey) was uncertain to the very last. The Giro had itself a cliffhanger and, in the Finestre, a rare and beautiful precipice. At the top of the climb, the hairpins and respite become scarcer, their pitches more severe, yet di Luca's pace remained relentless. Simoni pleaded with him – the road to the stage finish in Sestriere was still long – but he paid no attention. It would be a costly mistake, not so much for him as for Simoni: di Luca's cramps when they reached the bottom of the descent brought the self-styled Killer to a standstill. Without him in their number, Simoni and Rujano could forge ahead to a famous stage win for Rujano, but the Giro was Savoldelli's. Simoni's scant consolation was second place overall in one of the closest and, thanks to the Finestre, most spectacular Giri in the event's history.

Fond memories and a small stone monument to di Luca, the first man over the summit, aren't all that remain of that day. Those black and white images were broadcast around the world and, in an instant, the Finestre had taken its place alongside the Stelvio, the Fedaia and the Ghisallo, Italy's historical mountain meccas. Castellano's successor, Angelo Zomegnan, immediately made it his priority to search out another unpolished, unpaved gem in time for the 2006 race. And so Plan de Corones in the Dolomites became the Giro's next high-altitude Eldorado – albeit one with a rather manufactured feel.

The real beauty of the Finestre, by contrast, was that it seemed drenched in history, as though it had stood forever both among the snow-glazed peaks of the Alpi Graie and Alpi Cozie and in cycling mythology. The climb had everything: length, altitude, average gradients on the edge of the exclusive ten per cent club, plus dazzling good looks. Chamois bounded across the rocks, badgers foraged in the woods and eagles circled overhead; streams bubbled and rhododendrons bloomed; unobstructed views stretched further than the most distant horizon.

The Finestre next appeared on a Giro route in 2011, but in the meantime had become a rite of passage for climbing connoisseurs. Some came and were disappointed or rather appalled by the state of the *sterrato* white road. Others showed up at the weekend and found the mountain overrun with tourists and quad bikes.

Most, though, agreed that the Finestre was stupendous, unforgettable, incomparable. Castellano called it his 'greatest achievement'; Rujano said simply that the Finestre was 'too beautiful'. Together, and with a little help from a few others, in the space of a few hours on one sunny afternoon in 2005, they had created cycling's newest mountain legend.

PREVIOUS PAGE: High on the Colle delle Finestre, the last of the 45 hairpins that wind up the mountainside from Meana di Susa.

RIGHT: The condition of the *sterrato* varies greatly according to weather conditions. These photos were taken days before the Giro d'Italia's second visit to the Finestre, in 2011.

BELOW: The tightly packed windings that characterize the Finestre, particularly in its lower and middle portions.

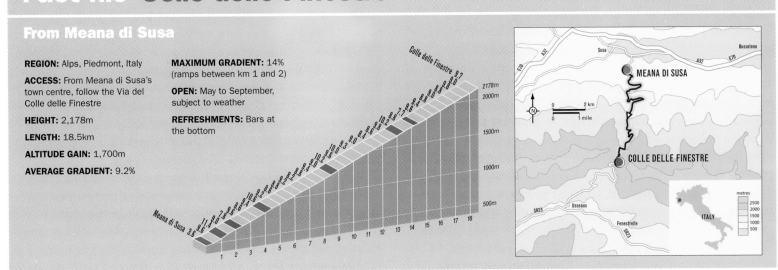

Fact file Colle delle Finestre

From Meana di Susa

REGION: Alps, Piedmont, Italy

ACCESS: From Meana di Susa's town centre, follow the Via del Colle delle Finestre

HEIGHT: 2,178m

LENGTH: 18.5km

ALTITUDE GAIN: 1,700m

AVERAGE GRADIENT: 9.2%

MAXIMUM GRADIENT: 14% (ramps between km 1 and 2)

OPEN: May to September, subject to weather

REFRESHMENTS: Bars at the bottom

Ordino–Arcalis
2,223m
Andorra

If Andorra remains a mystery to many people today, for travellers before the principality embraced tourism in the latter half of the 20th century it was hard to imagine a more bamboozling place on earth.

Thirty kilometres long and wide, consisting entirely of wild Pyrenean summits and narrow valleys, as recently as 1928 Europe's sixth smallest country was described by Bernard Newman in *All Around Andorra* as a land where change was 'almost unknown', the natives were 'simple-minded, superstitious and slow to move' and 'agriculture and smuggling' represented the mainstays of the economy. Newman's extensive travels in what Louis the Debonair had dubbed the wild valleys of Hell had provided ample evidence: the first Andorran Newman ever met, he said, was a mountain-dweller on the Port de l'Envalira who had never seen an Englishman and couldn't grasp the concept of a boat. Newman's 'inquisitive friend' had come across the odd motorcar, but naturally only on one of the two mountain roads that serviced Andorra at the time. This had led the man to form some interesting conclusions about the rudiments of internal combustion: 'He believed that the necessary power was obtained by the driver turning the handle – that is to say the steering wheel,' Newman wrote. 'One must remember that he had only seen cars ascending or descending the zigzags of the pass – that is to say when the driver was turning the steering wheel continuously.'

Andorra and its winding roads – namely the pass over the 2,408-metre Envalira – would leave their mark on professional cycling and the Tour de France in 1964. That year, having already correctly forecast the assassination of John F. Kennedy, a fortune-teller named Belline had another premonition: the winner of four Tours between 1957 and 1963, France's sporting *chouchou* Jacques Anquetil, would also die unexpectedly. Belline even named the date – Tuesday, July 6, 1964. The day, precisely, when Anquetil and the Tour peloton would head back into France via the Envalira.

Twenty-four hours earlier Anquetil had thought better of training on the Tour's rest day. The error would cost him dear: his eternal rival Raymond Poulidor was one of several riders to attack almost from the gun on the Envalira, and Anquetil withered. He would later admit to sensing the beat of death's drum: 'I was suffocating. I couldn't breathe.' Whatever the malaise, a water bottle filled with an unidentified magic potion – some said whisky, others champagne – revived him, and Belline and Poulidor went back respectively to the ouija and the drawing board.

You'd think that this episode would have enshrined the Envalira among cycling's iconic passes, but a young Andorran pretender was to usurp it in 1997. Opened in 1983, the Arcalis resort formed half of the Vallnord ski complex and was accessed via a fine, at times twisty 17.4-kilometre, 5.3 per cent road from Ordino, the town on the lower slopes of the 2,740-metre Casamanya mountain. Arcalis had successfully hosted a stage of the Vuelta a España in 1994. Now, three years later, it was the Tour de France's turn. Perched high in the remote northwest corner of the principality among the 'grey, gaunt' mountains described by Newman, and with a ring of menace and mystery to its name, Arcalis would be Andorra's perfect showcase.

It was also about to receive a baptism of fire, and power, like no other.

Ben Johnson in Seoul

The German Jan Ullrich had shocked the cycling world by finishing second in his debut Tour at just 22 years of age in 1996. After a series of brief and severe undulations in Andorra La Vella, La Massana and Ordino, the road to Arcalis climbs straight and steadily northbound alongside the Valira del Nord, and here Ullrich and his Telekom team-mate Udo Bölts set a ferocious pace. On a left-hand bend in El Serrat, Ullrich accelerated again and finally his opponents could take no more. As he steamrollered to a runaway victory and a yellow jersey he would never relinquish, former five-time Tour winner-turned-TV commentator Bernard Hinault gasped. 'This kid will win the Tour for the next ten years,' Hinault said.

Ullrich's legend was still in its infancy. It would burn itself out amid all sorts of private and professional woes over the next decade. What couldn't be erased was what the German had done at, or rather to, Arcalis. Antoine Vayer was the coach of one of the world's leading teams at the time, Andorra-based Festina, and later calculated that Ullrich's average power output of 497 watts on the climb to Arcalis constituted the single most powerful performance ever in the Tour. When Festina's rampant use of the illegal drug EPO was exposed in 1998, Vayer reinvented himself as an ardent critic of drug-taking in professional cycling.

Even in 1997, though, when he was in on the sport's sordid secrets, Vayer believed that Arcalis represented the pinnacle of cycling's pharmaceutical excess. He called it the sport's 'Ben Johnson' moment.

'To me, Ullrich at Andorra is the zenith of the EPO era. It's Ben Johnson running the 100 metres in Seoul,' Vayer reflected in 2010. 'You can make quite good comparisons between hundred-metre-races and Tour mountain stages: in terms of watts, 450 watts or more over more than half an hour is like a nine-second 100 metres. Admirable? Impressive? Sure, it's impressive to look at Ben Johnson on the start line in Seoul, with his deltoids practically bursting through his skin. But from a sporting point of view it's absolutely detestable.'

If hindsight hasn't been kind to Jan Ullrich, an almost vaudeville nostalgia may have benefited Arcalis. Widespread excitement greeted the news that the Tour would return in 2010. As it turned out, the strong headwinds that are common on the climb led to a rather turgid affair and victory for the young Frenchman Brice Feillu. Back down the mountain, though, what would develop into a thrilling and sometimes unsavoury rivalry between Alberto Contador and Lance Armstrong had flickered for the first time with Contador's late attack. 'That wasn't part of the plan, but then I didn't expect him to follow the plan,' Armstrong sniffed.

Andorra's national climb

The Briton Bradley Wiggins was among the best climbers that day. Indeed, Wiggins enjoyed the climb to Arcalis so much that he named the mountain among his favourites in his 2010 book *On Tour*. 'The first time [I rode Arcalis] was a time trial in the Tour of Catalunya and everybody was dreading it but I absolutely flew up it,' Wiggins recalled. 'Long and steady, set your gear and go to work, it is exactly the kind of climb that suits my physique and physiology.'

Decidedly unlovely in its first eight kilometres to Ordino, the Arcalis ascent becomes more attractive the higher it climbs. Four kilometres from the summit and 2,000 metres above the sea, a dizzying sequence of 12 hairpins, none of them more than a few hundred metres apart, offers redress and respite from the thinning air. By now criss-crossed by the Arcalis pistes, the mountainside is also dappled with firs and overhung by glowering peaks – the 'fearful monsters rather than the friendly hills of Wales' that Newman described in 1928.

The road continues for a few hundred metres beyond where Ullrich won in 1997 and Feillu in 2010 to the Port du Rat, an old border crossing into France. It has now travelled 26.1 kilometres from Andorra La Vella and gained 1,202 metres in altitude. To the right lies France, to the left the whole of Andorra, with its now thriving economy, developed resorts and population of 80,000 – 74,000 more than in Newman's day.

A symbol of prosperity and modernity, of Andorra's mountains and their enduring mystery, and of an age that professional cycling would rather forget, Arcalis is many things to many people. Above all, in importance if not elevation, it has become Andorra's national climb.

Fact file Ordino–Arcalis

From Andorra La Vella

REGION: Andorra

ACCESS: From Andorra La Vella town centre, follow the CS-340 (Carretera del Coll d'Ordino)

HEIGHT: 2,223m

LENGTH: 26.1km

ALTITUDE GAIN: 1,202m

AVERAGE GRADIENT: 4.61%

MAXIMUM GRADIENT: 12% in El Serrat

OPEN: From May to October, subject to weather

REFRESHMENTS: Bars in Ordino, El Serrat and at the summit

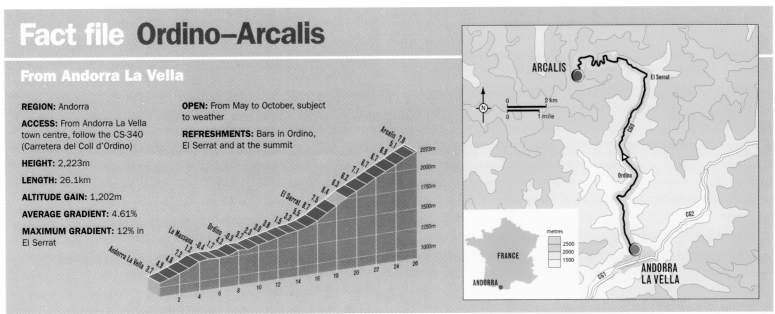

Passo Giau
2,236m
Italy

It seems extraordinary that the Passo Giau has appeared on the route of the Giro d'Italia only four times. Or, rather, it seems inexplicable that, having been used so sparingly in the only real arena that can consecrate a Dolomite climb, the Giro d'Italia, the Giau is still routinely bracketed with classics such as the passes of the Fedaia and Pordoi.

The Giau's status with the cognoscenti may appear even more surprising given that historical necessity – in other words how useful a pass is – can make or break a pass. Not that a journey over the Giau is some whimsical leisure drive – it's just that another mountain route, the Passo Falzarego, predates the Giau and more than adequately serves the same purpose of linking the valleys of Ampezzo and Livinallongo. Even the Giro has favoured the Falzarego, having first crossed its 2,109-metre summit in 1946. In recent years, race organizers RCS have gravitated towards the Giau for one reason only – it is far steeper than the Falzarego and so panders to the same hedonistic impulse that has given the Giro the Monte Zoncolan, the Zoncolan's neighbour Monte Crostis and the Plan de Corones.

This partially solves the mystery of why the Passo Giau is considered a Dolomite legend. Moreover, if ever a climb was both a beast and a beauty, the Giau has solid claims on both counts; many, indeed, consider the Giau the most attractive pass in the range, peaking as it does in a vast and beautiful mountain pasture at the foot of the Nuvolau Alto. The Nuvolau's otherworldly 2,647-metre turret is also but one of the wild and wonderful Dolomite summits visible from the Giau, including the Tofane, Monte Cristallo and the Sorapis.

These are peaks that have inspired endless hyperbolic descriptions but to which, equally, only extravagant and brilliant illustrations could ever do justice. John Murray made a good attempt in his *Handbook for Travellers in Southern Germany*, written in 1837:

'Sometimes they take the appearance of towers and obelisks divided from one another by cracks some thousand feet deep; at others, the points are so numerous and slender that they put one in mind of a bundle of bayonets or sword-blades. Altogether they impart an air of novelty and sublime grandeur to the scene, which can only be appreciated by those who have viewed it.'

A slap in the face

Alexander Robertson, author of the 1903 tome *Through The Dolomites*, commented generally of the range that 'What Venice is among cities, these Dolomites are among mountains'. Robertson went on, 'In line and colour, form and behaviour, they are unlike other mountains. They resemble reefs, over which may have broken, throughout long ages, the billows of an angry ocean.'

In their forms, reflections and even names there is, most people agree, something unique and mystical about the Dolomites. Today Cortina di Ampezzo, the town at the northeastern end of the Giau, is best known as a destination for winter sports, the main filming location of the 1963 *Pink Panther* film and as a magnet for millionaires in mink, but the resort also lies at the heart of a magical kingdom chronicled in folk tales. The Austrian Karl Felix Wolff spent years at the beginning of the 20th century piecing these stories together from the accounts of the mountains' inhabitants, spoken to him in their ancient Ladin language. The result was his legend of the Kingdom of Fanes – the epic story of an avid king and his beautiful daughter, Dolasilla. Several of the saga's key episodes played out close to the Giau and in particular on the Nuvolau Alto and the 2,709-metre Croda da Lago to the south of the pass. The neighbouring Falzarego, meanwhile, is said to take its name from the treacherous king of Fanes, the so-called *fàlza régo*, or false king, who was turned to stone for betraying his people.

In 1966, the Croda da Lago was the last mountain ever climbed by one of the great Italian novelists of the 20th century and some-time Giro correspondent, Dino Buzzati. When he reached the summit that day, Buzzati shed a tear. He died in 1972. Buzzati's ashes are now scattered over the mountain's stunning, serrated ridge.

Professional cycling is yet to furnish the Giau with narratives worthy of Buzzati or Wolff, but it may be only a matter of time. On those five occasions that it has appeared on the Giro route, the Giau has never failed to make waves. On its Giro premiere in 1973, the Giau, still unpaved at the time, lived up to its billing by *La Stampa* as a horrific obstacle. The winner in Auronzo that day was José Manuel Fuente; the Italian Franco Bitossi collapsed completely, losing over half an hour.

By now in the twilight of his career, the two-time Tour de France winner Laurent Fignon endured a similar ordeal on the Giau in 1992.

On the 'terrible Giau, so high, so muscular and so dark' as *La Stampa* described it that year, Fignon cracked spectacularly, reaching the snowbound summit over half an hour behind the leaders. The Frenchman stopped to catch his breath and composure, guzzled energy bars and drinks, but was still in such a pitiful state that team-mate Dirk de Wolf had to push him even on the descent. By the time the pair of them made it to the finish in Corvara in Badia, the roadside barriers were being dismantled and what fans remained greeted Fignon with either sympathetic applause or hoots of derision. For Fignon, the contrast with three years earlier, when he had ridden over the Giau en route to Giro victory, must have been sobering to say the least.

The Giro returned in consecutive editions in 2007 and 2008, this time as an *antipasto* for stage finales on the Tre Cime di Lavaredo and Passo Fedaia. Here, too, the Giau made up for in difficulty what it lacked in history. The Italian rider Ivan Basso said that the Giau was like 'a slap in the face'. His compatriot and rival Damiano Cunego gasped, 'The Giau never ends. You lose count of the hairpins.'

Had he done his sums, Cunego would have counted to 29 on the Selva di Cadore side. This is the classic and harder ascent of the Giau, the one most commonly adopted by the Giro and also, every July, as the penultimate of seven climbs in the Maratona dles Dolomites, among the hardest and most famous amateur mass-participation rides in the world. Over 20,000 people now apply for entry to the Maratona every year – approximately 11,000 more than there are starting places.

While the Selva di Cadore route alternates sections of pine forest with open pasture and unobstructed views, the slightly longer and more gradual incline from Pocol, just outside Cortina, has fewer hairpins and a thicker treeline. Consistency is the hallmark of both climbs – not that it's a good thing when the gradient hovers around ten per cent. Relentless and merciless are adjectives frequently used in relation to the Selva di Cadore climb, in particular.

In summary, the Giau surely won't have to wait long to build a cycling heritage that measures up to its majestic 2,236-metre stature. The ingredients are all there; a new, ancient legend already lurks in the peaks above Cortina, on a road beneath the Nuvolau Alto and the Croda da Lago.

RIGHT: Like a cresting wave, the rocky expanse of the Croda da Lago shadows the Giau road. The ashes of one of the leading Italian authors of the 20th century, Dino Buzzati, are scattered on the mountain.

FAR RIGHT: Looking up the steep lower slopes of the Giau on the Pocol side.

Fact file Passo Giau

From Pocol

REGION: Province of Belluno, region of Veneto, northern Italy

ACCESS: From Pocol follow the SR-48 and then the SP-638

HEIGHT: 2,236m

LENGTH: 8.6km

ALTITUDE GAIN: 716m

AVERAGE GRADIENT: 8.3%

MAXIMUM GRADIENT: 11% (ramp in km 4)

OPEN: April to October, subject to weather

REFRESHMENTS: In Pocol and at the top

From Selva di Cadore

REGION: Province of Belluno, region of Veneto, northern Italy

ACCESS: From Selva di Cadore follow the SP-251 to Codalonga then the Via Bacalin and the SP-638

HEIGHT: 2,236m

LENGTH: 10.12km

ALTITUDE GAIN: 922m

AVERAGE GRADIENT: 9.1%

MAXIMUM GRADIENT: 10.4% (ramp after km 6)

OPEN: April to October, subject to weather

REFRESHMENTS: At the bottom, at the Rifugio Fedare (km 7.4), Hotel Enrosadira (km 8), Rifugio Piezza (km 9) and the top

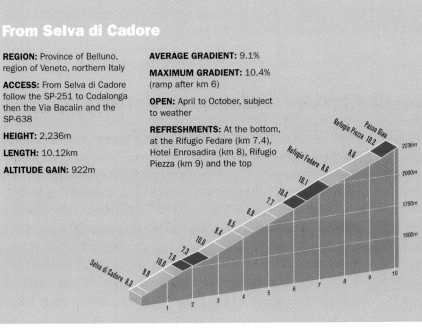

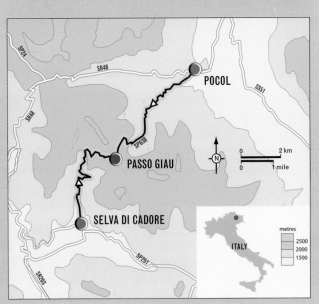

Passo Pordoi
2,239m
Italy

There are many harder climbs in the Dolomites than the Passo Pordoi, but none as essential or, for that matter, quintessential. There are more beautiful passes, but perhaps none more beguiling. There are older and more strategic roads in northeast Italy, and greater feats of engineering, but none, for the cyclist, whose name falls more mesmerizingly from the tongue.

The Pordoi is unmistakable. Moseying steadily upwards out of the Val di Fassa and Canazei in the west and the Val Cordevole and Arabba in the east, its trajectories unite in the shadow of the immense Gruppo del Sella and the Sasso Pordoi, commonly known as the *terrazza delle Dolomiti* or the terrace of the Dolomites. Much in the way that Table Mountain both envelops and towers over the South African Cape, the Gruppo del Sella sprawls the length of the Pordoi while peering nosily over another rocky massif at the northern face of the Marmolada, the Queen of the Dolomites and the highest mountain in the entire range at 3,343 metres.

It was to the vista from the Pordoi – particularly the craggy, almost gothic silhouette of the Rosengarten group to the west – that Charles L. Freeston was referring here in *The High-Roads of the Alps* in 1910:

'The most splendid view of all… is from the summit [of the Passo Pordoi] itself, just before turning the last corner. There is a noble expansiveness in the outlook which has few parallels elsewhere. There is less snow and ice in the height of summer than is seen from the summits of certain Swiss passes, but infinitely more variety of outline; while paramount among the many charms of the Dolomites, is the wonderful effect of the rising or setting sun upon the mountains, which respond to its rays with a vivid glow of marvellous and awe-inspiring effect.'

Bartali's blunder, Coppi's capitulation

The Giro d'Italia quickly discovered that there were few better ways to showcase the Dolomites than via the Pordoi. Completed in 1904, the Passo had already been the scene of intense and deadly bloodshed before the Giro arrived with its own version of mortal combat in 1940. Today, a circular ossuary containing the remains of over 9,000 German and Austro-Hungarian soldiers killed in the First and Second World Wars rises chillingly from the green pastures near the eastern side of the summit. At the pass itself stands a different tribute – to Fausto Coppi, the man whose legend seemed almost symbiotically linked to that of the Pordoi.

Another monument to Coppi can be found where the road forks left to the Passo Sella (2,214 metres; 11.4 kilometres at 6.6 per cent average) and right to Pordoi, five kilometres up from Canazei on the western side. Its location is significant, for it was here in 1940 that, on their descent off the Pordoi, Coppi turned right onto the climb of the Sella while his then team-mate but future nemesis Gino Bartali absentmindedly carried straight on towards Canazei. By the time Ginetaccio had realized his mistake and turned around, Coppi was fading. He would have to rely on Bartali to literally push him up the Sella's steepest sections and even to revive him by stuffing snow from the side of the road down his neck.

A picture taken on the Col du Galibier in the 1952 Tour de France and showing the two rivals sharing a water bottle remains possibly the most famous image in Italian sport – albeit one that was staged by the photographer who took it. Here on the Pordoi and Sella, their union may have been less photo-friendly but it was real and spontaneous – and the reason why Coppi won that 1940 Giro.

OPPOSITE: The Gruppo del Sella provides the unmistakable décor for the Passo Pordoi, particularly for the climb from Arabba.

BELOW: One of the 28 hairpins on the Canazei climb, which emerges from the pines after the turn-off to the Passo Sella into open Alpine pastures.

ABOVE: Three contented mountain dwellers on the road out of Arabba and towards the Pordoi.

ABOVE RIGHT: Thick pine forest on the lower portion of the climb from Canazei. As it does on the neighbouring Sella, the road eventually emerges from the trees to serve up memorable views of the Gruppo del Sella.

OPPOSITE (LEFT): Souvenirs and a touch of local colour on the Passo Pordoi.

OPPOSITE (RIGHT): Inside the funnel that runs from Arabba, parallel to the Gruppo del Sella and over the pass.

The five-times champion

Il campionissimo went on to develop a near-monopoly over the Pordoi. 'In 1940, when I was struggling and Bartali helped me to defend the pink jersey, I didn't think the Pordoi would go on to become my mountain,' he said later. 'I was first over the summit there five times, maybe because whenever I was in that area I could breathe beautifully.'

Coppi crested the Pordoi first in three straight Giri from 1947, the first and last of which he won, again during his victorious 1952 campaign, then once more in 1954. There was just one blip – on the stage from Vicenza to Bolzano in 1950, he fell and fractured his pelvis. First over the top that day was the Frenchman, Jean Robic. Robic would probably also have held on to win in Bolzano were it not for his insistence on eating only tomatoes in races – a vice that cost him many a bouquet in an otherwise illustrious career.

Coppi's death from malaria in 1960 set the Giro organizers thinking about how to honour their fallen five-times champion. They settled on a prize, the Cima Coppi, which would be awarded to the first rider over the highest summit in each edition of the Giro. As one of the tallest main road passes in the Dolomites, that often turned out to be the Pordoi. Indeed, the mountain that *La Gazzetta dello Sport* once dubbed *la Maracanà rosa* – cycling's equivalent of Brazil's most famous football stadium, tinted pink for the Giro – had served as the Cima Coppi 13 times up to 2011, more than any other climb.

Regular, almost rhythmic in its vertical progress on both sides, the Pordoi has not always been decisive. It proved just that in 1991, propelling Coppi-lookalike Franco Chioccioli towards his one and only

Giro success, but has more often provided a stepping stone rather than a launchpad to overall glory. So it transpired in 2001, when Gilberto Simoni wrested the pink jersey from compatriot Dario Frigo, but lost out to the Mexican Julio Pérez Cuapio in the sprint for the stage victory. As a child, Simoni had ridden to and climbed the Pordoi on the day of his idol Francesco Moser's victory in the 1984 Giro. 'The Pordoi is like my life force,' he said in 2003. 'This mountain has given me so much, right from when I used to come here as a ten-year-old kid, and we'd throw a blanket on the grass and have a party…'

Wriggling first through cool and fragrant pine forest, then Alpine meadow dappled with edelweiss, the road from Canazei arrives at the pass via 28 hairpins and is the lovelier of the two ascents. Certain glimpses of the vast Sella group and Sasso Pordoi to the left on this approach are breathtaking, even if a gradient that never creeps above eight per cent is not. From Arabba on the eastern side, the Sasso Pordoi's neighbour, the Piz Boè, to the right and its mirror image to the left form a majestic natural arcade, although the Marmolada remains stubbornly hidden from view as the road funnels through a grassy swathe and towards the pass. To see the Queen of the Dolomites, the cyclist will have to abandon his bike and walk five or ten minutes towards the Piz Boè. From here, noted Hugh Merrick in *The Great Motorways Of The Alps*, 'the Marmolada, with her beautiful snow cap and pale-blue glacier-shield streaming valleywards – the only sizeable sheet of ice in the Dolomites – lifts into view to the east.' A view, in short, fit for a king – or The Queen.

Fact file Passo Pordoi

From Canazei

REGION: Trentino Alto Adige, Dolomites, Italy

ACCESS: Follow the Via Pareda along the river and go left at the roundabout to the Via del Col de Pin

HEIGHT: 2,239m

LENGTH: 13km

ALTITUDE GAIN: 786m

AVERAGE GRADIENT: 6%

MAXIMUM GRADIENT: 7.7% (km 2)

OPEN: June to September

REFRESHMENTS: Bars at the bottom and at the top, depending on the weather

From Arabba

REGION: Veneto, Dolomites, Italy

ACCESS: From Arabba, follow the SR48 (Via Palluva)

HEIGHT: 2,239m

LENGTH: 9.4km

ALTITUDE GAIN: 637m

AVERAGE GRADIENT: 6.8%

MAXIMUM GRADIENT: 9.7% (km 1.5)

OPEN: June to September, depending on the weather

REFRESHMENTS: Bars at the bottom and at the top

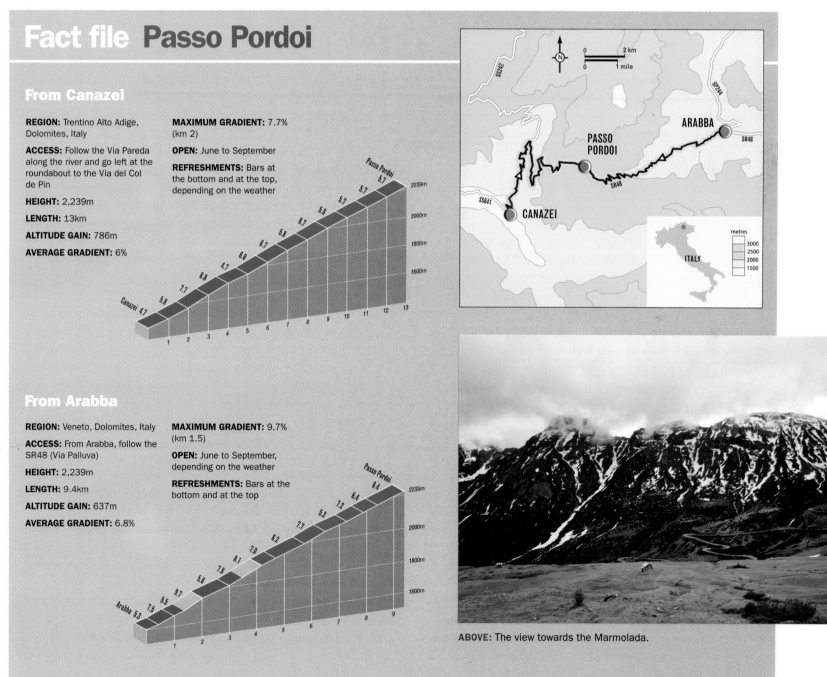

ABOVE: The view towards the Marmolada.

Cirque de Gavarnie 2,270m

France

Some climbs can and indeed have attained mythical status even without the blessing of professional racing. It takes exceptional beauty, outrageous difficulty or perhaps a combination of both, as well as the special cachet inherent to all forbidden fruit; the legs, like the heart, tend to ache for what they can't have, even if they'll ache when they get there – and for at least a while longer it seems that the most beautiful mountain backdrop in France will also remain out of bounds to the protagonists of the sport's most famous race.

The Cirque de Gavarnie has figured in at least one Tour de France – the poet Victor Hugo's in the 19th century. Hugo famously discovered at Gavarnie 'the most mysterious architecture by the most mysterious of architects, the coliseum of nature'. His contemporary Gustave Flaubert believed more simply that, 'Garvarnie is the most beautiful thing there is'. Over a century later, in 1997, UNESCO seemed inclined to agree, declaring Gavarnie a World Heritage Site and thereby helping to make this spine-tingling landscape one of the most visited sites in France – just not, clearly, by the Tour de France.

Gavarnie is among the best examples anywhere of what geologists classify as a cirque – an amphitheatre-like valley head formed over centuries by glacial erosion. A marvellous, six-kilometre, semi-circular wall of 3,000-metre peaks, its escarpments are home to France's tallest waterfall, the 423-metre Grande Cascade de Gavarnie. It is, in short, exactly the kind of natural, national treasure to which the Tour de France would normally make a beeline, particularly given the relative paucity of truly legendary venues in the surrounding mountains and valleys. For decades now, the Tour organizers have hopped from one uninspiring Pyrenean ski resort to another, without unearthing anything to remotely rival the jewel in their Alpine crown – l'Alpe d'Huez. They have the Tourmalet and the Aubisque, but those are passes – that is, designed to be passed, traversed. Since the Alpe became the race's first summit finish in 1952, a whirligig of wanderlust has given the Tour the Plateau de Beille, Piau Engaly, Guzet Neige, Ax 3 Domaines, Luz Ardiden, Superbagnères and perhaps the best of a mediocre bunch, Hautacam, without ever finding a new cosmic grandstand.

Gavarnie's ongoing absence seems all the more puzzling given that where there's a will there's usually a way – in this case, the wide and perfectly surfaced road out of Luz-Saint-Sauveur towards and past Gavarnie to the Col de Boucharo, on the D921. Which begs the question: is there a will? It appears or at least appeared so in the middle of the 1980s, when, according to Pierre Carrey in *Légendes du Tour de France – 100 ans de Pyrénées*, a file codenamed Gavarnie was one of several dossiers in a secret vault at the Tour's Parisian HQ. A potential finish line was even identified, 1,700 metres above sea level at Les Especières, six kilometres short of the Boucharo, at the doorway to Spain. After 19 kilometres of relatively gentle climbing towards Gavarnie and into the Cirque, the road and riders would veer right and into a new arcade of summits in the Vallée des Especières. The gradient in these last six-and-a-half kilometres hovered consistently between 6.5 and 11 per cent. Put another way, the spectacle, both natural and sporting, would be guaranteed.

Forbidden fantasy

It seems probable that whatever plans existed ran aground, perhaps definitively, in the spring of 1995. The previous winter, Tour boss Jean-Marie Leblanc had unveiled a route featuring a first-ever finish at the Pont d'Espagne, at the end of another Pyrenean valley. The problem, Leblanc's and the Tour's, was that the proposed finish line was situated in a national park, the Parc National des Pyrénées. As the Société du Tour announced in a *communiqué* on April 3, 1995, '[this poses] multiple constraints, some legal, some organizational, considering the size and the enthusiasm of the expected crowds'. The finish was duly moved down the mountain to Cauterets. A stage that seemed ill-fated from the outset then turned into a genuine tragedy with the death of Fabio Casartelli on the descent of the Col du Portet d'Aspet.

The same constraints that foiled Leblanc and the Pont d'Espagne today seem even harder to overcome at Gavarnie. This is especially true now that it has UNESCO World Heritage as well as national park status to honour and preserve. The custodians of the former have already taken a dim view of recent developments in the area. In 2007, a UNESCO report was fiercely critical of the theatre festival that takes place in Gavarnie every July, at precisely the same time as the Tour. Volunteers working at the event had even been violently attacked, some with car bombs, by militant locals upset at the festival's environmental impact. Needless to say, the bike race known fondly as *la fête du mois*

de juillet and the tens or perhaps hundreds of thousands of people it would attract might be even less welcome visitors.

On the Tour's part, too, all desire or at least hope appears to have evaporated. 'There was a project, a plan to go to Gavarnie, just like for the Pont d'Espagne, but both had to be discarded because they are protected sites,' the Tour's long-serving competitions director Jean-François Pescheux confirmed in 2011. 'There are all sorts of regulations regarding noise and traffic which would make it impossible to go there. I know the place, I know it's beautiful, but at the moment it looks like a definitive *non*.'

This left one leading professional, the Irish climber Daniel Martin, who often holidayed at Luz-Saint-Sauveur in his youth, ruing what might never now be. 'It's a really big shame. Gavarnie is an awesome location, like nothing else you'll see.'

The world's greatest cyclists then, may never grace one of France's and the world's most memorable mountain settings, at least not while they're racing. At all other times, they, like us, are at liberty to savour and suffer all the way to the Boucharo. And as we do we'll gaze in wonder at the Cirque and the Brèche de Roland, the 100-metre-high gap in the rock face said to have been cut by the blade of Count Roland in a famous 778 battle, and now part of the Franco-Spanish frontier – and we'll think perhaps that the Tour de France will have a similar void in its panoply until the day it finally ventures here.

One of Flaubert and Hugo's contemporaries, the historian and naturalist Hippolyte Taine, perhaps best summed up the compulsive allure of Gavarnie, and what the Tour is missing, in his 1867 *Voyage aux Pyrénées*.

'Anyone who can mount a horse, a mule or any kind of quadruped is duty-bound to visit Gavarnie: if he doesn't have anything else, he ought to put shame to one side and straddle a donkey...' Taine wrote.

'Otherwise, imagine what you'll face when you're home.'

'You're coming from the Pyrenees. Did you see Gavarnie?'

'No.'

'Why, then, did you go to the Pyrenees?'

'You bow your head and your friend triumphs... You are bombarded with stories and superb similes; you're charged with laziness, of heaviness of spirit, and as certain English travellers would say, of unaesthetic insensitivity.'

'There are,' Taine concluded, 'only two solutions: you either learn a description by heart or you make the journey.'

One hundred and fifty years on, the Tour de France would do well to remember: where there's a will – and a road – there is surely a way.

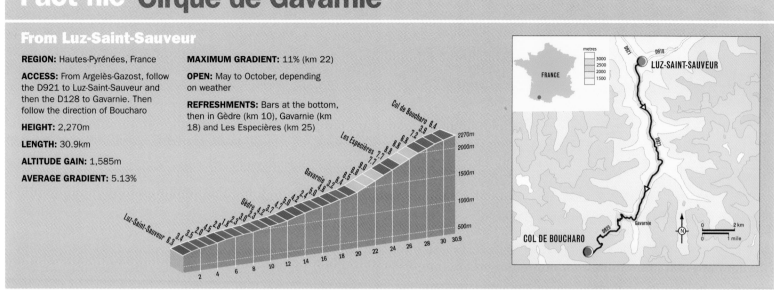

Fact file Cirque de Gavarnie

From Luz-Saint-Sauveur

REGION: Hautes-Pyrénées, France

ACCESS: From Argelès-Gazost, follow the D921 to Luz-Saint-Sauveur and then the D128 to Gavarnie. Then follow the direction of Boucharo

HEIGHT: 2,270m

LENGTH: 30.9km

ALTITUDE GAIN: 1,585m

AVERAGE GRADIENT: 5.13%

MAXIMUM GRADIENT: 11% (km 22)

OPEN: May to October, depending on weather

REFRESHMENTS: Bars at the bottom, then in Gèdre (km 10), Gavarnie (km 18) and Les Especières (km 25)

Tre Cime di Lavaredo 2,320m

Italy

Not for the first or final time in his career as organizer of Italy's greatest bike race, Vincenzo Torriani expected applause and all he got was scorn. By taking the Giro d'Italia to the Tre Cime di Lavaredo, Torriani believed that he'd pulled off a masterstroke, his umpteenth *capolavoro* (masterpiece). If the Dolomites were Italy's Giza, the Tre Cime were their Great Pyramids. The road from Misurina to the Rifugio Auronzo, 2,320 metres above the sea, was also about to become one of the Giro's fabled climbs. At least that was the theory. Instead, on the morning of June 9, 1967, Torriani glanced at a copy of *La Gazzetta dello Sport*, no less than the paper that had founded and still funded the race, and winced. 'The mountains of dishonour' was the front-page headline.

The previous afternoon, the Tre Cime had played host to a sporting debacle, a *disgrazia*. Mountaineers had been hurting and killing themselves on the Tre Cime for decades, but this was a calamity of a different order. The whole of Italy, it seemed, was in uproar, if not at the shameful spectacle of the Giro riders being pushed by fans all the way to the Rifugio Auronzo, then at Torriani's decision to declare the stage null and void. And if not at that, then at his hairbrained plan to bring the Giro to the Tre Cime in the first place.

The eventual winner of that year's race, Felice Gimondi, had been the first to the Rifugio Auronzo and the first to decry a form of audience participation which, in the Italian's eyes, had 'damaged [him] enormously'. The 'despicable pushes', as *La Stampa* deemed them, had arguably penalized Wladimiro Panizza even more; Panizza blubbed and threatened to go home. The foreign riders, many of them among the main beneficiaries, did likewise. Only the wily Jacques Anquetil, a five-time Tour de France winner, saw the funny side. 'They even pushed me,' Anquetil winked, clearly tickled by the Italian *tifosi*'s uncharacteristic largesse.

Either a glutton for punishment or a man with the strength of his convictions, Torriani was adamant that Le Cime were a Giro sensation in waiting, and he included them again on the 1968 route. But one effect of the previous year's fiasco was that, on the morning of stage 19, almost no one was talking about the horrific last four kilometres of the climb itself. Instead – and here connoisseurs of professional cycling's drug-addled history will laugh – some riders appealed for additional doping controls, mindful that gradient and temptation

THE TRE CIME HAD, OF COURSE, BEEN CAPTIVATING WRITERS, poets and painters, not to mention mountaineers and adventurers, for centuries.

ABOVE: The Tre Cime – in order, starting with the closest to the camera, the Cima Piccola, Cima Grande and Cima Ovest.

LEFT: Oddly, from the road, only two of the Tre Cime, or Three Summits, are visible on the approach to the Rifugio Auronzo from Misurina.

tended to rise together, and perhaps with Tom Simpson's death on
Mont Ventoux in the 1967 Tour de France still fresh in the memory.
Meanwhile, the local press neglected race reports and previews in
favour of a hysterical appeal to fans to curb their enthusiasm.

As they had been 12 months earlier, the conditions were biblical.
'The Tre Cime were hidden like three watchmen in their cloak
of clouds. Then came a snow storm, and wind to freeze your
muscles and your heart...' brrred *La Gazzetta*. But the fans behaved
themselves and in Eddy Merckx, the young Belgian who would go on
to become cycling's greatest rider, Torriani and Le Cime were blessed
with a regal winner. In interviews thereafter, Merckx would state
without hesitation that his ride on Le Tre Cime that day was the finest
of his career.

· The next time the Giro braved the Tre Cime, in 1974, a contrasting
performance saw Merckx lose his pink jersey to Gibì Baronchelli,
albeit temporarily. Meanwhile, the Spanish featherweight José
Manuel Fuente frisked away to victory. Another Latin climber, the
Colombian Luis Herrera, won at the Tre Cime in 1994. And on the
Giro's next visit in 2007, the soon-to-be discredited Italian Riccardo
Riccò triumphed on a wretched day.

Riccò later talked about 'the inhuman suffering' wreaked by the
Tre Cime, which again brought the best and most poetic out of the
Gazzetta. 'Dear Tre Cime, little sisters of a magic mountain, I won't
forget you as long as I'm on this earth,' gushed Candido Cannavò in
his editorial the following day.

The Tre Cime had, of course, been captivating writers, poets
and painters, not to mention mountaineers and adventurers, for
centuries before the advent of the Giro. One 1989 *La Stampa*
article said that its three spires were 'like three border guards
made from stone' – a reference to their historical importance as a
frontier separating Italy and Austria up to 1919. Earlier still, local
legend has it that they had come to form the dividing line between
the towns of Auronzo and Dobbiaco after a particularly wacky
race – a woman from each village leaving home at the cock's crow
and the pair supposedly meeting in the middle to establish the
boundaries of the two territories. The lady from Auronzo cheated
and left before dawn, meaning the border ended up much further
north than originally intended.

❝ WHAT CAN NEVER BE VIOLATED ARE
THE SUMMITS THEMSELVES – a 250-
million-year-old precursor to Gaudí's
Sagrada Familia in Barcelona. ❞

ABOVE: The savagely steep hairpins leading to the Rifugio Auronzo, in the shadow of the Tre Cime.

ABOVE RIGHT: The peaks around Auronzo and Misurina have inspired writers and mountaineers down the ages.

'Not a climb for our époque'

The Tre Cime and the surrounding peaks have spawned countless other myths. According to one, the Lago di Misurina, where the eight-kilometre cul-de-sac to the Rifugio Auronzo begins, was formed from the tears of a beautiful young maiden, Mesurina, who had been spurned by a knight in golden armour. In more recent times, mountaineering folklore has grown around the northern face of the 2,999-metre Cima Grande, the middle of the three peaks and among Europe's most coveted and elusive summits. Emil Solleder, the German who, in 1925, was the first to conquer the northwest flank of the nearby Civetta, declared after one failed attempt that the north face of the Tre Cime 'was not a climb for our époque'. Eight years later, the Italian Emilio Comici proved him wrong; the ascent took Comici three days and was hailed as one of the finest feats in mountaineering history. So great was the hype surrounding his exploit, in fact, that Comici would later claim that it had made his life unbearable.

The undisputed king of modern mountaineering, Reinhold Messner, has also been mesmerized by the Tre Cime. In 1989 and again in 2007, Messner welcomed the Giro as a brilliant advert not only for the Tre Cime – but also for his campaign to ban cars from the road to the Rifugio Auronzo. 'All of those vehicles which in July and August try to claw their way up the steep and narrow hairpins steal an important part of this spellbinding location's charm from tourists,' Messner argued, not without a point, given the stench of burning clutch and cacophony of tooting horns that can fill the valley on summer weekends. Sadly, at the time of writing, the Auronzo council said they had no immediate plans to implement Messner's proposal.

What can never be violated are the summits themselves – a 250-million-year-old precursor to Gaudí's Sagrada Familia in Barcelona, with similar forms but a better architect in Mother Nature. For the cyclist, even after a four-kilometre slog to the summit as abrupt and spectacular as anything they'll ever face, this backdrop is the real attraction of the Tre Cime.

Already wonders of the Italian landscape and the skyline of climbers' dreams, the 'mountains of dishonour' have become a cyclist's delight. Well, perhaps 'delight' is the wrong word.

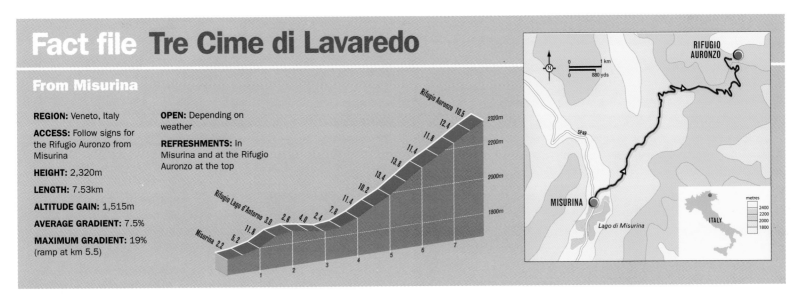

Fact file Tre Cime di Lavaredo

From Misurina

REGION: Veneto, Italy

ACCESS: Follow signs for the Rifugio Auronzo from Misurina

HEIGHT: 2,320m

LENGTH: 7.53km

ALTITUDE GAIN: 1,515m

AVERAGE GRADIENT: 7.5%

MAXIMUM GRADIENT: 19% (ramp at km 5.5)

OPEN: Depending on weather

REFRESHMENTS: In Misurina and at the Rifugio Auronzo at the top

Col d'Izoard
2,360m France

By the time the Col d'Izoard was built in 1897, mountaineers had conquered the west flank of the Eiger, Mont Blanc and the Matterhorn, tarmac roads criss-crossed the highlands of Europe, and the image of the Alps as a sinister and inhospitable expanse was slowly eroding. In May 1877, Henry Gotch had assured his colleagues at the Alpine Club: 'Goblins and devils have long since vanished from the Alps and so many years have passed without any well-authenticated account of the discovery of a dragon that dragons too may be considered to have migrated.'

There were, though, certain landscapes that still defied terrestrial comprehension, and the summit of the Izoard was one of them. Perforated with the sepia-coloured spires of *cargneule* rock, the mountain's upper reaches were, if anything, even more surreal, more haunting than the lunar contours of Mont Ventoux. Some thought the Izoard beautiful, others diabolical. And a third group, among them Jacques Goddet, Tour de France director from 1936 to 1986, had a foot in both camps. Goddet once dubbed the Izoard 'a new version of Hell'.

Goddet's predecessor, Henri Desgrange, had sent the Tour over the even higher Col du Galibier (2,645 metres) in 1911, but knew when he included the Izoard on the route 11 years later that he was venturing into not only uncharted territory, but also new and otherworldly terrain. The Casse Déserte, where the mountain bore its craggy fangs, was and still is unlike anywhere else in France. The sting in the tail of a formidable 274-kilometre stage from Nice to Briançon first scaling the Col d'Allos and the Col de Vars, the southern face of the Izoard inspired terror. 'The task at hand is so hard that our men won't even think about battling each other until the finish line,' Desgrange presaged. 'With their racing instinct, they've sensed that they first have to survive, to finish, and that with such difficulties and such suffering ahead of them, it would perhaps be a consolation to have comrades with whom to share their misery.'

With this description ringing in their ears and jangling their bones, the leaders huddled together on the lower slopes, fearful of what was to come. The Belgian Philippe Thys ran out the winner, but the talk that evening and the following morning revolved around the Izoard. Desgrange was captivated – so much so that he immediately began plotting a return visit 12 months later. 'The Izoard didn't disappoint,' he effused after Henri Pélissier's 1923 stage win in Briançon. 'At first, it allows itself to be climbed with elegance and urbanity, just hard enough to bend the back [Desgrange was almost certainly referring to the first 17 kilometres after Guillestre]. But then, everything must come to an end. And it was splendid because, bit by bit, you realized that the Izoard had fooled us [...] The Izoard is unnerving like a story that will keep you up all night and which lasts forever. Because the Izoard never ends – it's interminable: it seems somehow tame or dozy, which makes you think you're beating it and then, nothing of the sort, on a hairpin, at the exact moment when you're about to breathe a sigh of relief, it hits you in the legs with a ramp that would make a mule nicker.'

One man alone...

Anyone who has attempted the Izoard from pretty Guillestre knows exactly the wicked game to which Desgrange was alluding. The 17 kilometres hugging the Guil gorge are indeed but a tantalizing *hors d'oeuvre* before the D902 intersects with the D947 and the fortress of Château Queyras slides into view along with the first of the steep stuff. From here, 14 kilometres of unrelenting climbing await, particularly as the road javelins sharp and straight out of Arvieux, through La Chalp, then hitches into a series of tight hairpins after Brunissard. After four kilometres among the pines, the rider emerges into the Casse Déserte. Here the pass looks depressingly distant, the heat stifles, and the wind blows fiercely. A glance at the monument to Fausto Coppi and Louison Bobet (of which more later), a short descent, and the final two-kilometre grind begins where the Casse Déserte ends.

It was this more demanding and photogenic side of the Izoard that quickly became a Tour de France icon, long before smooth asphalt and colour photography had softened the climb's ferocious features. Having watched the French climber René Vietto's imprudent choice of gears on the Izoard cost him several minutes and maybe overall victory in the 1939 Tour, the journalist Robert Perrier sketched this portrait: 'It was because of his incredible vanity in not wishing to resemble other men, and because he refused to be a mortal champion, that Vietto vanished, a poor child sacrificed by the fire of his senseless ambition on this Izoard with the face of a bull.'

Gino Bartali's performance on the same escarpments a year earlier had, of course, distorted everyone's view of the Izoard. On his

LEFT: The view north from the Izoard
summit, towards the Refuge Napoléon.

RIGHT: The Guil gorge through which the Izoard road threads on its way out of Guillestre, before the tough stuff begins in Arvieux.

PREVIOUS PAGE: The monument to Louison Bobet and Fausto Coppi in the Casse Déserte, a landscape that prompted journalist Robert Perrier to speak of 'this Izoard with the face of a bull'.

Fact file Col d'Izoard

From Briançon

REGION: Hautes-Alpes, southern Alps, France

ACCESS: Follow the D902 along the Cerveyrette in the direction of Guillestre and La Combe de Queyras

HEIGHT: 2,360m

LENGTH: 19.2km

ALTITUDE GAIN: 1,136m

AVERAGE GRADIENT: 5.92%

MAXIMUM GRADIENT: 8.6% just before km 13

OPEN: May or June to November

REFRESHMENTS: At Refuge Napoléon (km 18), open from 1 June to 30 September

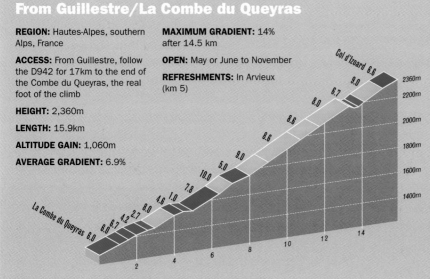

From Guillestre/La Combe du Queyras

REGION: Hautes-Alpes, southern Alps, France

ACCESS: From Guillestre, follow the D942 for 17km to the end of the Combe du Queyras, the real foot of the climb

HEIGHT: 2,360m

LENGTH: 15.9km

ALTITUDE GAIN: 1,060m

AVERAGE GRADIENT: 6.9%

MAXIMUM GRADIENT: 14% after 14.5 km

OPEN: May or June to November

REFRESHMENTS: In Arvieux (km 5)

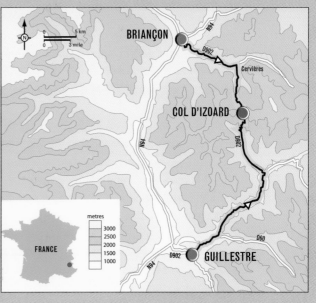

way to a staggering 17-minute victory margin in Briançon in the 1938 Tour, the Italian had been so far ahead on the Izoard that he began to betray signs of boredom. It was reported that, on one set of hairpins, he spied two coloured dots that looked like his countryman Mario Vicini and the Luxembourgeois Mathias Clemens on the hairpins below his feet, and raised an arm in jovial salute.

The Izoard seemed to ignite Bartali and incite his countryman Fausto Coppi, all the while stoking the embers of their crackling rivalry. Having claimed in 1938 that the glass of milk his masseur would have waiting in Briançon was his main motivation on the Izoard, ten years later no less a person than the Italian prime minister Alcide De Gasperi provided Bartali's spur. On the morning of stage 13 from Cannes to Briançon, with Bartali languishing 21 minutes behind leader Louison Bobet on the Tour's overall standings, De Gasperi called Bartali with grave news: the communist party leader Palmiro Togliatti had been assassinated and Italy was in uproar. Bartali asked De Gasperi what he could do. 'You can do a lot by winning stages,' the Italian leader replied.

Bartali went on to complete a clean sweep of the next three Alpine stages, seizing the yellow jersey from a shell-shocked Louison Bobet. He sealed victory in Paris on July 25, ten years after his first Tour win.

That man alone, in the wild gorge

The following spring, Bartali was back on the Izoard for what turned out to be an equally famous stage of the Giro d'Italia from Cuneo–Pinerolo. This time, though, the hero was another Italian: Coppi attacked alone on the Colle della Maddalena and forced Bartali into furious and fruitless pursuit over the four remaining passes on the day's epic Alpine route, including the Izoard. It was the stage that gave rise to the most famous piece of radio commentary in Italian sport – Antonio Ferretti's 'One man is alone at the head of the race; his jersey is white and sky-blue; his name is Fausto Coppi' – and also the following snapshot of the Izoard and another solitary figure, Bartali, by Italian novelist Dino Buzzati:

'He was caked in mud, his face grey with earth and static in effort. He pedalled, pedalled, as though something horrendous was giving chase and he knew that getting caught would mean all hope was lost. Time, nothing but irreparable time was giving chase. And what a spectacle it was, that man alone in the wild gorge, fighting a desperate battle against the years…'

Up to the time of writing, Italians had led across the Izoard's summit only six times in its 30 appearances on the Tour route, yet there is something about the mountain that clearly enchants them. In the 1949 Tour, the old foes Coppi and Bartali were again to the fore, with Coppi so dominant that he was suddenly overcome with generosity: having decimated his rivals for overall victory, he offered Bartali the stage win as a 35th birthday 'gift'. Four years later, his largesse was less evident when, having sat out the Tour to spend July with his new lover Giulia Locatelli, the infamous White Lady, he chose the Casse Déserte as the venue for a romantic getaway. The monument there now marks the spot where the lovebirds watched

Louison Bobet swish by en route to first place in Briançon and in Paris. 'Thanks for coming!' Bobet chirped on spying Coppi, his frequent nemesis but also his hero.

Another Italian icon, Marco Pantani, rekindled his homeland's love affair with the Izoard in 2000. A failed blood test at the 1999 Giro had plunged Pantani into a drug- and depression-fuelled spiral that would ultimately result in his death in 2004, but il Pirata had stirred briefly back to life with a brilliant display on the Izoard in the 2000 Giro. At the Tour de France a few weeks later, he had then stomped angrily to a stage win at Courchevel 24 hours after parrying Lance Armstrong's attacks on the Izoard. 'I didn't appreciate him attacking in my face like that. I wanted to give him a beating,' he seethed. Thus, the Izoard came to symbolize the toxic cocktail of genius and stubbornness that led Pantani to his grave, the brilliance and infidelity of Coppi, and the full parabola of Bartali's illustrious career.

Almost all of cycling's nonpareils have indeed left their mark on the Izoard, despite a lessening influence as the Tour's visits have become gradually more sporadic. In the 1960s, tourism on the Côte d'Azur exploded, and with it the possibility of closing roads to accommodate annual stages heading north towards Briançon. Suddenly, Raphaël Géminiani's old adage – 'The Tour is won at Briançon before it's won in Paris' – seldom applied.

Eddy Merckx, the greatest cyclist of all time, for instance, fulfilled one of his sport's great rites of passage – leading the Tour through the Casse Déserte – only once, in 1972. And even then it was an anticlimax: 'People talked to me about the Casse Déserte and Fausto Coppi's monument, fixed to a rock. I didn't see any of that. I'm sorry, but I was too busy…' Merckx shrugged on accepting his bouquet in Briançon.

While the Tour did return via the neighbouring Colle dell'Agnello in 2011, the opposite, north–south route up the mountain is now an even rarer excursion for the Grande Boucle. And yet, this is the classic approach to the Izoard, at least for motorists if not cyclists, figuring as it does on the Grande Route des Alpes traversing 16 of the great Alpine passes between Thonon-les-Bains on the southern shore of Lac Léman and the French Riviera. Larch woods carpet the Izoard on this side, dissipating only in view of the Refuge Napoléon shortly before the summit, as the vast and daunting Pic de Rochebrune looms high to the left. Ten kilometres shorter than the road to the pass from Guillestre, but four kilometres longer than the real northbound slog beginning on the D902, this is the steadier and more sheltered rendition of the Izoard.

Either way, from Guillestre or Briançon, Jacques Goddet was perhaps right when he identified the pinnacles of the Casse Déserte and the Izoard as staging posts on the cyclist's journey into a new dimension of torture. 'This terrible exigency,' as he called it, 'which establishes the border of the difficult and the terrifying.'

OPPOSITE: The D942 hugs the cliffs on one side, the Guil river on the other, on its way towards the legendary Izoard.

Col du Grand Saint Bernard
2,469m

Italy/Switzerland

❝ THE RIDE FROM AOSTA BEGINS AGAINST THE SUBLIME BACKDROP of the 4,314-metre Grand Combin to the north, and generally offers more scenic variation than the Grand Saint Bernard's northern side. ❞

The Col du Grand Saint Bernard is a little like the dogs to which it gives its name: certainly grand, quite beautiful, not as daunting as it first appears, and a little less practical than was once the case.

One of the great Alpine passes now also functioning as border crossings, in this instance between Switzerland and Italy, the Grand Saint Bernard is also the most ancient of all the routes through and over the western Alps. Archaeologists have unearthed strong evidence that humans first passed through and across the Val d'Entremont from the north, following the course of the modern road, as early as the Bronze Age. At least a thousand years later, in 390BC, two Celtic tribes, the Boii and Lingones, piled over the top on their way to invade what is now Italy.

Over the next 2,000 years, the corridor between Grande Chenalette at 2,889 metres and Mont Mort at 2,867 metres became a high-mountain hall of fame for adventurers and conquistadors. Julius Caesar didn't come in person but did order his best commander, Servius Galba, to seize the pass in 57BC; when Galba failed, Emperor Augustus avenged the defeat a few years later. One of Augustus's successors, Claudius, then built the first road over the saddle in the first century AD. By this time the mountain also had a name – the Mons Jovis, so called after Jupiter, the king of the Roman gods. The pass would take on its current identity with the foundation of a hospice at the summit in 1049 by Saint Bernard of Menthon.

The most famous journey over its brow was, though, and will probably forever be Napoleon Bonaparte's in 1800. On his way to ambush an Austrian army that had taken control of Genoa on the Mediterranean coast, the Little General dispatched 6,000 troops every day over a week in May from Martigny, to march in single file over the Grand Saint Bernard. Bands played rousing martial choruses as they ascended, punctuated with drum rolls to warn the soldiers of impending dangers. On reaching the pass, the men were each handed two glasses of wine and some cheese by the monks living in the hospice. Napoleon was the last to arrive and last to begin his descent, reportedly sliding down the snow and into Italy on his backside. By all accounts, he'd also been in a jovial mood on the way up; having spent much of the journey nattering to his young guide and mule driver, Pierre Nicholas Dorsaz, Napoleon succumbed to a sudden bout of largesse and agreed to buy Dorsaz the farm he had

always dreamed of. Records from the following October confirm that he tipped Dorsaz the princely sum of 1,200 francs – roughly the going rate back then for a cow, a field and some stables.

'What is possible is within everyone's range, I want to attempt the impossible,' Napoleon had snapped back at advice not to brave the Grand Saint Bernard. He gambled and won, but many over the years have not been so fortunate. The kennels opposite the hospice today house no more than four dozen animals and are principally a tourist attraction, but from the 17th century until relatively recently the dogs formed a crack mountain rescue team. Known for their gentle disposition, patched coats and the brandy barrels they carried around their neck (a hot dram could supposedly revive stricken climbers), the Saint Bernards were, above all, perfectly suited to bounding through deep snow and scenting out missing persons. And there were plenty of those, some of whom lived, some of whom wound up in the ossuary alongside the hospice.

The morgue had, mercifully, been removed before T. G. Bonney wrote this in his 1912 *The Building Of The Alps*: 'Here the bodies of those who perished on the journey were laid for identification, the mountain air keeping them from putrifying. In many cases they were never claimed. So a mass of bones covered the floor, and round the walls were ranged a number of corpses, propped against it; the flesh all shrivelled up and of a dark-brown colour, giving a hideous aspect to the faces.'

Road to greatness

While the Grand Saint Bernard is a very different proposition today, this should be a chilling reminder that, like the dogs, the pass also has a bark and a bite. How could it not from its height of 2,469 metres, which makes the Grand Saint Bernard the third highest pass in a country, Switzerland, where road travel often feels like a form of aviation?

What the Grand Saint Bernard most definitely is, whether from Martigny in Switzerland or lovely, luminous Aosta in Italy, is long. Epic, even. That's at least how it feels, whether because the echoes of past glories and tragedies fill the valleys and senses, or because the cross-border passes have a certain grandiosity, a prestige that other, even much prettier mountain passes, can't quite match.

Of 'commonplace' scenery and 'stupid' people

The Grand Saint Bernard is not, it's true, in the same league as the other Swiss passes such as the Furka, Splügen or the Grimsel, purely in aesthetic terms. Hugh Merrick, for one, wasn't particularly taken with the route from Martigny in his *Great Motor Highways of the Alps*. Merrick described the Entremont valley that serves as décor on the Martigny side as 'somewhat barren', the final few kilometres through the Combe des Morts as 'dreary' and bemoaned the lack of a 'surprise view' at the summit. That, though, was glowing praise by comparison with the English mountaineer and pioneer Edward Whymper's verdict in 1860: 'Martigny, by daylight,' Whymper wrote, 'looks worse than Martigny by moonlight.' He then added of climbing the Grand Saint Bernard from the north: 'I have not had any day so devoid of interest and barren of incident, neither have I walked over so uninteresting a road.' And of descending into Italy: 'The scenery is very commonplace and the people on the whole very stupid and somewhat uncivil.'

Whymper's journey, of course, predated the first ascents by bike, and 'uninteresting' is not an adjective that many cyclists would use in relation to the Grand Saint Bernard. In his Tour de France travelogue *On Tour*, Bradley Wiggins seemed to have confused the Grand Saint Bernard with its smaller sibling, the Petit Saint Bernard, when he talked about the 'staggering view' and 'lovely long sweeping corners' (the Grand Saint Bernard has few hairpins or even kinks on the Martigny side, which Wiggins climbed on the same day as the Petit Saint Bernard in the 2009 Tour de France), but the challenge of a 30.6-kilometre, 5.7 per cent climb is nonetheless absorbing. Some have also called the five kilometres in a cloistered tunnel between Bourg Saint Pierre and Bourg Saint Bernard frightening. A longer, paying road tunnel measuring nearly six kilometres and threading

BELOW: The road out of Aosta and the towering silhouette of the 4,314-metre Grand Combin. The Grand Saint Bernard passes below and to the right of the Grand Combin as we look at it.

underneath the summit begins in Bourg Saint Bernard – but this one can and indeed must be avoided by cyclists. The ride from Aosta begins against the sublime backdrop of the 4,314-metre Grand Combin to the north and generally offers more scenic variation than the Grand Saint Bernard's northern side. The villages of Gignod and Etroubles, with fine views to the northeast of the 3,734-metre Mont Vélan (which Merrick said '[more than the Grand Combin] is the true showpiece of the Saint Bernard Road'), are typical of the Valle d'Aosta. After Saint Rhémy en Bosses the road begins climbing in broad zigzags across lush mountainside mottled with grey rock and puddles of snow, steepening between the 24th and 28th kilometre.

Forced to choose, most would agree this is the more attractive, if slightly easier, of the two approaches to the hospice and the pass.

The Tour de France has taken on the Grand Saint Bernard just five times, most recently in 2009, and the pass last featured in the Giro d'Italia early on an uneventful mountain stage to Domodossola in 2006. It may never become one of the *hauts lieux* of professional cycling, but that won't matter; to paraphrase Shakespeare, some mountain roads are born great, some achieve greatness, and some have greatness thrust upon them. And however it got there, no one would argue that the Grand Saint Bernard road doesn't live up, very high up, to its 1,000-year-old name.

Fact file Col du Grand Saint Bernard

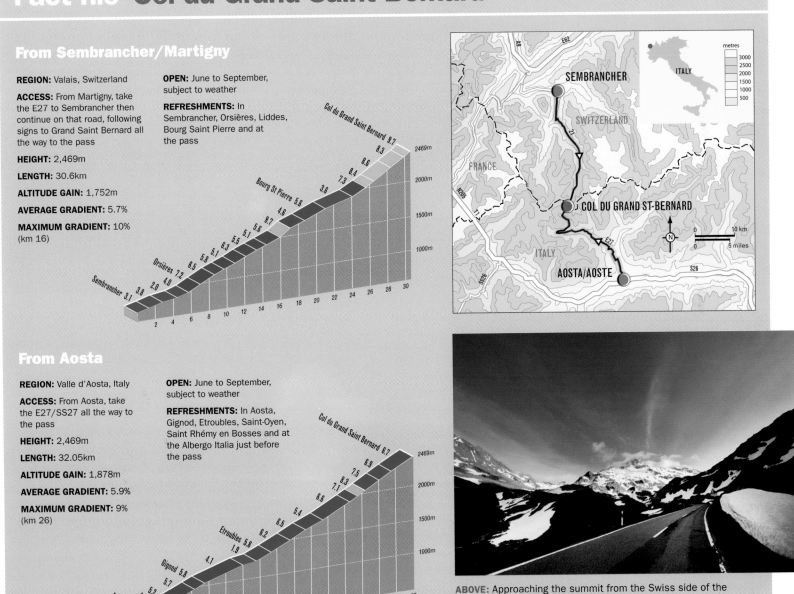

From Sembrancher/Martigny

REGION: Valais, Switzerland

ACCESS: From Martigny, take the E27 to Sembrancher then continue on that road, following signs to Grand Saint Bernard all the way to the pass

HEIGHT: 2,469m

LENGTH: 30.6km

ALTITUDE GAIN: 1,752m

AVERAGE GRADIENT: 5.7%

MAXIMUM GRADIENT: 10% (km 16)

OPEN: June to September, subject to weather

REFRESHMENTS: In Sembrancher, Orsières, Liddes, Bourg Saint Pierre and at the pass

From Aosta

REGION: Valle d'Aosta, Italy

ACCESS: From Aosta, take the E27/SS27 all the way to the pass

HEIGHT: 2,469m

LENGTH: 32.05km

ALTITUDE GAIN: 1,878m

AVERAGE GRADIENT: 5.9%

MAXIMUM GRADIENT: 9% (km 26)

OPEN: June to September, subject to weather

REFRESHMENTS: In Aosta, Gignod, Etroubles, Saint-Oyen, Saint Rhémy en Bosses and at the Albergo Italia just before the pass

ABOVE: Approaching the summit from the Swiss side of the Grand Saint Bernard. This is a journey which, in the 19th century, didn't impress Edward Whymper.

Großglockner
2,571m
Austria

The lack of rich cycling heritage in Austria is a mystery to anyone who hasn't ever ridden a bike there. Whereas the great Italian, Swiss and French engineers cast their gaze towards Alpine summits and envisioned a game of road-building snakes and ladders, their Austrian counterparts apparently saw anything but the most direct route to the top as needless shilly-shally. Not for them the sweeping hairpins of Alpe d'Huez or the Stelvio. Instead, they built their passes straight and steep – and if some fool wanted to ride up on his push-bike, well, that was his stupid fault.

In this sense, the most famous and highest of Austrian mountain climbs, and indeed mountains, the Großglockner, is untypical. True, it serves up gradients in excess of ten per cent on both its Fusch and Pockhorn sides, but for the most part the Großglockner Hochalpenstraße's (or Großglockner High Alpine Road's) 36 hairpins are more reminiscent of the ample whorls of the Galibier or Grand Saint Bernard than the steeper pitches found in the Italian Dolomites. Together with the pristine road surface and the mountain's imposing name (which, literally translated, means The Big Belltower) and history, they combine to give the Großglockner a regal feel.

Now a magnet for just under a millon visitors a year, making it Austria's most visited tourist attraction after Schönbrunn Castle in Vienna, a road slicing across the 3,798-metre Großglockner once seemed a fanciful, and indeed farcical, notion. The idea was first proposed in 1924, but ridiculed largely on financial grounds. The Austrian economy had been decimated in the First World War, and the prospect of what appeared little more than a frivolous tourist attraction was greeted with scorn and a firm *nein* from the Austrian government. At the time, Austria, Germany and Italy could muster only just over 150,000 cars and 2,000 kilometres of tarmacked road between them. Yes, there were other, even higher and more ambitious mountain highways in Europe, but they had been built for good and practical reasons. Or if they hadn't, they were at least the trophies of hedonistic men and times, aeons away from Austria in the wake of the Great War.

Oddly, it wasn't an improvement but a further deterioration that ended up salvaging the project. In 1929, the New York stock market crashed and the aftershocks deepened Austria's misery. The government racked its brain for ways to stop the

rot... and remembered the Großglockner Hochalpenstraße. The construction alone would provide jobs for 3,200 people, and the 900 or so million schilling cost could be recouped in toll fares once the pass was opened.

It took five years. Around 870,000 cubic metres of earth had been shifted and 115,750 cubic metres of wall erected, as well as 67 bridges. On August 3, 1935, the road opened and with it the floodgates to tourism and money beyond Austria's wildest expectations. Within three years, the Hochalpenstraße was attracting nearly 400,000 visitors a year – over three times what it was expected to entice to the Hohe Tauern range. In his book, *The Great Motor Highways of the Alps*, Hugh Merrick called the road 'truly stupendous' and a worthy, if in his view slightly inferior, challenger for the Stelvio's title of King of the Alpine Passes.

Second only to Mont Blanc

It certainly wasn't hard to see why it proved such a draw to tourists. The Großglockner's proud pinnacle had beguiled Austrians for centuries, and became a cult landmark when Belsazar Haquet, a

ABOVE: The famous view of the Paterze glacier from Franz Josefs Höhe, reached via a short detour on the Großglockner Hochalpenstraße's southern side. The summit of the Großglockner itself is draped here in woolly cloud.

ABOVE LEFT: Close to the summit of the two-kilometre cul-de-sac to the Edelweißspitze, accessed via a left turn off the Großglockner Hochalpenstraße's northern side.

" TACKLED FROM THE CHOCOLATE-BOX VILLAGE OF HEILIGENBLUT ON THE SOUTHERN SIDE, it would be hard to make a case for the Großglockner ripping off anything but your legs. "

professor from Ljubljana, travelled there in the late 18th century and claimed in his 1783 *Unterricht für Bergreisen* ('Lessons in Mountain Travel') that the mountain hadn't yet been conquered. The ensuing race to the summit lasted 17 years, its unlikely winners four carpenters and a local priest. The day after their successful ascent, the carpenters and other members of their original 62-man expedition returned to the peak to install the cross that still stands today.

The Großglockner's height and form weren't its only distinctive features. Although retreating fast, the Pasterze, Austria's longest glacier, still stretches for a mind-boggling eight kilometres down the mountain's eastern side. The Großglockner is also second only to Mont Blanc in Europe in terms of prominence or relative height – in other words, the independent height of its summit. As you'd expect, the vantage points are sublime, with more than 30 of Austria's 242 3,000-metre-plus peaks visible from its northern side.

Unknown monster

From the cyclist's viewpoint, the Großglockner is irresistible for a multitude of reasons, despite the dense traffic in summer. In 2010, motorists paid a princely 28 euros to access the Hochalpenstraße, but this still didn't deter 178,000 car drivers and 5,400 coaches from belching up its northern and southern flanks. It is some indication of the climb's allure that 20,000 cyclists still saw fit to make the same pilgrimage. Less heartening news, early in 2011, came with the announcement that, as of May that year, those on bikes would be asked to shell out five euros for their painful privilege between the hours of 9am and 3pm. A similar tax had existed when the Hochalpenstraße opened in 1935 but was scrapped in 1967. Purportedly, 44 years on, its re-introduction was necessary due to a surge in cycle traffic and in accidents, or at least the risk thereof. Unimpressed, environmentalists and online cycling communities threatened large-scale protests.

Tackled from the chocolate-box village of Heiligenblut (1,301 metres) on the southern side, it would be hard to make a case for the Großglockner ripping off anything but your legs. Save for a lightly descending two-kilometre section beginning in Kasereck, just short of where a stage of the Giro d'Italia was due to finish in 2011, the

14 kilometres between Heiligenblut and the Hochtor, 2,503 metres above sea level, are brutish. Slopes constantly above nine per cent are formidable enough; what makes matters much, much worse, is the oxygen debt that starts to kick in shortly after the toll-booth just beyond Wegscheider.

One of the best professional cyclists Austria has ever produced, Peter Luttenberger, agreed in 2011 that altitude was the Großglockner's secret, or at least its underestimated, weapon.

'Above 1,800 metres, you start to feel it,' Luttenberger said. 'The Kitzbüheler Horn is one of those typical Austrian climbs that go straight up and are really steep; the Großglockner isn't as steep or straight but it might be harder because of the altitude. The weather is another thing people overlook. It's very changeable on the Großglockner. It actually cost me victory in my first Tour of Austria, in 1991, when I was still a teenager. I was in good shape when we got to the Hochtor, but then I decided to put a rain jacket on for the little descent before the road climbs back up to the Edelweißspitze. The problem was that the jacket had frozen rigid and I couldn't get it on. I lost contact with the leaders and couldn't regain contact in the four kilometres that go back up to the summit.'

While the Tour of Austria often visits the Großglockner – the official crown of King of the Großglockner going to the first rider over the summit – the pass and indeed the whole of Austria is otherwise largely shunned by professional racing.

The Giro d'Italia did, it's true, take on what *La Stampa* called the 'unknown monster's' shorter but more linear and severe northern side from Bruck on stage 17 in 1971. A winner in Tarvisio the previous day, the clown prince of the Italian peloton, Dino Zandegù, wouldn't forget the ordeal in a hurry.

'Giro d'Italia 1971, Tarvisio–Großglockner, there was a bloke from my village who said, "Dino, after this curve, you've made it". He was right, but I could have killed him: I turned the corner and saw 12 kilometres of dead straight road in front of me, all uphill.'

If it comes as any reassurance, Zandegù was almost as famous for his exaggeration as he was infamous for his climbing. 'I've got another 9,995 stories,' he boasted, 'and every one of them is 90 per cent true.'

OPPOSITE: Another view of the Edelweißspitze, scene of summit finishes in the Tour of Austria.

LEFT: Left to the Edelweißspitze, straight on to the Hochtor: the Tour of Austria has varied its ascents of the Großglockner.

Fact file Großglockner

From Fusch an der Großglocknerstraße

REGION: Land of Salzburg, Austria

ACCESS: From Fusch, follow the 107 road to the summit. Take care not to use the Zeller Fusch road from Fuscher Ache

HEIGHT: 2,571m

LENGTH: 21.4km

ALTITUDE GAIN: 1,766m

AVERAGE GRADIENT: 8.3%

MAXIMUM GRADIENT: 11.9% (km 17)

OPEN: May to October/ November

REFRESHMENTS: Several bars and *Gasthöfe* from the bottom to the top

Profile graph: Edelweißspitze — Fusch 2.1, 9.9, 4.4, 9.9, 10.0, 10.9, 11.0, 11.9, 8.6, 9.8 — 2571m, 2000m, 1500m, 1000m — 2, 4, 6, 8, 10, 12, 14, 16, 18, 20

From Pockhorn

REGION: : Pockhorn village, Land of Kärnten, Austria

ACCESS: From Pockhorn, follow the 107 Road via Wolkersdorf, then turn left at the junction with the Schareck road, and keep following the 107 road

HEIGHT: 2,571m

LENGTH: 25.7km

ALTITUDE GAIN: 1,468m

AVERAGE GRADIENT: 5.7%

MAXIMUM GRADIENT: 11.8% (km 7)

OPEN: May to October/ November

REFRESHMENTS: Several bars and *Gasthöfe* from the bottom to the top

Profile graph: Edelweißspitze — Pockhorn 6.6, 9.7, 10.6, 11.8, 3.7, 10.7, 9.3, 5.9, 5.9, 8.7, 5.2, 10.1 — 2571m, 2000m, 1500m — 2, 4, 6, 8, 10, 12, 14, 16, 18, 20, 22, 24

ABOVE: Hairpin number 14 on the road from Fusch towards the Edelweißspitze and the Hochtor.

Map: metres 3000 2500 2000 1500 1000 — AUSTRIA — FUSCH — Bad Fusch — Edelweißspitze — POCKHORN — 107 — 0 5 km / 0 3 miles — N

Passo di Gavia
2,621m

Italy

The Stelvio's ever so slightly younger and smaller brother, the Passo di Gavia is also the *enfant terrible*, if you will the *bimbo terribile*, of Italian climbs.

Introduced to the Giro d'Italia in 1960, the Gavia has since then proven to be the Giro's showstopper *per eccellenza*, just not always in the manner that the race chiefs hoped or expected. In over half a century of Giri, this behemoth of an Alpine climb (frequently, falsely, both it and the Stelvio have been attributed to the Dolomites) has alternated scenes of delirium with debacle, moments of exquisite drama with complete, quite literal whitewashes. Stated simply, in May or early June, at the time of the Giro, the Gavia's altitude means that its summit is invariably caked in snow and, often, unnavigable. Or, in a third scenario, that it is impassable but pass the Giro still does, with dramatic and controversial repercussions.

Hampsten's triumph, Bernard's ordeal

The road itself, or at least a rugged antecedent, is said to date back at least to the 18th century. In those days, it was used mainly by Venetian merchants on the way to Bormio and, beyond that, Germany. Later, the pass gained in importance as an access route from the Republic of Venice to the Duchy of Milan. In the First World War, the Gavia's strategic position, like many of the great passes, made it the focal point of intense fighting; the Cima di Vallombrina peak that overlooks the Gavia on the eastern side, in particular, is still littered with fortifications used during that conflict.

Predating all of that, at the summit of the pass, is the Lago Bianco, or White Lake. Locals say that the name derives from the milky shade of the lake's waters, itself the result of glacial lime in the inflowing stream. At least that's what most claim; others still maintain that the Lago Bianco and its neighbouring Lago Nero, or Black Lake, are surviving testimonies to an ancient and ill-starred romance that took place on the Gavia. Without recounting the full, convoluted tale, the legend states that a passionate love between the young Bianchina and her beau Nerino was interrupted by the jealous Pinotta and the evil magician Viz, who unleashed a fierce storm upon the couple, turning them to statues of ice. On seeing them, *Lo Spirito delle Acque* or The Ghost of the Waters showered the figurines with such force that they finally melted, forming the two lakes we see today. One was white, like the colour of a woman's veil, the other black like the eyes of a man. Even nowadays, mythologists would have us believe, Bianchina and Nerino emerge from their respective lakes at nightfall to resume their courtship.

The Giro and the Gavia have, as we've already hinted, endured an equally tempestuous 50-year affair. That first trip up the pass in 1960 was applauded by many but disparaged by others such as *La Stampa*'s Giro correspondent for 'not living up to the frenetic expectations' despite 'a beautiful and majestic course'. The winner was Charly 'Angel of the Mountains' Gaul; the star an emerging Italian climber by the name of Imerio Massignan. Massignan surely would have triumphed were it not for three punctures on the Gavia's atrociously dangerous descent.

Not that Giro chief Vincenzo Torriani could have known it at the time, but in future years both he and his successors would be grateful if the race even made it to the summit of the Gavia. The 1984 Giro, when the Stelvio was airbrushed from the route due to snow at the last minute, outraging French pink jersey contender Laurent Fignon, heralded the start of a depressing pattern. The 1988 stage up the Gavia has been celebrated and endlessly relived by fans, but was something akin to a human rights atrocity from the riders' point of view. Stories from that day are legion: of the blizzard; of Hampsten's Giro-winning attack two kilometres from the summit, the sheets of ice on his shins as he rode clear; of the breakaway leader Johan van der Velde stopping at a refuge on the way down and eventually losing 48 minutes; of the Dutchman Erik Breukink taking the stage in Bormio but admitting later 'don't ask me about the climb – I didn't see it'; and of more than one rider descending the Gavia in their team car, and the race referees either not realizing or turning a blind eye.

Shivering uncontrollably as he glugged whisky and scalding coffee at the finish line, the pre-Giro favourite Jef Bernard said he was 'happy to be alive'. 'I couldn't care less how much time I lost,' the Frenchman shuddered. 'All I know is that I won't be a cyclist for much longer. Winning races is no compensation for this much suffering.'

BELOW: The snowdrifts that invariably still border the Gavia road when the Giro d'Italia visits in May and early June, and that prompted *La Gazzetta dello Sport* to describe the Gavia ascent as 'a voyage, an adventure, a novel – a Nordic, northern, polar journey'.

Bimbo terribile

Carmine Castellano, who was to inherit stewardship of the Giro from Vincenzo Torriani in 1989, had, then, been warned. The day after the Gavia fiasco in 1988, Torriani had even erased the Stelvio from the route of the 15th stage under pressure from teams and riders. Regardless, Castellano included the Gavia again on the '89 route and paid a high price: the day of the race came and so did the snows, forcing him to outright cancel, not just modify, what should have been the race's queen stage.

Having taken control of the Giro months earlier with the firm intention of making the Stelvio and Gavia the race's alternating mountain obelisks, Castellano was now ready to discard them forever. 'I'd had enough of the worry and the sleepless nights they caused me,' Castellano reflected in Herbie Sykes's *Maglia Rosa – Triumph and Tragedy at the Giro d'Italia*. 'Every time we went there we seemed to be at the mercy of the weather, and of pedantic safety officers… We'd grafted for nine months to build a beautiful race, only to see our work undone by the vagaries of the Dolomite [sic] climate. Worse still, we'd been slaughtered in the media through no fault of our own.'

It would be years before Castellano forgave the Gavia and included it again, in 1995. In the meantime, at least some good (or bad, if you were a rider) came out of the 1989 fudge: that same night, a local journalist had suggested a valid and nearby alternative that could outdo both the Gavia and the Stelvio in future Giri – the Passo di Foppa, better known as the Mortirolo.

'One of those climbs where, when you start, you're never sure you'll make it to the top' according to two-time Giro winner Gilberto Simoni, the Gavia has now reclaimed its place in Giro folklore as well as its favour. From Ponte di Legno, the Giro's preferred starting point, in the words of Andy Hampsten, the Gavia is 'super hard and long' (17.3 kilometres) with 'steady, steep grades' (7.9 per cent average, but with multiple pitches of 15 per cent and worse) and 'tons of switchbacks'. The road is also, Hampsten didn't mention, barely wider than a bike path. Just as narrow, whether ascended or descended, the Bormio side is longer and only marginally less thuggish (25.6 kilometres at 5.5 per cent average). In 2010, *La Gazzetta dello Sport* described the whole Gavia, kit and caboodle, as 'a voyage, an adventure, a novel – a Nordic, northern, polar journey'.

While anyone who has watched the Giro scale the Gavia on TV will recognize the vast walls of snow on either side of the road across the summit, only those who have set foot on this mercurial mountain will be aware of the incomparable 360-degree view from the summit: to the north the 3,678-metre Punta San Matteo and the Ortler group; to the east the immense rock face of the Corno dei Tre Signori; to the south the Val delle Messi and the aforementioned Lago Nero; and to the west, the 3,223-metre Monte Gavia.

It is a vista that, in 1989, the Giro d'Italia risked never seeing again. As long as the *bimbo terribile* behaves himself, fingers crossed, that's a prospect that neither we nor the *Corsa Rosa* will ever have to contemplate again.

LEFT: The snows tend to remain on the Gavia until the late spring and even summer, meaning Giro stages here are often fraught with the risk of disruption.

OPPOSITE: The descent back towards Ponte di Legno from the Gavia summit, with the Lago Nero or Black Lake off the road to the right.

Fact file Passo di Gavia

From Ponte di Legno

REGION: Lombardy, Italy

ACCESS: Turn off the SS42 (Via Nazionale) at Ponte di Legno and take the SS30 (Via Trento). Continue on the SS30 (Via Statale Passo Gavia) to the top

HEIGHT: 2,621m

LENGTH: 17.3km

ALTITUDE GAIN: 1,363m

AVERAGE GRADIENT: 7.9%

MAXIMUM GRADIENT: 16% (short section between km 7.6 and km 8)

OPEN: June to September

REFRESHMENTS: Bars at the bottom at Pezzo (km 12). The Rifugio Bonetta is at the top

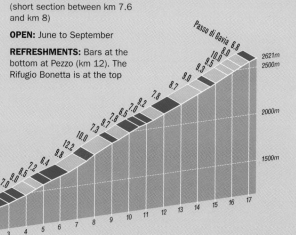

From Bormio

REGION: Lombardy, Italy

ACCESS: Follow the SS300 from Bormio to the top

HEIGHT: 2,621m

LENGTH: 25.6km

ALTITUDE GAIN: 1,404m

AVERAGE GRADIENT: 5.5%

MAXIMUM GRADIENT: 11% (short section between km 20.8 and 21.2)

OPEN: June to September

REFRESHMENTS: Bars at the bottom, at San Nicolo (km 3), at San Antonio (km 4.2), at Santa Catarina (km 12.2), at Rifugio Plaghera (km 17.5) and Rifugio Berni (km 23.6). The Rifugio Bonetta is at the summit

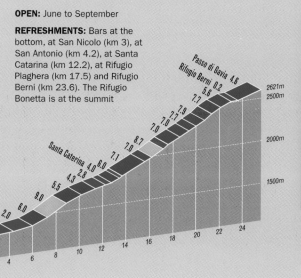

ABOVE: The Rifugio Bonetta overlooking the Lago Bianco, or White Lake, on the Gavia's summit. The Lago Nero or Black Lake lies around a kilometre to the south.

Col du Galibier
2,642m
France

BELOW: The road wriggles back down the Galibier's southern side and towards the Col du Lautaret, with the Massif des Ecrins yawning in the distance.

How high is too high? Tour de France director Henri Desgrange must have asked himself the same question a fair few times in the spring of 1911, but in the end probably sought and found comfort in what had occurred 12 months earlier in the Pyrenees. Desgrange mysteriously left the 1910 Tour on the eve of the race's first ever ascent to over 2,000 metres on the Col du Tourmalet – most assume for fear of retribution, either from nature or the riders – but the following day had breathed a sigh of relief; yes, Octave Lapize had called Desgrange a 'murderer' and his cohorts 'criminals', but by finishing the stage in Bayonne that day, Lapize and his fellow convicts of the road had also proved that where there was a road over the mountains, however primitive and however high, there was also a way.

Desgrange had never hidden his preference for the Alps over the Pyrenees, so having taken on the Tourmalet, it seemed only natural that he should also take aim at the mythical 2,000-metre barrier in France's other great mountain range. The Galibier, though, was a different and bigger beast – half a kilometre in altitude bigger, to be precise. There wasn't, and indeed still isn't, a single permanent resident above (the aptly named) Bonnenuit, 12 kilometres below the summit on the northern side, or above the Col du Lautaret in the south. As Philippe Bouvet of L'Equipe later put it, on the Galibier the Tour truly was 'entering a new dimension'.

The road itself, or at least some early precursor, had been known and used for decades and maybe even centuries. A Col du Galaubier appeared on the first ever complete map of France, the Carte de Cassini, in the middle of the 18th century, its name apparently deriving from galaubié, a provençal word for ravine. At around the same time, in the war of the Austrian succession, the Spanish prince Don Felipe and his army marched cheerfully and peacefully to what they hoped would be glorious conquests on the other side of the Alps. According to Henri Ménabréa's Histoire de la Savoie, so hungry and thirsty were the invaders after scaling the Galibier that they proceeded to eat and drink the people of Valloire out of house and home. Writing in 1909, Ménabréa claimed that 'a hour was all it took for the people of Valloire to see all their provisions disappear and to develop a hatred of the Spaniards, traces of which can still be found today.'

The Galibier continued to be a route of ill repute in the 1800s, when pedestrian traffic both created and followed the first substantial track over the mountain. Among the most frequent users in this period were smugglers cashing in on the difference in the price of salt between France on the northern side of the pass and Savoy to the south. Also in the 19th century, the Galibier's green and fertile northern flanks began to attract leading botanists, who invariably described both the pass and its plant life in evocative detail. One, Alphonse Gacogne, waxed poetic about the view from the summit – 'How imposing and grandiose this landscape is when lit up by radiant sunshine! How the soul is lifted by sweet emotion towards the Creator of such marvels! How easily one breathes, so far from the tumult of the town, in the middle of beautiful nature, how pathetic all human ambition seems before this grand canvas' – having earlier dispensed the following, rather more down-to-earth advice: 'You should also take care to have your dinner [elsewhere], because all you find in this sad place is bad wine, butter and bread!'

Tourists crossing the Galibier at the end of the 19th century at least enjoyed the relative, very relative, luxury of the road opened in 1891. To complete it, a tunnel had been blasted through the top of the mountain at an altitude of 2,556 metres, 89 metres below the ridgeline. The tunnel measured exactly 365 metres, or, as the locals said, one for every day of the year. The first man over the summit

on that maiden ascent in 1911, Emile Georget, took two hours, 38 minutes from Saint Michel de Maurienne, but didn't lose his sense of humour on the way. 'Listen, if they wanted a tunnel at the top of the Galibier, the fellows who did that, they could have done it at the bottom, with making us climb up into the snow,' Georget said. 'I wouldn't have minded doing a touch of bike riding on the metro.'

Others weren't quite so amused. The champion-elect of that year's Tour, Gustave Garrigou, offered a subtle variation on Lapize's 'murderers' diatribe on the Tourmalet, calling Desgrange and his men 'bandits', most likely not in some *savant* reference to the Galibier's nefarious past. Another star of that era, Eugène Christophe, protested, 'It's not sport anymore, it's not racing, this is just hard labour.'

Nothing, though, could persuade Desgrange that the Galibier wasn't the jewel in his and the Tour's crown. The Tour director was besotted, calling the inclusion of the Galibier his 'act of adoration' towards the Tour. 'Oh Sappey, oh Laffrey, oh Col Bayard, oh Tourmalet!' he wrote in *L'Auto*, itemizing climbs that now shrunk by comparison with his new talisman, 'I will not shirk from my duty in proclaiming that compared to the Galibier you are no more than pale and vulgar babies; faced with this giant we can do no more than tip our hats and bow!'

Higher and harder

Only for the Col d'Aubisque, years later, would Desgrange ever reserve such lavish and overwrought praise. When he did, it perhaps said more about the race chief's profound awareness that he and the Tour had to innovate to survive – which, after all, was why he'd taken the race up the Galibier in the first place – than his true feelings. Or maybe Desgrange really was just fickle. His frisson for the Aubisque in 1919 certainly carried echoes of his earlier odes to the Galibier: 'The Col d'Aubisque on its own is worth all of the other difficulties in France... I saw, and I've seen only there, in ten years of us going over mountains, the unforgettable spectacle of gigantic eagles flying 200 metres over us, majestic and almost motionless.'

Whatever he said, it was no secret that the Galibier was always Desgrange's favourite. Neither is it a coincidence that a large monument to the Tour's founder was built at the summit in 1949, nine years after his death. Its dedication reads simply, 'To the glory of Henri Desgrange (1865–1940), former director of the newspaper *L'Auto*, founder of the cyclists' Tour de France.'

This hasn't been the only change or addition to the road over the years. In 1947, the south–north route over to the Galibier was altered dramatically to accommodate anti-avalanche barriers above the Lautaret. A new, longer and more gradual summit road was built some distance to the west of the old track, with which it intersected by the Desgrange monument. Looking south towards the Guisane valley, the line of the old road is still just about visible, weather permitting, which can never be taken for granted on the Galibier.

On the other and more 'classic' side of the pass, the hamlet of Bonnenuit and its 14 per cent ramp before Plan Lachat are now bypassed, although the old road does still exist. Plan Lachat, many will know, marks the start of the Galibier in earnest from the north side. Having barely deviated since Valloire, at Plan Lachat, the road crosses a bridge eight-and-a-half kilometres from the top and flicks right to the other side of the giant natural funnel pointing towards the pass. From here on in, the gradient is almost permanently above eight per cent and the oxygen begins to drain from the air.

To make matters worse, the Galibier now climbs 89 metres higher than was the case up to the 1970s. The reason is that the 365-metre tunnel through the ridge had to be closed for safety reasons in 1979. A further tortuous kilometre was tacked on to the existing road as a deviation and today is the only permitted route for cyclists, although the tunnel has been fully refurbished and reopened.

While professional riders consistently stress how tough the Galibier is on that northern side – some, indeed, calling it the hardest climb that regularly features in the Tour – sometimes in the modern era the pass's length, height and severity have worked against it. Put simply, the Galibier is too intimidating to coax Tour riders to go for broke, coming as it almost inevitably does before another major challenge – very often l'Alpe d'Huez. A rare, recent stage, and indeed Tour-winning move, came in 1998, when the Italian Marco Pantani attacked in freezing conditions at Plan Lachat and rode 47 kilometres to the finish in Les Deux Alpes alone. Wearing the yellow jersey, his face bloated and contorted in pain, the German Jan Ullrich rolled over the line nine minutes later. Pantani would go on to conquer the Tour and Ullrich to squander the best part of the next decade.

Fact file Col du Galibier

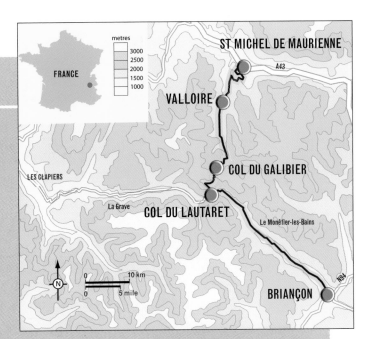

From Saint Michel de Maurienne, via Col du Télégraphe

REGION: Savoie, Rhône-Alpes, France

ACCESS: Follow the E70-A43 (l'Autoroute de la Maurienne) from Saint Jean de Maurienne to Saint Michel de Maurienne, turn right and follow D902 to the top

HEIGHT: 2,642m

LENGTH: 35.25km

ALTITUDE GAIN: 1,933m

AVERAGE GRADIENT: 5.48%

MAXIMUM GRADIENT: 15% (short section at km 6.5)

OPEN: June to October

REFRESHMENTS: Bars at the bottom, at Valloire (km 17) and at Les Verneys (km 19.5)

From Col du Lautaret

REGION: Hautes-Alpes, Provence-Alpes-Côte d'Azur, France

ACCESS: From the Col du Lautaret, take the D902 to the top

HEIGHT: 2,642m

LENGTH: 8.52km

ALTITUDE GAIN: 585m

AVERAGE GRADIENT: 6.9%

MAXIMUM GRADIENT: 12.1% (short section in the last 200m)

OPEN: June to October

REFRESHMENTS: None

ABOVE: The 3,983-metre Meije, as seen from the Galibier road. The Meije was the last major Alpine summit to be conquered by mountaineers.

From Valloire

REGION: Savoie, Rhône-Alpes, France

ACCESS: From Saint Michel de Maurienne follow the D902 to Valloire and to the top

HEIGHT: 2,642m

LENGTH: 18.1km

ALTITUDE GAIN: 1,241m

AVERAGE GRADIENT: 6.9%

MAXIMUM GRADIENT: 10.1% (short section in the last kilometre)

OPEN: June to October

REFRESHMENTS: Bars in Valloire and at Les Verneys (km 2)

ABOVE: Saint Michel de Maurienne is a fitting starting point for the calm before a storm.

Cycling's Meije

La Gazzetta dello Sport's coverage the next day was, in places, as overblown as anything written by Desgrange. The Galibier, it was clear, could have that effect even on the *transalpini*, the Italians' sworn enemies, the French: 'Among the French Alps battered by the storm, above the clouds of imagination, rises a god of sport: he's called Marco, the strong name of an evangelist,' wrote the *Gazzetta*'s editor Candido Cannavò in his first-page editorial. 'He went up, on a duplicitous day in July, to preach on the mountains the eternal mystery of man in the confines of the most merciless suffering.'

The Galibier had featured 59 times in the Tour up to 2011, the hundred-year anniversary of its first appearance, which race chief Christian Prudhomme celebrated with a double ascent and summit finish. In that century, the Sacred Monster of the Tour had given us innumerable, magical battles, some terrible collapses and the odd mystery. Debate in Italy still rages over who passed the water bottle to whom on the Galibier's slopes in 1952 – Gino Bartali to Fausto Coppi, or vice versa. For the annals, Coppi, like Pantani, attacked at Plan-Lachat and wasn't seen again by his rivals until the finish line over the border in Sestriere.

Steadier in its upper portion, with just an evil final kilometre above the tunnel through the summit, the south–north route from the Lautaret is less famous but equally awe-inspiring. Towards the top, in particular, the giant rocky wedge of the 3,228-metre Grand Galibier commands the view.

But it's perhaps another mountain dominating the skyline when you look towards the Lautaret that best mirrors the Galibier that cyclists know and love. Rising to 3,983 metres, the Meije is a mythical mountaineering destination due to its difficulty and the fact that it was the last major Alpine summit to be conquered.

Edward Whymper, the first man to climb the Matterhorn, said that the view of the Meije from La Grave, 11 kilometres west of the Lautaret, had 'only one worthy competitor' – the Ortler Spitz as seen from the Stelvio.

For long years the Meije, like the Galibier, seemed so high and savage that reaching the top was a completely far-fetched and preposterous notion. As it would later turn out, all it took in the latter case was a bit of imagination and some rare feats of human endurance – that, and Henri Desgrange's 'act of adoration'.

Colle dell'Agnello
2,744m
Italy/France

If the Colle dell'Agnello had a metre for every time someone claimed that Hannibal and his elephants had swept across its brow in 218BC, it would be by far the highest mountain pass in the Alps, and not only one of the most beautiful. As it is, the Col d'Iseran just over the border in France and the Stelvio back over the Agnello's right shoulder in Lombardy top it by 26 and 14 metres respectively – and the mountain of myths continues to dwarf all three.

It is over 2,000 years since Hannibal's march from the south of Spain, over the Pyrenees, then the Alps and towards the last obstacle to Carthaginian domination of Europe: Rome. Two thousand years, and still no one has a definitive answer on where he descended to the plains, for all that half a dozen Alpine valleys still trumpet the same claim to fame. Hannibal's contemporary, Polybius, presented a strong case for the pass now known as the Petit Saint Bernard, 150 kilometres back up the Alpine chain, but more theories have zeroed in on the area around the Agnello. One legend, the least probable of the lot, states that Hannibal himself used timber and vinegar to burn a hole in the Monviso, the famous mountain overlooking the Agnello, and in so doing created the aperture of the 2,950-metre Colle delle Traversette. Others have proposed the footpath over the 3,071-metre Colle dell'Autaret, the border crossing 14 kilometres southwest of the Agnello; a report in *La Repubblica* newspaper in 2010 said it was the 2,491-metre Colle Clapier (Col du Clapier), 70 kilometres to the Agnello's north; others still maintain it was the 2,184-metre Colle del Piccolo Moncenisio, just underneath the Petit Saint Bernard; and there are those who stick resolutely by the Agnello, whether out of ignorance or exhaustion with the insolvable debate.

The writer and painter William Brockedon – whose visits to the Petit Saint Bernard in the 1820s led him to conclude, 'The character of this part of the country is entirely adapted to the events of Hannibal's passage as related by Polybius' – probably said it best with his weary final word on the matter: 'The inquiry into this historical event, to determine the line of Hannibal's march, has carried his name into almost every pass of the Alps.'

Those with the patience may want to investigate speculation that Attila the Hun's journey over the Alps also took him to and through these parts, but most at this point would rather just enjoy the cycle ride or at least the view. The Giro d'Italia had crossed the Agnello just three times up to 2011, but one glimpse of the pass from Pontechianale on the day of the 2007 stage from Scalenghe to Briançon, won by Danilo di Luca, was enough to convince *La Gazzetta dello Sport*'s Paolo Condò that the Giro had rarely gorged on such a visual feast. 'Seen from the base,' Condò wrote, 'just the other side of Pontechianale, the Colle dell'Agnello is one of the most beautiful places we've ever seen, a majestic green cliff-face so glorious it could be a Japanese painting.'

The Agnello on the Italian side is truly among the most handsome of Alpine passes. Fifty-one kilometres long from Piasco at the end of the Valle Varaita, which threads in and then out of Europe's largest Arolla pine forest, the climb is a continual escalation ending with a *pièce de résistance* – the gradual unveiling of the 3,841-metre Monviso to the north. The story popular in these parts – even more popular than tales of Hannibal – is that Paramount Pictures based the design of their famous logo on this mountain. When the Piedmont regional tourist board sought confirmation from Paramount in 2010, it never came, but the theory still conjures a useful mental picture of the fang-like pyramid which is among the Alps' most isolated – and therefore visible – grand summits. Not dissimilar in form or mystique to the Matterhorn, the Monviso was first climbed in 1861 by a quartet including the Frenchman Michel Croz, who died on his way down from the first successful expedition to the Matterhorn's pinnacle four years later. Even before that, partly because the Po river originates from a tiny trickle down at Pian del Re on the Monviso's northern side (the water is the coolest and most delicious you will taste), and partly because of its prominence, the Monviso had already captured the attention of illustrious writers and poets, including the Italian Petrarch and Geoffrey Chaucer.

Chaucer's *Canterbury Tales* contained the following verse:

A poem to describe those lands renowned,
Saluzzo, Piedmont, and the region round,
And speaks of Apennines, those hills so high
That form the boundary of West Lombardy,
And of Mount Viso, specially, the tall,
Whereat the Po, out of a fountain small,
Takes its first springing and its tiny source
That eastward ever increases in its course
Toward Emilia, Ferrara, and Venice;
The which is a long story to devise.

The hardest Alpine crossing

A long story is also what the climb of the Agnello can be, whether tackled from Guillestre in France (where it is known as the Col d'Agnel) as it was in the 2008 Tour de France, or from Piasco. The former professional rider Miculà Dematteis was born in Sampeyre in 1983 and has spent his entire life in the Valle Varaita, at the foot of the Agnello. Although it lasted just two years, Dematteis's career was memorable if only for a letter he wrote to *La Gazzetta dello Sport* in 2007. Earlier the same week, exasperated by the doping scandals that had decimated a generation of Italian champions, the newspaper's editor had written a column lamenting that there was not a single rider he could be confident was not taking drugs. Dematteis replied two days later, at length and with great eloquence, explaining that he had and never would have recourse to doping. When *La Gazzetta* published the letter, Dematteis was deluged with messages of support from fans – and with ambivalence from his fellow riders.

In retirement, Dematteis became a world cup champion in mass-participation *cyclosportive* or *granfondo* events and still rode the Agnello regularly in training. He described the climb as 'beautiful but one of the hardest there is'.

'The Italian side is the classic side, and the last section after Chianale the classic climb,' Dematteis explained. 'The real Agnello starts there, where up until about ten years ago there was a bar across the road and a border posting. If you start from the bottom of the Valle Varaita, up until that point it's already 40 kilometres of climbing, although for the most part it's only false flat, particularly up to Sampeyre. In a race, you'd be going at 35km/h on that section, to give you an idea. After Casteldelfino, there are two hard parts, lasting for four kilometres between them. But the hard stuff, as I said, starts at Chianale. From there it's very steep and relentless; the only let-up comes with three kilometres to go when the gradient lessens for half a kilometre to around four per cent. You also have to remember that those last ten kilometres are almost all above 2,000 metres, so the altitude is a major factor. There's also no vegetation, no shelter on this part – it's a landscape a lot like the top of the Izoard. The view is stunning; you can't see the Monviso as you ride through the valley but then, after Chianale, the higher you climb, the better the view. At the top, it feels so close you could reach out and touch it.

'On the French side it's the length that's the problem, as well as the lack of shelter and the altitude,' Dematteis continued. 'It's very wild on that side, too. The Agnello is, I'd say, the hardest of the main transalpine passes linking France and Italy. It's harder than the Maddalena or the Colle di Tenda, much harder than the Moncenisio. The Colle della Lombarda on the Italian side is the closest to it in difficulty... but the Agnello is still higher, harder and more handsome.'

High, hard and handsome – three adjectives to perfectly sum up the Colle dell'Agnello. Whether Hannibal or Attila the Hun ever graced these slopes or not...

PREVIOUS PAGE: Still ten kilometres short of the Agnello's summit on the French side. Less famous and in many ways less difficult than the Italian ascent, the climb from Guillestre is no less beautiful.

LEFT: As the Monviso peaks over the closer ridges on the right of the road, so the Agnello climb from Chianale settles into a steady ten per cent gradient.

OPPOSITE: High among the snowfields towards the final hairpins on the Agnello's French side. Did Hannibal cross into Italy here? Some locals think so.

Fact file Colle dell'Agnello

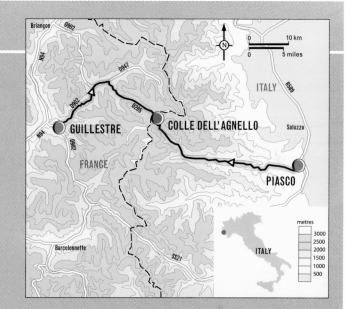

From Piasco

REGION: Piemonte, Italy

ACCESS: Leave Piasco on the SP8, which becomes the SP105 in Sampeyre, then the SP251 in Castello

HEIGHT: 2,744m

LENGTH: 51.36km

ALTITUDE GAIN: 2,178m

AVERAGE GRADIENT: 4.2%

MAXIMUM GRADIENT: Multiple ramps at 15% in last 10km

OPEN: May to late September

REFRESHMENTS: Bars in Piasco, Sampeyre, Casteldelfino (where there is also a fountain on the right of the road), at Pontechianale and at Chianale. The final opportunity is at the Malga di Grange del Rio 6km from the top

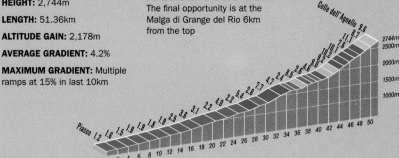

From Guillestre

REGION: Hautes-Alpes, Provence-Alpes-Côte d'Azur, France

ACCESS: From Guillestre follow the D902, then D947 and D205 to the top

HEIGHT: 2,744m

LENGTH: 42km

ALTITUDE GAIN: 1,008m

AVERAGE GRADIENT: 4.1%

MAXIMUM GRADIENT: Multiple ramps above 10% (short sections at km 22, 25.7, 34.8, 39 and 40.5)

OPEN: May to late September

REFRESHMENTS: Bars in Guillestre and at Molines en Queyras (km 27)

ABOVE: Ascending from the French side, parallel to the Aigue Angelle stream.

Passo dello Stelvio
2,758m

Italy

If Fausto Coppi thought he 'was going to die' while climbing the Passo dello Stelvio during the 1953 Giro d'Italia, the man the Italians dubbed *campionissimo* could have perished in worse places. Robbed of its status as Europe's highest road pass by the Col d'Iseran in 1937, the Stelvio nonetheless remained and remains today arguably the purest, most exhilarating, most spellbinding mountain playground accessible to cyclists. Not that either of the eastern (from Prato allo Stelvio) or western (from Bormio) ascents offers much in the way of recreation; one Italian rider who scaled the Stelvio in the 2005 Giro, Marco Pinotti, called it 'an ascetic experience' – an act of self-denial and quasi-religious devotion.

In one sense, though, ascetic may be the wrong word, with its connotations of austerity and abnegation, because the Stelvio is also a treat. There is something spiritual about any journey to its summit – and any time the Giro d'Italia braves the snows that can linger all through the summer. 'The gods live on the mountains,' wrote *La Gazzetta dello Sport*'s Claudio Gregori in 2005. 'The Indians had located them on the mythical Muru. The Greeks on Olympus. The sherpas on the Himalayas. The Japanese on Mount Fuji. The Stelvio is the sacred mountain of the Giro d'Italia.'

Long before cycling and the Giro, the Stelvio was one of Italy's great national landmarks. Not that modern-day Italy was even a recognized entity when, by virtue of the 1815 Treaty of Vienna, the Habsburg Empire took control of Lombardy and

immediately began hatching plans to connect the region to the neighbouring Tyrol. Their solution would be a road crossing from Valtellina in Lombardy to the Val Ventoso, and the man to bring it to fruition was a renowned architect from Brescia, Carlo Donegani. Donegani spent a year plotting his 49-kilometre masterpiece, and it took 2,500 hardy souls five years to complete. The Stelvio was officially opened in 1825, with a delighted Emperor Ferdinand the guest of honour but the plaudits all for Donegani. Twelve years later, Ferdinand would award him two titles – Knight of the Austrian Empire and the arbitrary Nobleman of the Stelvio. Donegani died in 1845 due to heart problems reportedly aggravated by his gruelling work in the Alps.

His legacy was of the very highest order, not only literally. Over a century later, that seasoned connoisseur of mountain passes Hugh Merrick's musings about the Stelvio were drenched in superlatives: 'Most of the great passes have their individual and varied glories, of engineering skill and scenic beauty. For me the Stelvio has everything any of them has, and more than all of them put together.'

OPPOSITE: The 'serpent of asphalt' described by *La Gazzetta dello Sport* in reference to the Bormio side of the Stelvio pass.

RIGHT: Reputations, as well as buildings, have been ruined on the interminable climb to the Stelvio from Bormio.

FAR RIGHT: In sight of the summit on the Bormio side – the less famous, but scarcely less arduous or interesting, ascent of the Stelvio.

Many others have come, seen and concurred. Over nearly two centuries, the Stelvio has inspired not only cyclists, mountaineers and skiers (the World Cup course is one of the most demanding anywhere), but also writers, artists and poets. Having visited the Stelvio in the late 19th century, the esteemed literary translator F. A. Malleson even speculated that Charles Dickens may well have been referring to the village of Trafoi – 'a place of perfection' according to Malleson – in a famous passage in *David Copperfield*. 'I had found sublimity and wonder in the dread heights and precipices, in the roaring torrents, and the wastes of ice and snow,' Dickens wrote.

A serpent of asphalt

Trafoi nestles high up the eastern (some call it northern) face of the pass, the more famous and photogenic of the two ascents. From Prato allo Stelvio at the bottom to the summit, the road coils mazily through 48 hairpin bends, 27 more than Alpe d'Huez, maintaining a relatively steady gradient of between seven and nine per cent after a gentler approach to Gomagoi. From here, two works of art, Donegani's and nature's, do-si-do all the way to the top, 20 kilometres away. Having listed sections of the Gottard, Iseran and Susten passes as fine examples of 'marvellous windings up steep mountain flanks', Merrick concluded that, 'Nowhere in all these varied victories over verticality is there anything as sensational, from the engineering point of view along, as the desperate defeat of the Stelvio north face by road. Set, as it is, within a stone's throw, across the chasm, of the tremendous upsurge of mountain and glacier scenery which faces and dominates its heroic traceries, the effect is overwhelming.'

It is also on this side of the Stelvio that some of the Giro d'Italia's most famous chapters have been written. In 1953, the Giro attacked the pass for the first time, thus pitting its greatest athlete, Fausto Coppi, against his homeland's most magnificent mountain. Wearing the pink jersey of the race leader, Hugo Koblet buckled when the *campionissimo* attacked 11 kilometres from the summit. Not even the Swiss's superb descending could prevent Coppi from winning the stage and, effectively, the Giro. A similar, virtuoso performance on the Stelvio saw Charly Gaul, the Angel of the Mountains, triumph in Bormio in 1961. On that occasion, however, it wasn't enough to overhaul Arnaldo Pambianco and bring Gaul overall victory in Milan the next day.

The 1956 and 1972 Giros took on the Stelvio from Bormio in the west – an ascent *La Gazzetta dello Sport* called a 'a serpent of asphalt, five tunnels, 21.9 kilometres and 1,560 metres of climbing'. Aurelio del Rio and José Manuel Fuente were, respectively, the first and second over the summit, snake charmers for a day.

Those western slopes have indeed often been decisive, but usually on the way down. In 1980, the legendary French *directeur sportif* Cyrille Guimard gathered his men on the morning of stage 20 and announced that the Stelvio represented their captain Bernard Hinault's last hope of seizing the pink jersey. On hairpin number 34, 'the Badger', as Hinault was known, seized his chance and left pink jersey Walter Panizza reeling. But it was the descent into Bormio, and more specifically his team-mate Jean-René Bernaudeau's work as pathfinder that won Hinault the Giro. 'I rode down with Jean-René Bernaudeau in the tunnels, but he didn't brake once, the fool!' Hinault said, having graciously gifted Bernaudeau first place in Sondrio and himself obliterated Panizza to tie up overall victory.

Weeks earlier, Bernaudeau's brother had drowned in a canoeing accident. Partly for this reason, the Stelvio held a special poignancy for Bernaudeau, so much so that in retirement the Frenchman would open a restaurant in La Chataigneraie in the west of France and call it Le Stelvio.

Four years later, history seemed sure to repeat itself, with another Frenchman, the late Laurent Fignon, poised to kill off his Italian rival Francesco Moser on the slopes of the Stelvio. Alas, to Fignon's everlasting disgust, race organizer Vincenzo Torriani scrubbed the Stelvio from stage 18, citing snow at the summit – snow that was curiously invisible in television pictures filmed from a helicopter. By far the superior climber, Fignon moped. Predictably, he then relinquished his pink jersey to Moser in a time trial into Verona on the final day of the Giro.

The Stelvio's inclusion on the Giro route is, then, fraught with risk. In 1988, snow again forced its cancellation, this time legitimately. Fourteen years had therefore elapsed between Hinault's escape to victory in 1980 and *la Corsa Rosa*'s next visit in 1994. That day, Francesco Vona crested first to claim the Cima Coppi prize, awarded to the first man over the highest peak in the Giro. Both Vona and, for once, the Stelvio, however, were overshadowed by the young Marco Pantani's stage-winning exploits on the Mortirolo.

The most horrible descent

One of the unsung survivors that day was former Motorola pro Brian Smith. Smith told *Rouleur* magazine in 2007 that he remembered the long crawl up from Prato allo Stelvio well – and the divebomb into Bormio even better.

'Your eyes are watering, you're freezing cold, but what I was told to do was to close one eye,' Smith recalled. 'The tunnels are unlit, and they're so long you can't see the end when you're inside: it's pitch black. It's disorientating.

'So you enter the tunnel in the middle of the road, try and hold your line, and just hope you don't hit the side. But if you close one eye before you enter the tunnel, then open it again once

BELOW: The famous Trafoi windings leading to the Stelvio summit on the Ponte di Stelvio side.

you're inside, then at least your eyesight has half adjusted to the darkness.

'It was the most horrible descent I've ever done,' Smith continued. 'I was never one to get scared on a descent. But coming down the Stelvio that day, with my hands freezing, having to close one eye for the tunnels, and then hope for the best once you were inside, is something I'll never forget. I was petrified.'

Ivan Basso will also have mitigated memories of the Stelvio, for different reasons: the favourite for overall victory as the 2005 Giro left the Dolomites and headed for the Alps, the Italian succumbed to a deadly cocktail of stomach troubles and the Stelvio's intestinal contortions to lose 42 minutes and all hope of overall glory.

Glory, though, is what awaits anyone who earns the reward of a summit vista as awe-inspiring as anything in the Alps. Particularly when, of the many delicacies that make up that visual feast, it is not the giant snow-clad dome of the Ortler mountain (the view of which from the Stelvio was the greatest in the Alps, according to the celebrated British climber, Edward Whymper), the distant Zillertal Alps, or the gorgeously verdant Adige valley that overwhelm the senses – but a glimpse of Donegani's creation unravelling into the valley.

If gods really did inhabit the mountains, they would access them via roads like this. As it is, after 200 years, the Stelvio stands proud and unchanged, Italy's most perfect of passes.

Fact file Passo dello Stelvio

From Bormio

REGION: Lombardy, Italy

ACCESS: Follow SS38 from Tirano to Bormio and turn off left on Via Stelvio

HEIGHT: 2,758m

LENGTH: 21.9km

ALTITUDE GAIN: 1,560m

AVERAGE GRADIENT: 7.12%

MAXIMUM GRADIENT: 14% (short section at km 10.5)

OPEN: May to October

REFRESHMENTS: Several bars at the bottom, at Bagni Vecchi (km 4), at km 15 and at the top

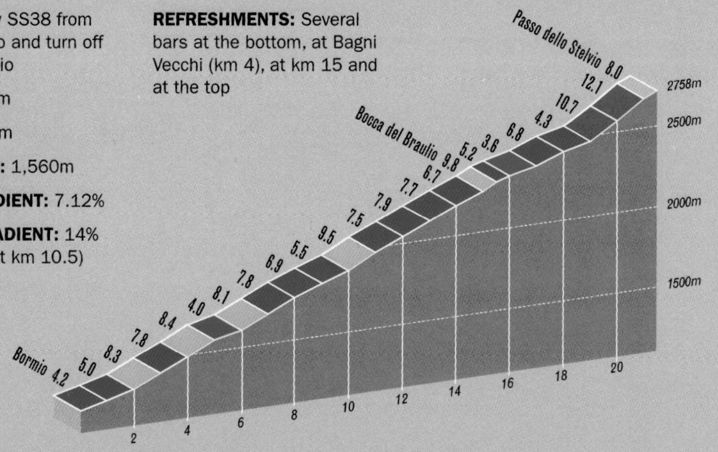

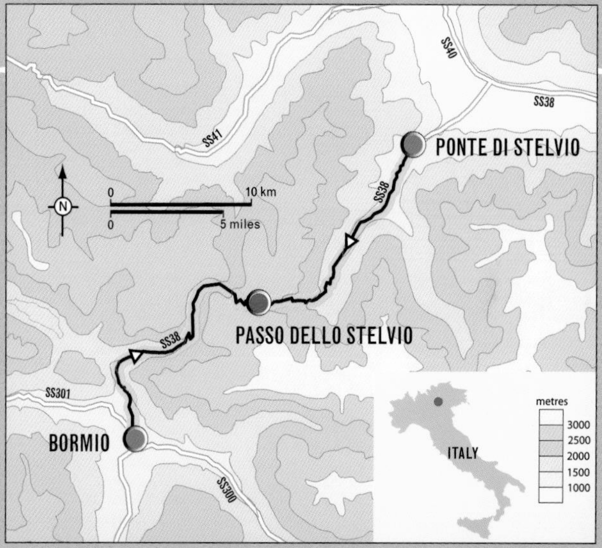

From Ponte di Stelvio

REGION: Trentino-Alto Adige, Italy

ACCESS: Follow SS38 from Bolzano to Prato allo Stelvio

HEIGHT: 2,758m

LENGTH: 24.3km

ALTITUDE GAIN: 1,808m

AVERAGE GRADIENT: 7.4%

MAXIMUM GRADIENT: 9.2% (short sections between km 17 and 18)

OPEN: May to October

REFRESHMENTS: Several bars at the bottom, at Gomagoi (km 7), at Trafoi (km 8), at km 18 (Berghotel Franzenshöhe) and at the top

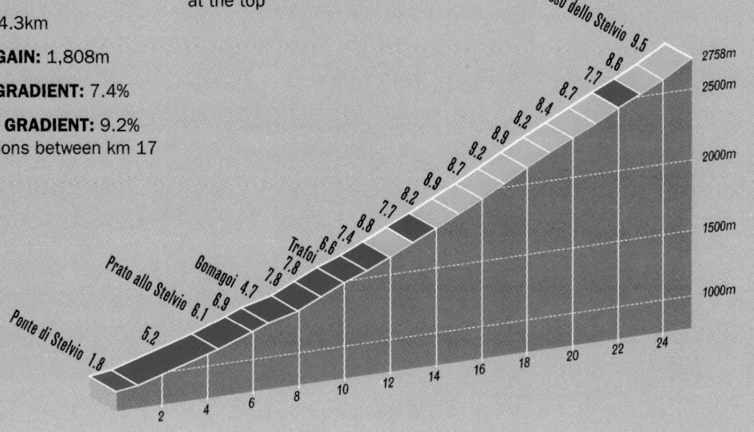

ABOVE: The Piccolo Tibet (Little Tibet) hotel on the Stelvio – an incongruous, yet somehow appropriate, landmark.

Col de l'Iseran
2,770m
France

BELOW: Val d'Isère acts as base camp for the final push to the Iseran's summit on the northern side.

The title of highest pass in the Alpine range somehow seems a lofty distinction for the Col de l'Iseran, a mountain highway that Hugh Merrick describes thus in his 1958 opus on the great roads of the range:

'There is something about the Iseran, quite apart from the exceptional bleakness of its summit sectors, which leaves one with a feeling of artificial contrivance and of having, in a way, been 'sold the pass'. For this manifestly major triumph of engineering enterprise goes up – very far up – and it goes down again, rather like the noble Duke of York, without a shred of that sense of essential purpose which is the hallmark of the great mountain passes.'

In one respect, Merrick was right: the Iseran was built not out of necessity and indeed almost on a whim. As he went on to point out, 'The fact is that if it were not there as a show-piece the civilian motorist would hardly have missed it, for it leads not across a frontier, nor across the main chain of the Alps…' The impression that emerges, rather like the stunning vistas of the Chalanson and Albaron glaciers as one nears the summit from the southern side, is of a feat of roadbuilding that was also in part a vanity project.

Murmurs of a Route des Alpes stretching from Thonon-les-Bains on the shores of Lac Léman in the north to Nice on the Côte d'Azur first swirled through the corridors of French government in 1904, but it wasn't until February 1912 that an edict formalized what, in the context of the time, seemed a grandiose and improbable venture. 'Passing altitudes reached by very few roads in Europe,' said the official proposal, 'the Route des Alpes will show off unfamiliar and inaccessible marvels of nature, connecting them to the southwest region of France, which is frequented by tourists and foreigners.'

Mystery of Mont Iseran

The very wording of the document reinforced a sense of otherworldliness that still characterized perceptions of the mountains, and none more so than the Iseran. For decades and perhaps even centuries, even in the communities clinging to both the northern and southern flanks, confusion had reigned as to the existence of a Mont Iseran, not to mention its altitude. In 1811, the French colonel Courtaboeuf had climbed the pass and, based on who knows what system of measurement, reported that Mont Iseran

soared to an altitude of 4,045 metres – an identical height to the Gran Paradiso just across the border in Italy. Nearly a century later, a famed British mountaineer would scramble to the same spot, only to forlornly deduce that Courtaboeuf's calculations and those of the cartographers who'd taken him at their word were somewhat wide, or rather high, of the mark. About 1,300 metres high, to be precise.

These weren't the only mysteries to have played out here. Archives recall that a young man from Tignes, now one of two prominent ski resorts on the northern side along with Val d'Isère, was the victim of a robbery and murder that both captivated and terrified locals in November 1783. The same records make no mention of whether the killer was ever caught. A far more prolific claimer of lives did for a 12-year-old girl from Val d'Isère in 1745, a 14-year-old boy a few years later, then a pair of soldiers in 1848 and 1871. This heavy toll even by Alpine standards, plus other tragedies, gave rise to an adage that has entered common parlance in Bonneval-sur-Arc: 'If all of the people dead on the Iseran linked hands, they'd form a chain from here to Val d'Isère.' In 2007, the Dutch professional Kai Reus narrowly avoided joining their number in a training crash that left him in a coma for 11 days.

Sumptuous spaghetti

It was on a more festive note that French president Albert Lebrun had officially opened what became and remains the highest of all Alpine passes in July 1937. The first work on existing access routes had begun as the First World War ended, then accelerated in the early 1930s with the arrival of 600 Italian migrant workers. Within months of its inauguration, the Col had been been hailed as both a social and commercial triumph, having doubled the summertime population in Val d'Isère and Tignes and halted an exodus from the surrounding villages.

Soon it would also find its way onto the pages of sporting annals. Stage 14 of the 1938 Tour de France took the peloton from Digne to Briançon, over a cardiogram of climbs including the Iseran, and while the Belgian Félicien Vervaecke was the first over the summit, the Italian Gino Bartali would later credit his brilliant slalom down the northern side with his overall Tour victory in Paris a week later: 'I won my jersey on the descent of the Col de Vars. I saved it on the descent off the Iseran,' Bartali observed. A component manufacturer had soon celebrated the exploit with a new model of brakes – l'Iseran.

The Tour would return to the Maurienne and the Iseran a year later, this time for a mountain time trial dominated by the Belgian Sylvère Maes, much as he dominated that year's race overall. The Grande Boucle's meagre five subsequent visits have been dramatic more for the splendour of the backdrop than the racing, mainly because the climb's isolation from major towns makes it impractical for the denouement of stages. Nonetheless, as he rode towards an astonishing and, with hindsight, dubious 230-kilometre breakaway win in Sestriere in 1992, the Italian Claudio Chiappucci applied his *coup de grâce* on the Iseran, ending the resistance of fellow show pony Richard Virenque and cresting the mountain alone.

That day, dense crowds packed the summit. At any other time it is an eerie and desolate place. There is no souvenir shop, monument or signpost serving notice of the Iseran's unique stature among Alpine roads. This seems particularly curious given what we know about why the road was built. All there is, in fact, is a small mountain inn and the grey-brick chapel of Notre Dame de Toute Prudence – a timely reminder of the caution required particularly on the open hairpins that toboggan thrillingly down towards Bonneval-sur-Arc. That and a view that barely redeemed the Iseran in Merrick's critical eyes: 'So high is the point at which the observer is standing that [the 11,830 foot Tsanteleina and the 12,325 foot Grande Sassière's] extra 2,000–3,000 feet of stature seems of little account; one appears to be hob-nobbing with them on very familiar terms. It is certainly impressive, but not one of the great summit views; and the Stelvio, beaten by 46 feet for height, need not lose any sleepless nights about it,' he concluded.

The climbs themselves are, of course, long, but not preposterously difficult if not for their altitude, with the southern ascent marginally more variable and demanding. In landscape, too, the ride up through the glaciers from Bonneval-sur-Arc is the grander of the two ascents, although the traffic thins almost as fast as the air as one passes through Val d'Isère on the northern side. Thereafter, a sumptuous spaghetti of hairpins worthy of even Merrick's admiration leads to the summit.

One of the iconic passes it may not be, but the Iseran is the quiet achiever of the Alpine class. Out of sight and out of mind, it is also, still, up and out on its own – the very highest mountain pass anywhere in the Alps.

RIGHT: Climbing towards the Iseran on the wilder and steeper southern side.

Fact file Col de l'Iseran

From Bourg-Saint-Maurice

REGION: Savoie, northern Alps, France

ACCESS: From Bourg-Saint-Maurice, take Avenue du Stade, Route du Col du Petit Saint Bernard, Rue de la Libération and Route de Val d'Isère

HEIGHT: 2,770m

LENGTH: 48km

ALTITUDE GAIN: 1,955m

AVERAGE GRADIENT: 4.1%

MAXIMUM GRADIENT: 6.9% (km 12 to 15 and km 21 to 24)

OPEN: June to October, depending on weather

REFRESHMENTS: Several bars, mainly in Sainte-Foy-Tarentaise (km 12), La Thuile (km 15) and Val d'Isère (km 31)

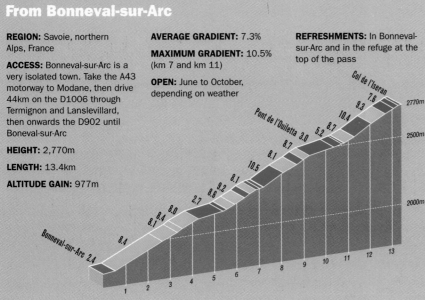

From Bonneval-sur-Arc

REGION: Savoie, northern Alps, France

ACCESS: Bonneval-sur-Arc is a very isolated town. Take the A43 motorway to Modane, then drive 44km on the D1006 through Termignon and Lanslevillard, then onwards the D902 until Boneval-sur-Arc

HEIGHT: 2,770m

LENGTH: 13.4km

ALTITUDE GAIN: 977m

AVERAGE GRADIENT: 7.3%

MAXIMUM GRADIENT: 10.5% (km 7 and km 11)

OPEN: June to October, depending on weather

REFRESHMENTS: In Bonneval-sur-Arc and in the refuge at the top of the pass

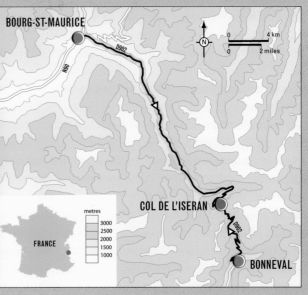

Col de la Bonette
2,802m

France

If you've ever heard of the Col de la Bonette, the chances are that you've also heard that its 2,802 metres make it the highest main road in Europe, not to mention the highest mountain pass, and the furthest above sea level that the Tour de France has ever planted its flag.

The truth is that only one of those statements is actually, well, true. The highest main road in Europe is, in fact, to be found on the Pico de Veleta, 3,392 metres up the Sierra Nevada in southern Spain, and even in the Alps there are several higher roads accessible to two- and four-wheeled modes of transport. The Tiefenbach above Sölden in Austria tops out at 2,829 metres at the southern entrance to the tunnel that threads though its eponymous glacier. The Pic de Châteaurenard (10.3 kilometres at 8.9 per cent from Saint Véran), a few valleys to the north of La Bonette, peaks at 2,990 metres via a serviceable 'white' road. And a sturdy bike, intrepid spirit and rudimentary but rideable gravel track will deliver you all the way to the Grand Col (2,935 metres) above the ski resort of Les Arcs 2000, the Col Sommeiller (3,009 metres) overlooking Bardonecchia on the Franco-Italian border, or the Col du Jandri (3,151 metres), approached from Les Deux Alpes.

The second point of contention is whether the road that climbs to 2,802 metres on the Bonette is a *bona fide* pass at all. The easy and correct answer is that it is not. The real col is actually to be found 2,715 metres above sea level – some way below its fellow skyscrapers, the Iseran, the Agnello and the Stelvio. From there, a two-kilometre loop wraps around the 2,880-metre Cime de la Bonette, a scree summit as exposed and windswept as it is unsightly – however breathtaking its vistas over a virgin Alpine landscape as far as the Monviso across the border in Italy to the north.

At the apex and pinnacle of the extension road, a brown roadsign wrongly proclaims, La Route de la Bonette – La plus haute d'Europe – alt. 2,802m. While the Bonette retains only two real claims to fame, those of the Tour de France's and indeed France's highest main road ascent, the propaganda continues to fool riders and writers alike. Articles perpetuating rather than debunking the myth of its status among Europe's mountain roads remain legion.

But the Bonette also has many redeeming features. Among the most *sauvage* and unspoilt areas in the range, the surrounding Mercantour National Park is an Alpine Eden bejewelled with rare flora and fauna, notably the wolf and the ibex. Nicholas and Nina Shoumatoff's *The Alps:*

Europe's Mountain Heart also notes that the Bonette is 'home to glacier crowfoot, creeping avens and other lovely, rare high-altitude flowers'. Maybe ironically, the glacier crowfoot is generally considered to be the highest-growing flower in the Alps, usually thriving above 4,000 metres.

The road itself, like many mountain passes, began life as a goat track. Heavily used for military purposes, it was widened in 1832 and officially classified as a *route impériale* by Napoleon III on August 18, 1860. A century later, work began on the current road and the extension which, in the locals' minds, edged the Bonette ahead of the Iseran and installed the pass as Europe's highest. Within two years, the Tour de France had taken on the climb for the first time, and in doing so scaled heights never reached before.

ABOVE: The Casernes de Restefond barracks, built between 1901 and 1906, are a reassuring landmark on the Jausiers side of the Bonette: the end is now in sight.

TOP: Glacier crowfoot flowers on the Bonette – one of numerous rare varieties of flower that grow here.

PREVIOUS PAGE: Halfway up the Bonette on the Jausiers side, the more varied of the two routes to the top.

Fignon's swansong

In six-times King of the Mountains Federico Bahamontes, the first to the top of the mountain's southern side from Saint-Étienne-de-Tinée in that 1962 Tour, the Bonette couldn't have been christened by a more illustrious climber. The Eagle of Toledo, as the Spaniard was known, was again the first to the summit in 1964, this time having ascended from Jausiers and the north.

The Tour's next visit, again from Jausiers in 1993, was remarkable for another eccentric climber, Robert Millar's solo break over the summit. Later that afternoon, though, while Tony Rominger was catching then passing the Scotsman en route to a stage victory at the Isola 2000 ski resort, a Tour legend was savouring his final hours as a professional cyclist on the Bonette's barren slopes.

'I can remember it very clearly,' Laurent Fignon, who died of cancer aged just 50 in 2010, recalled in his autobiography. 'I rode up the whole climb in last place. Because I wanted to. I put my hands on the top of the bars and savoured it all to the full... This col was all mine and I didn't want anyone to intrude. Climbing up over 2,700 metres above sea level like this gave me a host of good reasons to appreciate everything I had lived through on the bike. I had plenty of time to let my mind wander. It was a poetic distillation of the last 12 years... I pressed gently on the pedals, admiring distant views, weighing each second as if it were a tiny shard of a time that had taken flight, glimpsing amidst the horizon of blue sky and mountain peaks a whole new universe that was opening up before me, and a different way of seeing what lay ahead... It was a genuine moment of sadness and grace, intermingled.'

The following morning, French sports newspaper *L'Equipe* seemed less concerned with Fignon's decline than with the backdrop of La Bonette. 'They rode on the moon,' wrote journalist Philippe Bouvet.

The Grande Boucle didn't return to the Bonette until 2008, but that day, too, it invoked swoons. So, too, did the young South African John-Lee Augustyn. First over the summit, Augustyn plunged towards Jausiers and, almost, to his death, when he overshot a tight corner early on the descent. The pictures of the Barloworld rider and his bike cascading nine metres down the mountain – and of an unhurt Augustyn scrambling back up to the road to collect his spare bike – were among the most heart-stopping in the Tour's recent history.

'Coming over the top, at that altitude, my heart was pumping, the adrenaline was rushing,' Augustyn recalled in 2011. 'All you're thinking is, "I could win a Tour de France stage!" I was looking slightly to the side, and as I looked back I saw I was completely in the wrong line for the corner, and I thought: I'm not going to make it. I slammed on my brakes, but the next thing I saw was the sky. The first thing I thought was, when am I going to stop? Then I thought, how am I going to get back up?'

The difficulty of the descent towards Jausiers was further exemplified that day by the Russian Denis Menchov's floundering efforts, but the same northern flank is probably the easier of the two routes on the way up. Slightly shorter at 24 kilometres to the Saint-Étienne-de-Tinée side's 26 kilometres, gaining slightly less altitude (1,589 metres plays 1,658 metres), and slightly more consistent, this route also benefits from a prevailing tailwind. It's worth noting all the same that the sting in the tail, or rather the ring around that tail and the Bonette's summit, is even more venomous when tackled in this anti-clockwise direction. The final 800 metres from this side rise at an average of over ten per cent.

Both approaches are wild, exposed, in parts austere and strewn with traces of the Bonette's bellicose history. On the northern side, above the Lac des Essaupres (2,322 metres), stand the Casernes de Restefond barracks, built between 1901 and 1906. Even more striking and unnerving is what remains of the Camp des Fourches, eight kilometres from the summit on the opposite face of the Bonette. Constructed between 1896 and 1910, 26 shacks that once housed a 150-strong batallion of Alpine hunters now lie in disuse and disrepair, a miniature ghost town in an already surreal setting. Vague plans hatched in 1988 to turn the camp into a tourist village complete with hotel and restaurant have never left the Conseil Général des Alpes-Maritimes's drawing board.

As it is, this lonely aggregation of crumbling shacks somehow suits La Bonette. It is a mountain of unfulfilled promise, but one with an allure that's wonderfully raw.

Fact file Col de la Bonette

From Saint-Étienne-de-Tinée

REGION: Alpes Maritimes, southern Alps, France

ACCESS: Take the D2205 and D64 to summit from Saint-Étienne-de-Tinée

HEIGHT: 2,802m

LENGTH: 25.8km

ALTITUDE GAIN: 1,658m

AVERAGE GRADIENT: 6.4%

MAXIMUM GRADIENT: 15% between km 11.5 and 12 and also in the last kilometre

OPEN: May to October

REFRESHMENTS: Nothing very sure during the climb, so fill your bottles at the bottom

From Jausiers

REGION: Alpes de Hautes-Provence, southern Alps, France

ACCESS: Leave Jausiers on Les Caïres and continue on that road all the way to summit

HEIGHT: 2,802m

LENGTH: 23.4km

ALTITUDE GAIN: 1,589m

AVERAGE GRADIENT: 6.76%

MAXIMUM GRADIENT: 15% in km 22 and 23

OPEN: June to September

REFRESHMENTS: Nothing very sure during the climb, so fill your bottles at the bottom

ABOVE: The lake below the summit on the Bonette's northern side. The summit is but a few minutes of suffering away.

3,000m +

Pico de Veleta
3,384m
Spain

Somehow, it seems paradoxical yet also fitting: mainland Europe's highest main-road climb lacks in kudos what it offers in elevation precisely because of its height. The Pico de Veleta is, more simply put, too high. Too high for year-round access and too high, perhaps most to the point, to join the upper crust of professional cycling's most noble mountains.

And to think that one supposed and verified great advantage of the Vuelta a España moving from April to September in 1995 was improved access to climbs that were still snowbound in spring. Even in its new slot in the calendar, though, Spain's national tour deemed its fourth highest mountain and the ceiling of Europe's road network out of bounds. The arms race between major tour organizers raged on, but on a different front – that of steepness or difficulty. The record for the highest altitude reached by a major professional race, meanwhile, had remained stuck in a time warp since the Col de la Bonette's first appearance on the Tour de France route in 1962.

Yawning oblivion

The Veleta's loss was also the Vuelta's, particularly in an age when Spain's premier bicycle race has struggled to capture the public imagination. The event has, it's true, still traded on the Veleta's name, without ever venturing beyond 2,600 metres, some 800 metres vertically and 10,000 by road from where the tarmac runs its course. The Veleta's peak, the weather vane from which it takes its name, is just 11 metres higher, 3,395 metres above the sea.

The Veleta is, then, higher yet already less hallowed than Vuelta newcomer the Angliru; it is taller and tougher than almost anything in the Tour de France, while still dwarfed by the Ventoux's or Galibier's notoriety. Legendary status is a subjective privilege and one to which neither the Veleta's stature, its length nor its myriad beauties may ever hold the key. In some ways, it is better that way: the Veleta and the southern Spanish range to which it belongs, the Sierra Nevada, will retain a mystique and exclusivity in keeping with their elevation above all other European climbs.

Climbing into the Sierra, whether by car or bike, is a unique experience. All mountain ranges have to start somewhere, but in few places is access to over 3,000 metres so abrupt or theatrical as in the Sierra. The main A-395 road into the massif and its major ski

> **THE VELETA'S LOSS WAS ALSO THE VUELTA'S,** particularly in an age when Spain's premier bicycle race has struggled to capture the public imagination. **"**

> **6 THE HIGHEST MOUNTAIN IN THE SIERRA NEVADA** and anywhere in mainland Europe outside the Alps or Caucasus, the 3,479-metre Mulhacén is the next major peak along, six kilometres as the crow or, more likely, vulture flies from the Veleta. **7**

resort, Sol y Nieve (Sun and Snow), climbs out of Granada and almost immediately, it seems, into a different orbit. On a wide and often chaotic road, it continues to curl its way around the Sierra's western side on a ledge above and overlooking the Rio Genil and a yawning oblivion. The ascent up to kilometre 15 and the junction with the A-4025 is traffic-laden and somehow harder than its gradient suggests, yet still irresistible; while at times terrifying, those views to the left are the first in a kaleidoscope of unmissable vistas on the Veleta.

A figure of eight effectively connects two or, if you like, four roads to the Soy y Nieve ski resort, among Europe's highest. The A-395 continues all the way to Sol y Nieve on the same broad and bustling rim around the mountain; the other route is a combination of the 12.2-kilometre, 6.19 per cent climb to El Purche, a short interlude of six kilometres on the A-395, followed by a left turn on what's known as the old Sierra Nevada road at the El Dornajo visitors' centre. The bow is completed just before Sol y Nieve – although those wishing to bypass the resort and the three-kilometre descent to get there should keep left at the Collado de las Sabinas, 2,173 metres above sea level, and carry on climbing to the intersection with the Veleta road at 2,369 metres altitude.

This El Purche–Collado de las Sabinas–Veleta itinerary is the one that the Vuelta directors might feel inclined to chose for maximum drama – and maximum agony for the riders. Considerably steeper than the equivalent first section on the A-395, this route is also a good deal quieter and prettier. Monachil is the idyllic starting point, all white-washed Andalusian charm and Moorish heirlooms – including the Arab-influenced name. On the approach to the village and throughout the climb to El Purche, the Veleta's apex is but a distant spectator, disappearing and reappearing behind closer ridges in a game of perpetual peekaboo. In spring and autumn, when the mountain is green and lush below Sol y Nieve but completely white above its waistline, the rare glimpses of the Veleta from the Monachil road are superb.

Too high for the Vuelta

Alejandro Valverde effectively lost the Vuelta on this route in 2006, two years after the climb's 'discovery' by race chief Victor Cordero (in neither 2004 nor 2006 did the peloton continue to Soy y Nieve, instead descending from El Purche on the A-395 towards Granada). That day an attack from eventual Vuelta winner Alexandre Vinokourov finally unhinged

PREVIOUS PAGE: The Pico de Veleta, photographed from 2,400 metres above sea level in March 2011.

RIGHT: The military academy 2,550 metres above sea level on the Veleta. For much of the year, the road is clear only up to this point.

OPPOSITE: Looking down towards the Sol y Nieve resort, high on the Veleta. This is the last significant vegetation on the Veleta's southern side.

Fact file Pico de Veleta

From Huétor-Vega/Monachil

REGION: Andalusia, Spain

ACCESS: Take the GR-3202 from Huétor-Vega towards Monachil, pass through Monachil following signs to Sol y Nieve on the Carretera de El Purche. After 13km, turn right on the A-395 for 6km to El Dornajo. Bear left here. Now follow signs to Veleta all the way to the summit

HEIGHT: 3,384m

LENGTH: 46.62km

ALTITUDE GAIN: 2,662m

AVERAGE GRADIENT: 5.7%

MAXIMUM GRADIENT: 17% (km 11, just before El Purche)

OPEN: Up to 2,550m from March until October, subject to weather. June to September for the summit road, again depending on weather

REFRESHMENTS: In Monachil, at El Dornajo (km 19), in Sol y Nieve (km 30), in the kiosks next to the military academy at the Virgen de las Nieves (km 36)

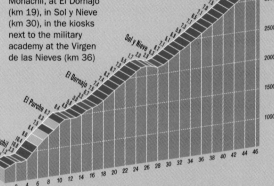

From Granada

REGION: Andalusia, Spain

ACCESS: Take the A-395 from Granada all the way to Sol y Nieve ski resort. Continue through resort on Urbanizaciòn de Sol y Nieve, continue 3km then bear right following signs to Veleta and carry on to summit

HEIGHT: 3,384m

LENGTH: 43km

ALTITUDE GAIN: 2,700m

AVERAGE GRADIENT: 6.2%

MAXIMUM GRADIENT: 15% (in final km)

OPEN: Up to 2,550 metres from March until October, subject to weather. June to September for the summit road, again weather dependent

REFRESHMENTS: Multiple options up El Dornajo (km 16), in Sol y Nieve (km 26), then in the kiosks next to the military academy at the Virgen de las Nieves (km 36)

ALTERNATIVE ROUTE: From Granada, via Pinos Genil and Güéjar Sierra on the GR-460 (44.3km at 5.77%)

ABOVE: Looking back towards Monachil, just short of El Purche. Some of the steepest slopes anywhere on the Veleta are here, close to the Collado del Muerto.

Valverde two kilometres from the summit at El Purche, where the road plunges into a beautiful moorland oasis before a final 13 per cent kick up to the 1,495-metre pass. Back at the foot of the mountain, the road clambers up a series of narrow and tightly packed hairpins, its gradient almost constantly above ten per cent between the second and fifth kilometres out of Monachil. After two relatively comfortable kilometres, it then rises from 1,300 metres altitude to 1,400 in less than a kilometre. The second short descent in quick order, this one just over a kilometre through cooling pines, leads back to the A-395 and the option of a right turn to Sol y Nieve and the Veleta or left and down to Granada.

A right here, then left after five kilometres of routine climbing on the A-395, takes you onto the A-4025 and yet another variant of the Veleta. It's on this road, after some nasty hairpins in the forest, that the panorama to the southwest begins to truly reveal itself for the first time. The end of this stretch also marks the end of the figure of eight and the point from which all roads, or rather just one, lead all the way to the Veleta, still 15 kilometres and 1,200 metres of elevation away.

If the Veleta's height has penalized its popularity, it does the same for its aesthetics from here on in; sadly, the Veleta is easiest on the eye when it is impossible to access, in spring and winter. Most of the time, when there are skiers on the pistes of Sol y Nieve and a thick layer of icing on the Veleta and neighbouring summits, the road is cleared up to the military refuge 2,550 metres up, but not further. Later in the year, the snows depart and with it a lot of the Veleta's conventional beauty; what's left is a dark and desolate moonscape, a deteriorating but still passable road and the sense of riding into a quarry – albeit one from which you can see Africa, Morocco and the Riff mountains on a clear day. The highest mountain in the Sierra Nevada and anywhere in mainland Europe outside the Alps or Caucasus, the 3,479-metre Mulhacén is the next major peak along, six kilometres as the crow or, more likely, vulture flies from the Veleta.

The last ten kilometres of road to the summit worm furiously at a gradient never below six per cent. At these altitudes, though, as everyone knows, it's the lack of oxygen as much as the angle of the road that causes problems. Cycling's physiological gurus have it that above 2,000 metres, altitude begins to significantly impair performance; at that height, it is estimated that an athlete has access to 80 per cent of the oxygen present in the air at sea level. At 3,384 metres, the finishing height of the Veleta, the figure falls to 67 per cent.

This statistic alone, more than any logistical concerns, may be enough to dissuade the Vuelta or any other professional race ever from venturing all the way to the Veleta. In 2009, they went as far as 2,520 metres to a finish line the Frenchman David Moncoutié was the first to cross. Two years later, the Tour de France raised the bar for major tour finales even higher with a stage ending on the 2,645-metre Col du Galibier.

This left a long way still to go just to break the mythical 3,000-metre barrier – and no one was holding their breath. Probably wise up here, where the air is thin and the sense of wonder anything but.

RIGHT: One of the first hairpins on the road out of Monachil. The landscape here seems to belong to a different universe to the snowy crests 2,000 metres higher up.

Index

Acknowledgements

In addition to Richard Green, Nick Clark, Paul Oakley and Emma Heyworth-Dunn at Quercus, Ivo Marloh and Vanessa Green at The Urban Ant, Alan Horsfield at Map Graphics and David Luxton at Luxton Harris, the authors would like to thank the following people, who made valuable contributions to *Mountain High* with their interviews or advice: Bernhard Eisel, Mark Cavendish, Magnus Backstedt, Kate Clarence, Tania Goding, Lucien Aimar, Peter Luttenberger, Miculà Dematteis, Richard Moore, Pierre Carrey, Peter Cossins, Filippo Simeoni, Jean-François Pescheux, David Millar, Giancarlo Andolfatti, Samuel Sanchez, Angelo Zomegnan, Mario Aerts, Dirk de Wolf, Fiorenzo Magni, Dan Martin, Giuseppe Saronni, Paul Godfrey, Marco Pinotti, Bruce Hildenbrand, Leon de Kort, Pier Maulini, Jeremy Whittle and last but not least Marcel Wüst for modelling for our cover photograph.

Daniel Friebe is one of Britain's leading cycling journalists and, at 31, a veteran of ten Tours de France. Daniel is the long-serving European editor of *Procycling* magazine. He collaborated with cycling superstar Mark Cavendish on the best-selling *Boy Racer – My Journey to Tour de France Record-breaker*.

Pete Goding is a formidable force in professional cycling photography, shooting some of the most influential personalities in the sport, while encapsulating awe-inspiring scenery for travel and sports features in journals worldwide. Pete has supplied images through agencies and via individual commissions to a wide range of national and international publications including *The Times*, *Guardian*, *Sunday Herald*, *Daily Telegraph*, *Procycling* magazine and *Cycle Sport*, to name a few. Currently Pete works with the UK Press Association who represent his sports content via www.paphotos.com.

All photography: Pete Goding
www.petegodingphotography.com

Except:
p167 bottom-right Andrzej Gibasiewicz/Shutterstock.com; p202 edella/Shutterstock.com; p203 bottom-right LianeM/Shutterstock.com.

Maps and illustrations:
Map Graphics Ltd
www.mapgraphics.co.uk

Except:
p6–7 The Urban Ant/Alan Horsfield

Quercus Editions Ltd
55 Baker Street
7th Floor, South Block
London
W1U 8EW

First published in 2011

Copyright © 2011 Daniel Friebe and Pete Goding
Design, layout and editorial by The Urban Ant Ltd, London
[www.theurbanant.com]

A catalogue record of this book is available from the British Library

ISBN: 978 0 85738 624 3

Printed and bound in China

10 9 8 7 6 5 4 3 2 1